TEXT AND TRANSLATION SOCIETY SERIES (TTS)

ELEVEN VOLUMES, REISSUED IN REPRINT, DEVOTED TO EARLY CHRISTIAN TEXTS, EDITED WITH INTRODUCTIONS, TRANSLATIONS, COMMENTARIES, AND NOTES

★ ★ ★ ★ ★

(1) BROOKS, E.W. (ed/tr): The Sixth Book of the Letters of Severus, patriarch of Antioch (†536) in the Syriac version of Athanasius of Nisibis... Edited, translated, annotated... 1902-04. 2 vols in 1. 1039 pages. Cloth bound, 8vo. (ISBN 90 6022 301 2)   *

(2) BURKITT, F.C. (ed/tr): Euphemia and the Goth, a legendary tale from Edessa, and the Acts of Martyrdom... Syriac texts, edited and examined, with introduction, translation, notes... 1913. 284 pages, plate, map. Paper bound, 8vo. (ISBN 90 6022 302 0)

(3) CHARLES, R.H. (tr): The Chronicle of John (7th century), Coptic bishop of Nikiu, being a history of Egypt before and during the Arab conquest of Egypt... Translated from the Ethiopic version edited by H. Zotenberg (*separately available*), with introduction, notes, index. 1916. 231 pages. Paper bound, 8vo. (ISBN 90 6022 303 9)

(4) CONNOLLY, R.H. & H.W. CODRINGTON (eds/trs): Two Commentaries on the Jacobite Liturgy... 1913. 275 pages. Bound, 8vo. (=90 6022 304 7=)

(5) CONYBEARE, F.C. (ed/tr): The Armenian version of Revelation, Apocalypse of John. Followed by Cyril of Alexandria's Scholia on the Incarnation... Edited, translated... 1907. 414 pages. Paper bound, 8vo. (ISBN 90 6022 305 5)

(6) GWYNN, J. (ed): Remnants of the later Syriac versions of the Bible... Edited, with reconstructed Greek text, introductions, notes... 1909. 339 pages. Paper bound, 8vo. (ISBN 90 6022 306 3)

(7) MARSH, F.S. (ed/tr): The Book of the Holy Hierotheos, ascribed to Stephen Bar-Sudhaile (c.500)... Syriac texts, edited, translated, annotated... 1927. 494 pages. Cloth bound, 8vo. (ISBN 90 6022 307 1)

(8) MITCHELL, C.W. (ed/tr): The Prose Refutations of Mani, Marcion and Bardaisan, by Ephraim Syrus, of Nisibis, c.306-373. Syriac text, edited, translated, annotated... 1912-21. 2 vols in 1. 756 pages. Cloth bound, 8vo. (ISBN 90 6022 308 X)   *

(9) RIEDEL, W. & W.E. CRUM (eds/trs): The Canons of Athanasius, patriarch of Alexandria (c.293-373). Arabic and Coptic texts, edited, translated, annotated... 1904. 249 pages. Paper bound, 8vo. (ISBN 90 6022 309 8)

(10) WINSTEDT, E.O. (ed/tr): Coptic texts on St Theodore the General (†c.306)... and on Chamoul and Justus. Edited, translated and annotated... 1910. 298 pages. Paper bound, 8vo. (ISBN 90 6022 310 1)

(11) WRIGHT, W.A. (ed): A Commentary on the Book of Job, by Berechiah, Mediaeval Jewish scholar... Hebrew text, edited, annotated, with a translation... 1905. 406 pages. Paper bound, 8vo. (ISBN 90 6022 311 X)

★ ★ ★ ★ ★

*Volumes are numbered in alphabetical order of editor's names. *Reprint editions not yet published; pre-publication orders will benefit 20% discount.*

APA   /   POSTBUS 122   /   NL-3600 AC MAARSSEN   /   HOLLAND

THE CHRONICLE OF JOHN,

COPTIC BISHOP OF NIKIU

(*c.* 690 A. D.)

ROBERT HENRY CHARLES

THE CHRONICLE OF JOHN

(*c.* 690 A. D.)

COPTIC BISHOP OF NIKIU

BEING A HISTORY

OF EGYPT BEFORE AND DURING THE ARAB CONQUEST

TRANSLATED FROM

HERMANN ZOTENBERG'S EDITION OF THE ETHIOPIC VERSION

WITH

AN INTRODUCTION, CRITICAL AND LINGUISTIC NOTES,

AND AN INDEX OF NAMES

APA - PHILO PRESS

AMSTERDAM

TEXT AND TRANSLATION SOCIETY, LONDON, 3

APA - ACADEMIC PUBLISHERS ASSOCIATED
(APA-UITGEVERS ASSOCIATIE)
PHILO PRESS-VAN HEUSDEN-HISSINK & CO / FONTES PERS
HOLLAND UNIVERSITY PRESS
ORIENTAL PRESS / UNIVERSITY PRESS AMSTERDAM

POSTBUS 1850   POSTBUS 122
NL-1000 BW AMSTERDAM & NL-3600 AC MAARSSEN

ISBN 90 6022 303 9
REPRINT OF THE EDITION LONDON 1916
PRINTED IN THE NETHERLANDS

INTRODUCTION

§ 1. John, Bishop of Nikiu and his Chronicle.

John of Nikiu [1] was probably born about the time of the Mohammedan invasion of Egypt. He was the Coptic bishop of Nikiu and 'rector' of the bishops of Upper Egypt who took part in the election of the successor of John of Samnûd in 690 A.D. In 696 he was appointed administrator general of the Monasteries, but was later deposed from these offices on the ground that he had abused his powers.

His *Chronicle*, though even imperfectly preserved, is of immense value to historians of Egypt. As Butler [2] remarks: 'It is the acquisition of John's manuscript by the British Abyssinian expedition which has made it possible to write a history of the Arab conquest of Egypt.' Unhappily, however, his *Chronicle* has suffered in the course of transmission. Large portions of it have been lost. That some of these losses were sustained after it had been translated into Arabic is shown by the fact that the rubrics (see pp. 1–14 of this book), which were prefixed by the Arabic translator, do not always correspond to the chapters they profess to summarize. Thus rubric CXIV (CXV) [3]: 'How the Moslem took Misr in the fourteenth year of the cycle and made the fortress of Babylon open its gates in the fifteenth year', has no relation to the actual contents of that chapter. Again, there is a lamentable gap of thirty years, from 610 to 640, from the accession of Heraclius to the arrival of the Arabs before Babylon in Egypt. Hence we are without John's account of the Persian wars,

---

[1] I have followed the general usage in England, using the Coptic form of the name. In the Ethiopic text, however, this form never occurs. Sometimes we have Nikius and at others Nakius (the Arabic form of the word). The Greek was Νικίου ; but see p. 15, note 2.

[2] *Arab Conquest of Egypt*, p. ix.

[3] See p. 13.

of the Persian occupation of Egypt, and of their evacuation of it early in 627 under pressure of Heraclius's victories : also of the ten years' persecution of the Copts by Cyrus, patriarch of Alexandria, and of the first acts of the invasion of Egypt by the Arabs. When John resumes his story Theodore the commander-in-chief of the Roman armies in Egypt has just learnt the defeat of the local levies under John and the death of that general.

Those who wish to gain a coherent and historical knowledge of the contribution made to the history of Egypt by John of Nikiu have only to read the resumé in Butler's *The Arab Conquest of Egypt*, pp. 8–27. But this work must be read as a whole for the new light it throws on Egyptian history of this date. In this field Gibbon fails us, since he often misconceives the rôle played by Egypt at this period. Seeing that Egypt took a prominent part in the revolution against Phocas and was one of the most turbulent countries in the whole Empire, as we now learn from John of Nikiu and other less authoritative sources, it is clear that he could not have described the rebellion of Heraclius against Phocas in the terms he did (v. 66–7, Bury's ed.) and declared that Egypt was 'the only province which had been exempt, since the time of Diocletian, from foreign and domestic war' (v. 71) if he had had John of Nikiu's *Chronicle* at his disposal.

§ 2. VERSIONS OF JOHN OF NIKIU.

John of Nikiu was written originally in Greek, but it is not improbable, as Zotenberg points out, that some chapters which dealt with purely Egyptian affairs were written in Coptic. This hypothesis is supported by the Coptic forms of proper names. But this question needs to be critically and fully threshed out. It is impossible at present to attempt to delimit the boundaries of the Coptic sections.

A Sahidic fragment was discovered in the Berlin Museum, which according to its discoverer, Dr. Schäfer, is closely related to John's *Chronicle*. Future investigation must determine whether this Sahidic fragment is derived directly from the original work or translated from one of its versions,

or whether it is merely an independent document dealing
with the same material as our *Chronicle*.

From Greek the *Chronicle* was translated into Arabic, and
from Arabic into Ethiopic in the year 1602. The Arabic
version is wholly lost, though Amélineau, in his *Vie du Patriarche Copte Isaac*, p. xxiv, *n.*, states that he knows of an
Arabic manuscript of John's *Chronicle*. But when asked for
further information by Dr. Butler, none was forthcoming (see
Butler, *op. cit.*, p. ix, *n.*).

The Ethiopic version gives the student the impression of
being a literal reproduction of the Arabic. It is rather of
a hybrid description. The Ethiopic itself is very late and
unclassical, and exhibits idioms impossible in the earlier period.
It contains many transliterations from the earlier languages
in which the *Chronicle* was written. Thus we have Ἰὼ μάκαιρα
transliterated in 22^4, πανόπτης in 33, ὁ πάνταρχος in 51^{62}, ἡλιακή
.. σεληνιακή in 74^6, ἀναγνώστης in 79^{13}, φιλαλήθης in 89^{53}, &c., &c.
The Arabic names of five of the planets are transliterated in
2^1, and other Arabic words in 84^{30}, $97^{2,\,16}$, 102^{10}, $107^{18,\,33}$, 109^3,
&c., &c. Amharic words appear occasionally, as 96^2, 107^{10},
108^{10}, but this is due to the Ethiopic translator's use of
Amharic colloquially. The Coptic article has survived in 31^1,
107^{14}, as Zotenberg has shown.

§ 3. THE ETHIOPIC MANUSCRIPTS.

There are only two manuscripts at present known of this
version, which for convenience are designated A and B.

A is No. 146 in Zotenberg's Catalogue of the Ethiopic
manuscripts in the Bibliothèque Nationale. It is written on
vellum, being about 368 mm. by 296. Each page has three
columns of thirty-two lines each. According to Zotenberg it
was written in the seventeenth century. Our *Chronicle* begins
on fol. 62 and ends on fol. 138.

B. This manuscript is Orient. 818 in the British Museum
(391^a in Wright's Catalogue of the Ethiopic manuscripts there).
It is written on vellum, being about $14\frac{7}{8}$ in. by 13, and contains 191 folios. Each page has three columns of thirty-six
lines each. It is well written, and belongs to the first half of
the eighteenth century.

John of Nikiu begins on fol. 48ᵃ and ends on fol. 102ᵇ. In the last column it is stated that it was translated from the Arabic version in 1602 by Gabriel the Egyptian, son of John of Kaljûb, at the order of the Abyssinian general Athanasius and of Mariam Sena (Malak Mogasa), the wife of Jacob, Malak Sagad the younger (1597–1603 A.D.).

These two manuscripts are not copies of the same manuscript, but are derived, and not distantly, from one and the same exemplar.

§ 4. ZOTENBERG'S ETHIOPIC TEXT.

Zotenberg's text (*Chronique de Jean, Évêque de Nikiou, Texte éthiopien publié et traduit*, Paris, 1883) is on the whole reasonably good as a first edition. Since there are only two manuscripts, and these are closely related, there was little difficulty experienced in forming the text. But Zotenberg's chief merit lies not in the making of the text, but in the great ingenuity he has shown in deciphering the very corrupt forms under which a considerable number of the proper names are disguised. The corruptions in question are due to the fact that the Ethiopic translators were using an unpointed Arabic text, and were largely ignorant of the historical persons and events described in John of Nikiu's *Chronicle*. But this merit should be dealt with rather in connexion with Zotenberg's translation than with his text.

We have observed that the text is reasonably good. This qualified praise will become more intelligible as we proceed. Thus, frequently, where the text is unquestionably and sometimes hopelessly corrupt, no attention is drawn to this fact either by the use of obeli in the text or footnotes, and not unfrequently the translation proceeds as if the constructions were quite normal. In footnotes in my translation I have called attention to some of these passages. Here I mention a few cases either where an absolutely corrupt text has been reproduced, or the text has been wrongly emended. First let us take the proper name መክስምያናስ፡ (i.e. Maximian), which is allowed to stand wrongly in 77[47, 48, 73, 74, 83, 88, 92], where it should have been emended into መክስሚኖስ፡ (i.e. Maximin).

On the other hand, he wrongly allows the latter to remain in $77^{2,\,25}$. In his translation, however, these errors are set right silently save in two instances. In 88^{69} Zotenberg omits the clause 'to set free her mother' (ይኅድግ፡ ላቲ፡ ለእማ፡), and thus fails to recognize the meaning of this verb in 88^{67}, where he renders it by *permettre*, i. e. 'de permettre à Vérine de demeurer dans le château d'Isaurie'. But this gives exactly the opposite sense to what we require. See my emendation on p. 117, note 4.

In the passage just dealt with we have a very common kind of error into which Zotenberg falls. He emends a passage in such a way as to make it inconsistent with its context or with the universal tradition on the subject. Thus in 88^{67} Zotenberg emends the *vox nulla* ይቀላ፡ into ይቅትላ፡ (= 'to put her to death'), but the rest of the verse suggests that Zeno only intended to keep the empress under guard. Hence we should read ይዕቀብ፡.

Another instance of Zotenberg's wrong restoration of the text occurs earlier in this chapter. In 88^{44} he renders his reconstructed text as follows, the words enclosed in brackets being Zotenberg's addition to supply an indubitable loss : 43. 'Quant au patriarche Pierre, on le transporta, chargé de chaînes, dans la ville d'Euchaïtès . . . . 44. [On nomma ensuite patriarche d'Antioche Étienne] qui proscrivait la secte de Nestorius. En conséquence tous les habitants de la ville le détestaient, et il fut massacré par la population d'Antioche et le clergé.' Here, according to Zotenberg's restored text, Peter the Fuller is transported to Euchaites, and his successor Stephen is put to death by the clergy and laity of Antioch because he had persecuted the Nestorians. Now the facts are exactly the opposite. Peter was a persecutor of the Nestorians, but Stephen was charged before a Council of Nestorianism and, when his enemies failed to prove their accusation, the inhabitants of Antioch, who were strong opponents of Nestorianism, took the law into their own hands and put Stephen to death. See my note on p. 113.

In 82^1 Zotenberg inserts ሐዘን፡ after ሁሉ፡, and በጽሐ፡ before ከመ፡. Thus he arrives at the following translation, in which he omits መጽአ፡ : 'Après la mort de Jovien, l'ami de Dieu, [régna] Valentinien. Comme il y avait une grande affliction parmi les officiers, à cause de la mort de l'empereur Jovien, [il était venu] pour pleurer avec les autres.' I have inserted in square brackets Zotenberg's additions. Now this is not John of Nikiu, but Zotenberg. John's text is literally as follows: 'And after the death of the Godloving Jovian, Valentinian, being the foremost amongst the officers, came to mourn with them over the death of the emperor Jovian.'

In 120[46] the text is not defective and is perfectly right historically and grammatically. The literal rendering of the text is: 'This letter was sent by Martina ... to David ... (urging him) ... to put down the sons of Constantine, who had been emperor with Heraclius, his brother.' The persons referred to are as follows: Heraclius I married first Eudocia and had by her Constantine III here mentioned, and married secondly Martina and had by her the Heraclius II here mentioned. Thus 'brother' in the text means in reality 'half-brother'. Again, 'the sons of Constantine III' in the text were Constantine (i.e. Constans II) and Theodosius. Now it is these grandchildren of Heraclius I that Martina requested David to remove in favour of her own children by Heraclius I. Zotenberg, however, misconceives the passage utterly and emends it. His rendering then is: 'Une lettre que l'on disait avoir été adressée par Martine ... à David ... pour l'engager ... à déposséder les fils de Constantin, c'est-à-dire Constantin (le jeune), qui gouvernait avec Heraclius et son frère.' The phrase 'c'est ... Constantin' is needlessly inserted by Zotenberg, and 'et', quite wrongly added before 'son frère'. This last addition makes the text unintelligible.

I will content myself with adducing another erroneous emendation. On p. 25 of his text Zotenberg quite rightly follows his manuscripts in reading ትጠፍእ፡ ፍጡነ፡ መንግሥት፡, but as a footnote on p. 236 of his translation, and in the list of 'Corrections' on p. 487, he writes that መንግሥት፡ must be emended into መንግሥተ፡ or መንግሥት፧. Thus he takes ትጠፍእ፡ to be a transitive verb and accordingly translates 'tu détruiras bientôt le gouvernement'. But ጠፍአ፡ is always intransitive. Hence the manuscripts are right, and the text should be rendered: 'the kingdom ... will speedily be destroyed.'

This list could be largely increased, but sufficient facts have been given to prove that Zotenberg's text needs to be carefully revised.

§ 5. Zotenberg's Translation and Index.

Though this translation is still more faulty than the text, the gratitude of all scholars interested in this subject is due to this scholar for the immense industry and the great learning he has shown in the illustration and explanation of his author. The student will find the results of such studies in the notes on the French translation as well as in the earlier ·contributions in the *Journal Asiatique*, t. x, 1877, p. 451 sqq.; t. xii, 1878, p. 245 sqq.; t. xiii, 1879, p. 291 sqq. I have learnt much from the notes, but I have preferred to work to a great extent independently with the help of the Greek chronographers. The translation is suprisingly faulty. I will confine my criticism to the later chapters, and select from these only a limited number of typical mistranslations.

In 120[44] the text is to be rendered 'whom Heracleonas had taken unto him (as colleague)', as is manifest from 120[43]. But Zotenberg renders 'qu' Héracléonas avait levé des fonts baptismaux' (!). In 82[4] he emends the text and reads ኢ፡ይተሥእ፡ ሕልያጊ፡ ወኢኣምኃ፡ (MSS. ወኢኣምኃኒ፡) በከንቴ፡. This='he did not accept gifts and bribes rashly'—a statement which would imply that he exercised great discretion in his acts of maladministration. But this is quite contrary to the context, and so Zotenberg abandons his emended text and likewise the manuscripts and simply writes 'il ne se laissait pas corrompre par des dons'. But በከንቴ፡ (='rashly') must be rendered. Hence we have only to emend ኣምኒ፡ into ኣምኒ፡ and we arrive at the following excellent sense: 'he refused bribes, and did not give his confidence rashly.'

In 84[97] በኣከይ፡ and ዘእንበለ፡ ነጢኣት፡ are omitted in his translation. In 88[51] he renders ረስይ፡ ሰሀገር፡ ሰዘይትኙ፡ ንጉሥ፡ by 'il ... y fit reconnaître la souveraineté de l'empereur Zénon'. This is an impossible rendering. If the Ethiopic means anything it is: 'he made the city of' (or 'to belong to') 'the emperor Zeno.' But, as I have shown in the note on p. 115 of my translation, the key to the text is given by

John Malalas, and the text must be emended accordingly. Of 88^{80} ከመ፡ ይኩን፡ ኅሩየ፡ ለትእዛዝነ፡ is given the strange rendering of 'pour être l'exécuteur fidèle de notre autorité'. The words are literally: 'that he might be chosen for our commands.' But the original form of the phrase occurs in 88^{82}, where Verina declares that she has chosen Leontius emperor 'that he may be *solicitous* after every good work'. Hence here ኅሩየ፡ is to be emended into ኅላዩ፡, and so we have 'that he might be solicitous as regards our commands'.

In 90^{31} ካልኣንሂ፡ እምአንስት፡ አውፅኡ፡ cannot under any circumstances be rendered 'certaines femmes firent paraître leurs enfants', but 'others (i. e. men) drew forth certain women'. It is extraordinary that Zotenberg should make እምአንስት፡ (feminine) the subject of the transitive verb አውጽኡ፡ (masculine termination) and omit ካልኣንሂ፡ (='others' (masc.)), which is the real subject of the verb.

In 119^{18} we have an instance of Zotenberg's paraphrasing the text—a thing he does frequently. 'Après la mort de Constantin, fils d'Heraclius, on fit monter sur le trône Heraclius, son frère *d'un autre lit*.' The italicized phrase is a rendering of እምአቡሁ፡, which should be rendered literally 'on his father's side'. Heraclius II was a half-brother of Constantine, son of Heraclius, by the same father. But 'd'un autre lit' does not express this fact.

I will only adduce one more of the many errors in translation. In 120^{13} we find an astonishing misrendering of the text. 'Il fit ouvrir (?) la citerne dans laquelle se trouvait la Sainte-Croix qu'il avait reçue avant son exil du général Jean.' It is true that the query after *ouvrir* is Zotenberg's. But አዕበዩ፡ cannot under any circumstances be rendered by *ouvrir*. It means 'extolled'. As Butler (*Arab Conquest*, 538 sq.) remarks, Cyrus was here 'recounting the story of the Invention of the Cross . . . with the Eastern Church the Invention and the Exaltation of the Cross were always celebrated on one and the same day, September 14.'

In his Index, which is admirable in its fullness, there are some errors. Constans II is not to be found in 120^{39-45} as appears in his index, though he is there named 'Constantine the younger' (120^{45}). Constantine (i.e. Constans II), son of

Constantine III, though expressly mentioned in $20^{38, 44, 45}$, is not given in the index. Under 'Jean l'Évangéliste' two personalities are confused, i. e. 'John the Fourth Evangelist' and 'John the Theologian or Divine', the author of Revelation. Under 'Jean (Talaïa), patriarche d'Alexandrie' lies another error. The John actually mentioned in 94^{23} had been patriarch of Alexandria under Tiberius, 578–582 A.D., whereas John Talaia was elected patriarch of Alexandria in 482, and is actually referred to in $88^{60, 61}$. Maximin is not mentioned in the Index, while Jeroboam, the son of Nebat (93^5), appears as Roboam. Apparently Zotenberg confuses him with Rehoboam.

§ 6. The Present Translation.

Since John of Nikiu is merely an annalist, who records in the simplest language the facts at his disposal, the present translator has made it his aim to translate the Ethiopic version as literally as possible. In this respect his translation differs greatly from Zotenberg's, which is of the nature of a paraphrase, and aims at giving a smooth and rather a literary version of a very rough piece of writing.

In the present translation the roughness of the Ethiopic version is reflected. Form has been sacrificed to accuracy. As respects accuracy, owing to the corruptness of the text this has not been achieved to the extent I could wish. Subsequent translators will carry forward the identification of corrupt proper names, as well as the further emendation of the text.

In the translation words enclosed thus ( ) are supplied by the translator, and words enclosed ⟨ ⟩ are necessary restorations; while words enclosed † † are treated as corrupt, and words enclosed [ ] are regarded as interpolations.

Amongst the Greek Chroniclers I have chiefly relied on John Malalas (the Bonn edition), John of Antioch (fragments of whose Chronicle are edited in Müller's *Fragmenta Historicorum Graecorum*, iv. 535–622), *Chronicon Paschale* (ed. Ducange). These were undoubtedly at our author's disposal. But I have found the Church History of Eusebius, as well as those of Evagrius and Socrates, of great service, and in a slight degree that of Theodoret. The Chronicles of Syncellus (Bonn ed.) and Cedrenus (Bonn ed.) have also been found helpful as preserving more accurate accounts of events recorded in our author.

On the later chapters regarding the Mohammedan invasion of Egypt, Butler's work—*The Arab Conquest of Egypt* (Oxford University Press, 1902)—is simply indispensable.

THE CHRONICLE OF JOHN,

COPTIC BISHOP OF NIKIU

(*c.* 690 A. D.)

THE CHRONICLE

OF

JOHN, BISHOP OF NIKIU

In the name of the Father and of the Son and of the Holy Spirit, one God. An introduction to this Chronicle with an enumeration of its one hundred and twenty-two chapters. These accounts of the primitive events which are past and gone (the author) has put together from the chronicles of primitive generations: i. e. (the events) from Adam to Tîw (= Dido) who reigned over the Greeks and over Africa, and from the time of Rômânôs (? = Remus) and Romulus, who reigned over Rome, of happy memory, to the end of the reign of the holy Constantine, first Christian emperor of Rome; from the accession of the sons of the great Christian emperor, the Godfearing Constantine, to the end of the Godloving emperor Jovian; and from the accession of Andejâs (? Valentinian) to the end of Theodosius, the great and blessed emperor; and from the time of Arcadius and Honorius, the sons of the Godloving emperor Theodosius, to the end of the blessed emperor Anastasius; and from the days of the emperor Justin to the days of the reign of Heraclius (even) to its end; and from the time of Theodore, chief prefect of the province of Egypt, to John, monk of the convent of Sinai, who believed in the faith of the Chalcedonians. And furthermore these accounts were put together in (their) completeness by John the ascetic and Maddabbar,[1] which is by interpretation, administrator, who was bishop of the town of Nakijus in Egypt, which is called Absai. And these he has put together from more extended histories, and these are (in)

---

[1] The text reads 'the Madabbar and Ascetic'. The meaning of Mastagaddal is doubtful here: it = ἀθλητής in its literal sense, and next in its metaphorical one.

chapters to the number of one hundred and twenty-two, which is
(thus) a chronography beginning with the generation of primitive
men.

CHAPTER I. Concerning the names of Adam and Eve and their
children and all creatures.

CHAPTER II. Concerning the names of the stars and of the sun
and of the moon and the things that are found in the books of
the Hebrews.

CHAPTER III. Concerning those who first began to make ships [1]
and went upon the sea.

CHAPTER IV. Concerning those who engraved astrolabes from
first to last.

CHAPTER V. Concerning the beginning of the building of
Babylon, and those who worship the image of the horse as a god,
and the beginning of the chase and the eating of animal food.

CHAPTER VI. Concerning those who first eat human flesh, and
him who first slew his sons, and likewise him who slew his father.

CHAPTER VII. Concerning him who first took his sister and
made her (his) wife.

CHAPTER VIII. Concerning him who founded the city of Nineveh
and who first took his mother and made her (his) wife.

CHAPTER IX. Concerning him who first wrought gold and
brought (it) from mines.

CHAPTER X. Concerning him who first made weapons of war.

CHAPTER XI. Concerning him who first made a furnace and who
married two women.

CHAPTER XII. Concerning him who built a city named the City
of the Sun.

CHAPTER XIII. Concerning him who built two cities, Abusir,
the one in upper Egypt, the other in northern Egypt.

CHAPTER XIV. Concerning him who built the city of Samnûd and
Elbarâbî, which is the house of idols.

CHAPTER XV. Concerning the Greeks, who were the first to
proclaim the glory of the coequal Trinity.

CHAPTER XVI. Concerning those who first made a plough in the
provinces of Egypt, and in what condition Egypt was at the first.

CHAPTER XVII. Concerning him who first levied taxes on the
country of Egypt and measured the land with a reed and made

---

[1] I have necessarily changed the order of the text here.

the inhabitants give (a return) to the king. And who it was that dug channels in the land for the water to flow in and the canal named Dîk.

CHAPTER XVIII. Concerning him who made the waters to disappear and drained the marshes of Egypt, so that they could build cities and villages thereon and plant plantations.

CHAPTER XIX. Concerning those who built three temples (? pyramids) in the city of Memphis.

CHAPTER XX. Concerning him who first made dyes for garments.

CHAPTER XXI. Concerning him who made beautiful statues and worshipped them. And concerning him who founded the cities of Iconium and Tarsus. And who named Assyria Persia, and who planted trees in Egypt, and who was the first to worship the sun and the moon and fire and water.

CHAPTER XXII. Concerning him who worshipped the moon only and built an altar to her as a goddess.

CHAPTER XXIII. Concerning him who named Libya. And who built Tyre and who named Canaan, and Syria and Cilicia.

CHAPTER XXIV. Concerning him who named the cities of Europe and built the city of Gortyna.

CHAPTER XXV. Concerning him who first put beams of wood to the feet of men.

CHAPTER XXVI. Concerning him who first built an altar to idols and worshipped them.

CHAPTER XXVII. Concerning Melchizedek the priest, the nature of his descent : and concerning those who built Sidon and Sion, which is called Salem ; and the naming of the Jews, that is, the Hebrews.

CHAPTER XXVIII. Concerning those who first invented the letters of the Greeks and the teaching of the writing of letters.

CHAPTER XXIX. Concerning the deluge in Attica,[1] and the cause of the long continuance (of the waters) upon it and of its becoming a desert.

CHAPTER XXX. Concerning the condition (?) of Pharaoh before Moses and his destruction with his own in the depths of the Red Sea.

CHAPTER XXXI. Concerning him who changed the name of the

---

[1] Text reads ደስ: ; corrupt for እንደስ:

town of Absâi and named it Nakijus, and the cause owing to which the river changed its course from the east and came to be on the west of the city according to the commandment of God.

CHAPTER XXXII. Concerning the building of Jerusalem, and the alteration of its name into Nâblôs, and concerning the house of God which was built in it.

CHAPTER XXXIII. He who first pursued a handicraft among the ancients.

CHAPTER XXXIV. Concerning him who was the first to find an inscription and communicate it to men : and concerning him who found the teaching and who interpreted the verses which were written on the table of stone.

CHAPTER XXXV. Concerning him who established the law of marriage, that men should take to wife young virgins and call them spouses : and concerning him who was the first to institute the (common) meal.

CHAPTER XXXVI. Concerning him who first among the Greeks believed in the Holy Trinity as coequal in one Godhead.

CHAPTER XXXVII. Concerning those who first practised medicine in the world.

CHAPTER XXXVIII. Concerning him who first built a bath in the world.

CHAPTER XXXIX. Concerning him who first played on the flute and like instruments such as the horn and the trumpet.

CHAPTER XL. Concerning the building of Cyzicum and the cause which led the spirits to confess the unity of the Holy Trinity and announce to all men that God should be born of a virgin.

CHAPTER XLI. Concerning him who established the sanctuary of Sosthenium and the building of a church by the command of the Godloving emperor Constantine.

CHAPTER XLII. Concerning the nails (of the cross) of our Lord Jesus Christ and the victory which the kings won by their means.

CHAPTER XLIII. Concerning him who gave their names to the two provinces Achaia and Laconia.

CHAPTER XLIV. Concerning him who named the Peloponnesus [1] and built in it a city called Peloponnesus.[2]

CHAPTER XLV. Concerning him who built Farmâ and Bûlkînûn.

---

[1] The Ethiopic is hopelessly corrupt here ; = island of Lûnânjâ.
[2] Ethiopic = Lûbânîjûn.

CHAPTER XLVI. Concerning him who first taught playing on instruments of music.

CHAPTER XLVII. Concerning him who named the island of Ephesus which is in Asia; formerly it was named Saqâlbah, but they changed its name and called it Iconia (*sic*).

CHAPTER XLVIII. Concerning him who built the city which is named Bûlmîz (= Palmyra), for[1] in its neighbourhood David conquered the Philistine.

CHAPTER XLIX. Concerning the cause of Nebuchadnezzar's conquest of the city of Tyre, which is an island.

CHAPTER L. Concerning the Ark of God and the tables and Aaron's rod which budded and the measure of manna and the fragment of hard rocks, and concerning him who hid them from men.

CHAPTER LI. Concerning the kingdom of King Cyrus and his sending back the captive children of Israel; and how Cambyses forbade them to build the temple and Yasîd the Commander of the Egyptian forces provoked Cambyses and Cambyses[2] slew the Egyptian officers and took away captives, which he had taken from Egypt, to his own country, and (how) the Egyptians returned a second time to their own land, and (how) after forty and one years Alexander of Macedon, called the conqueror of the world, became king.

CHAPTER LII. Concerning the building of the city named Lavinia.[3]

CHAPTER LIII. Concerning him who was the first to build a house and call it a palace.

CHAPTER LIV. Concerning him who built the city named Alba.[4]

CHAPTER LV. Concerning him who built Carthage.

CHAPTER LVI. Concerning him who built Rome and the reason they were named Romans: and concerning the origin of the formulas in demanding and decreeing, and the circuit of the courts,[5] and how the army went to battle on horseback: and concerning the establishment of a place of combat for women, and the administrative decrees for the army and concerning those who are sent and those

[1] Or, 'indeed'.

[2] Transposed to this clause: it wrongly occurs in the clause, 'which he had taken from Egypt'.

[3] Text = Lûnjâ.

[4] Text = Helvîn (A, Helvân B).

[5] So MSS. But I emend ዑደት፡ into ዐጸዱ፡ as in Chap. LVI, and translate 'and the courts'.

who minister to them; and the reason on account of which our Fathers the monks of Egypt celebrated the Eucharist on the first day of every month.

CHAPTER LVII. Concerning him who invented, as it appears, stamped money, which gave rise to selling and buying. And concerning the institution of prefects, magistrates, and judges.

CHAPTER LVIII. Concerning him who built the city of Thessalonica.

CHAPTER LIX. Concerning him who built the cities of Alexandria and Chrysopolis of Byzantium, i.e. Alexander. How he conquered Darius and took his daughter captive: and how queen Candace took Alexander prisoner when he came to her with spies (even) the messengers whom he had sent to her: and how he made her his wife.

CHAPTER LX. Concerning the epoch when the Scriptures inspired by God were translated, and how many translations there were.

CHAPTER LXI. Concerning him who built Antigonia, and Antioch, and Laodicea and Apamea, cities of renown.

CHAPTER LXII. Concerning him who first wrote chronicles and named them.

CHAPTER LXIII. Concerning him who persecuted the Maccabean saints.

CHAPTER LXIV. Concerning the birth of Julius Caesar, King of Rome: and the reign of Cleopatra, and the building of a great Church named Caesarion in the city of Alexandria.

CHAPTER LXV (LXVI). Concerning him who built Caesarea in Palestine.

CHAPTER LXVI (LXVII). Concerning him who built the Pharos of Alexandria and made a channel through the land in order to conduct the canal of Kariûn, which is by interpretation 'ditch', so that the water came from the great river Gihon to the great city Alexandria. And concerning the passage of the water to the skilfully constructed and deep reservoir. And at what time our Lord Jesus Christ was born in the flesh. And why the Romans made their months to begin with the sixth month of the year.

CHAPTER LXVII (LXVIII). Concerning him who fixed one of the 'changes'[1] on the sixth day of the month Ter. And how Ezra, the holy man, was unjustly rejected.

---

[1] Text reads አምርታት፥, which I emend into አምርያታት፥ See Dillmann, Lex. 169.

CHAPTER LXVIII (LXIX). Concerning the reign of the Emperor in which our Lord Jesus Christ was crucified : and concerning him who built the city Tiberias.

CHAPTER LXIX (LXX). Concerning that which befell the Emperor Nero and his bitter death.

CHAPTER LXX (LXXI). Concerning the Emperor Domitian and how he sent St. John the Evangelist twice into exile, and concerning his (St. John's) death : and how he built Domitianopolis, and concerning the grievous death of Domitian, and the abolition of (gladiatorial) combats and the smiting of men.

CHAPTER LXXI (LXXII). Concerning the death of Ignatius, clothed (?) with God and the women who became martyrs with him : and the building of a fortress in the Egyptian Babylon. And concerning him who named it Babylon and him who made the channel for the canal called by the name of Trajan which terminates in the Red Sea, and concerning ⟨him who built⟩ the fortress in Manûf.

CHAPTER LXXII (LXXIII). Concerning him who built Antinoê in the province of Rîf.

CHAPTER LXXIII (LXXIV). Concerning him who established the decree as to fathers that they should make wills in favour of their children : and the construction of two gates in the city of Alexandria in its east and west.

CHAPTER LXXIV (LXXV). Concerning him who introduced lions into Egypt and Palestine.

CHAPTER LXXV (LXXVI). Concerning him who founded the usage of writing accounts and pledges that a man might be made secure.

CHAPTER LXXVI (LXXVII). Concerning the reign of Diocletian the Egyptian and how he lost his reason and was exiled : and which of his sons wrought the evil. And concerning the pestilence which God brought on the idolaters till there were none to bury them. And concerning the reign of the Godloving Constantine and the achievement of the works which he wrought and the magnificence of the churches [1] in his days. And concerning him who was the first to make a qanâtra [2], i. e. a bridge. And concerning the finding of

---

[1] Zotenberg has rightly restored **ቤተ፡** here.

[2] A transliteration of an Arabic word ; while the word rendered 'bridge', **ድልድል፡** is Amharic, though wrongly vocalized.

the cross. And concerning the building of Constantinople and its designation by this name, being called aforetime Byzantium. And concerning the faith of Gelasinus (which was produced) by a wonder which he saw, i.e. the holy baptism, and his marvellous death: and in what way the Indians came to know our Lord Jesus Christ, one God. For the holy Athanasius, the apostolic, was the first to ordain for them a bishop of India and of Yemen. And (how) there had been visible to Constantine all the days of his life an angel of God who awaked him for prayer.

CHAPTER LXXVII (LXXVIII). Concerning the building of a qantarâh (sic), i.e. a bridge on the river named Pyramus: and the disaster at Nicaea, and the appearance of the holy cross at midday on Golgotha in the place where our Lord was crucified. And the tribulations which the holy Athanasius, the apostolic, had to endure at the hands of the Arians. And the exile of Liberius and the holy bishops who were with him through the evil devices of the Arians. And moreover concerning the emperor Julian, the apostate: and how he forsook the orders of the Church and became the general of the army until he acceded to the throne in the place of Gallus his brother: and how he persecuted the holy Athanasius, in order to slay him at the instigation of the heathen. And how Alexandria was deemed worthy to receive the body of St. John the Baptist, that it might dwell there and a magnificent building might be constructed for it by the command of the patriarch Theophilus.

CHAPTER LXXVIII (LXXIX). Through whom it is we know the city and family[1] of Theophilus, the patriarch of Alexandria and the place of the birth of Cyril, his sister's son.

CHAPTER LXXIX (LXXX). Concerning the consummation of the death of the holy martyr Domecius: and the vengeance which God brought upon Julian, the apostate, and how God punished him by the hand of the holy martyr Mercurius and how he died by an evil death.

CHAPTER LXXX (LXXXI). Concerning the reign of Jovian and how the Church became glorious: and how the holy Athanasius returned to his throne with great honour: and the Church everywhere was conspicuously in the orthodox faith.

CHAPTER LXXXI (LXXXII). Concerning the reign of Sallustius (? Valentinian) and his hatred of iniquity and his just and equitable

---

[1] The Ethiopic is very irregular here.

judgement : and his construction of stone gates, i. e. the Heracleotis, the gates of the great river of Egypt which he had caused to be made with excessive labour. And how the ocean tide rose to Alexandria to such a height that it would have submerged [1] the city had not the holy Athanasius the patriarch checked it by his prayers.

CHAPTER LXXXII (LXXXIII). Concerning the reign of the Godloving Theodosius the elder : and the address which he pronounced before Amphilochius bishop of Iconium on the unity of the Holy Trinity. And concerning the Council which the emperor convoked in Constantinople : concerning the strengthening of the Churches. And concerning Timothy, patriarch of Alexandria, who admonished Gregory bishop of Nazianzum [2] to leave the city of the emperor Constantine and go to his own city and nominated a man named Maximus patriarch of Constantinople. And further concerning the building of the church of Theodosius at Alexandria and the church of the holy martyrs Cosmas and Damian and the martyrs their brethren. And concerning the burning by fire of the city of Antioch by the command of the emperor : and the reproof which was sent to him by the holy monk of the desert of Asqêto on this matter and the grief of the emperor regarding it. And further concerning the wine-merchants and the brothels which were suppressed in his days : and the splendour of his reign in all places.

CHAPTER LXXXIII (LXXXIV). Concerning the accession of the emperors Arcadius and Honorius : and Arcadius was over Constantinople and Honorius over Rome. And concerning Arcadius' love of God and the devotion of Honorius. And concerning the revolt which Alaric raised in the city of Rome. And how the sister of the emperor Honorius was taken prisoner by him. And the plundering of all the treasures of the palace. And further how Honorius quitted Rome and went to Constantinople and became the colleague of the emperor Theodosius the younger, the son of his brother Arcadius, till the day of his death. And further concerning the empress Eudocia, the consort of the emperor Theodosius the younger—her family, and how the emperor made an alliance

---

[1] Here we must emend ኢየሥግም፡ (B) into የስግም፡

[2] The Ethiopic ብርየሱስ፡ is owing to a faulty transcription of the Arabic, as Zotenberg points out.

with her and took her to wife. And at what time they inscribed the name of St. John Chrysostom in the diptychs, after he had gone to our Lord. And concerning the anathema of Nestorius and the victory of Cyril. And further concerning a heathen woman of Alexandria and the tumults which she caused between the Jews and Christians in Alexandria. And how the holy Cyril took the Synagogue of the Jews and made it a church in consequence of his controversy with the Jews. And how they dragged the heathen woman through the streets till she died. And how they burned her body with fire by the command of the patriarch, Abba Cyril.

Chapter LXXXIV (LXXXV). Concerning the massacre made by the Jews in Qîmîtrâ: concerning the mockery they practised against the cross of our Lord Jesus Christ, when in mockery they crucified a young infant and put it to death.

Chapter LXXXV (LXXXVI). Concerning Fînkeser the Jew who presented himself to the Jews saying, I am Moses the chief of the prophets.

Chapter LXXXVI (LXXXVII). Concerning the apple which they brought as a present to the emperor Theodosius and the appointment of his sister Pulcheria: and the darkness which prevailed over all the earth from morning to evening on the day that Marcian the schismatic became emperor.

Chapter LXXXVII (LXXXVIII). Concerning the occasion when the heaven rained dîran, i. e. the lightnings on Constantinople, and the fire flamed from sea to sea: and the conversion of the heathen philosopher Isocasius to the orthodox faith. And from what place came the patriarch Timotheus. And concerning the terrible pestilence which prevailed in Constantinople: and the fall of the mountain in Syria and the apostasy of Basiliscus after the manner of the Chalcedonians for corruptible goods. And concerning the reign of the emperor Zenon over the imperial city of Constantinople, and the banishment of Basiliscus for life, and the death which was inflicted on the judges because of their negligence in the administration of justice. And concerning the reign of Zenon and his command that the letter should be read in every place. And concerning Verina his mother-in-law and her warring against him till death overtook her and her adherents.

Chapter LXXXVIII (LXXXIX). Concerning the reign of Godloving Anastasius in consequence of the prophecy of Abbâ

Jeremiah, an anchorite of the convent of Manûf: and the building of the stone gates of Elmûwrad and a trench in order to make a great bridge which should start from Babylon and terminate with the river. And concerning the naming of Philaletes, and the victory of the great patriarch Severus, and the banishment of Macedonius and the abrogation of the Chalcedonian Council.

CHAPTER LXXXIX (XC). Concerning the banishment of the holy Severus from his throne in Antioch through the instrumentality of heretics, and the prayer which he made to God on behalf of the inhabitants of Constantinople regarding the evil that the emperor Justin had wrought, and the admonition which he heard from God. And concerning the fire which raged in Antioch and in the cities of the East: and the destruction of many oratories of the Martyrs, and all kinds of marvels which befell. And concerning the baptism of the people of the Arians (?) and the kings of India and the Elmarîts, that is, the Nubians. And of what religion they had been formerly. And concerning the earthquake in Egypt: and the Huns [1] (?) without the city. And the Indians, that is the Elmâkûrîds, were formerly Jews.

CHAPTER XC (XCI). Concerning the manifestation of the towel and mandîl of our Lord Jesus Christ: they were found in the house of a Jew who lived in Alexandria.

CHAPTER XCI (XCII). Concerning the reason of us Christians being named after the name of Theodosius, and the appearance of the Athenâwjân and their doctrine. And concerning that which the chief officials published in the market-places that there should be a memorial with them till all who wished might take.

CHAPTER XCII (XCIII). Concerning the primitive building of the city of Rome.

CHAPTER XCIII (XCIV). The tumults which took place in the city of Constantinople concerning the holy body of our Lord and Saviour Jesus Christ.

CHAPTER XCIV (XCV). Regarding Aristomachus the son of Theodosius of the city of Absâi and the accusation which they brought against him ⟨before⟩ the emperor, so that he was put in bonds. And how Chosroes the King of the Persians believed and became a Christian.

CHAPTER XCV (XCVI). Concerning Galandûh, a woman of

---

[1] Text wholly corrupt. I have adopted Zotenberg's suggestion.

patrician rank—the name of a dignity—and the vision which she clearly saw in prison during her exile.

---

[1] Lit. 'cisterns' (or, 'wells') 'of the sepulchres'.
[2] Text quite corrupt = Anlejâ.

CHAPTER CVII (CVIII). Concerning Theophilus the Stylite and his prophecy to Nicetas [1]: 'Thou wilt conquer him and the kingdom of Phocas will speedily be destroyed and then Heraclius will reign.'

CHAPTER CVIII (CIX). Concerning the bridge which was in the city of Dafâsher near the church of St. Mînâs.

CHAPTER CIX (CX). Concerning the death of Phocas and the dispersion of the treasures of the palace: and the chastisement which Heraclius inflicted on Phocas because of the outrage he had done to his wife and daughter.

CHAPTER CX (CXI). Concerning the appearance of the Moslem on the confines of Fîjûm and the defeat of the Romans who dwelt there.

CHAPTER CXI (CXII). Concerning the first encounter of 'Amar with the Romans at the city of 'Awn (i. e. Heliopolis).

CHAPTER CXII (CXIII). How all the Jews assembled in the city of Manûf owing to their fear of the Moslem, the cruelties of 'Amar and the seizure of their possessions till (at last) they left the gates of Misr open and fled to Alexandria. And how wicked men multiplied in the beginning of wickedness and began to help ('Amar) to destroy the people of Egypt.

CHAPTER CXIII (CXIV). How the people of Samnûd so flouted 'Amar as to refuse to receive him: and concerning the return of Kalâdî to the Romans: and how they seized his mother and his wife—now he had hidden them in Alexandria—because he had joined and helped the Moslem.

CHAPTER CXIV (CXV). How the Moslem took Misr in the fourteenth year of the cycle and made the fortress of Babylon open its gates in the fifteenth year.

CHAPTER CXV (CXVI). Concerning the death of the emperor Heraclius and the return of Cyrus the Patriarch from exile and his departure for Mesr to pay tribute to the Moslem.

CHAPTER CXVI (CXVII). How God gave the Romans into the hands of the Moslem and rejected them because of their incredulity and their divisions and the persecution which they had brought on the Christians of Egypt.

CHAPTER CXVII (CXVIII). How 'Amar got possession of

---

[1] Text (= Yeftaṭâs) corrupt owing to a faulty transcription of a faulty Arabic form.

Absâdî, that is, Niqîjûs: and (concerning) the flight of the general Domitian and the destruction of his army in the river, and the great massacre which took place in the city of Absâdî, and in all the remaining cities—till 'Amar came to the island of Sawnâ— which were under the sway of Absâi and its island on the eighteenth day of the month Genbôt, in the fifteenth year of the cycle.

CHAPTER CXVIII. How the Moslem got possession of Caesarea in Palestine and the trials that overtook it.

CHAPTER CXIX. Concerning the great earthquake and the loss of life in Crete both in their island and in all their cities round about.

CHAPTER CXX. Concerning Cyrus the Patriarch of the Chalce-donians—the same who went to Babylon and to 'Amar the chief of the Moslem and took the tribute in a vessel and paid it into his hands. And further how 'Amar increased the taxes of the Egyptians: and concerning the death of Cyrus the Chalcedonian after he had repented of having delivered the city of Alexandria into the hands of the Moslem.

CHAPTER CXXI. Concerning the return of Abbâ Benjamin the patriarch of Egypt from his exile in the city of Rîf (where he had been) fourteen years, and of these (he had been there) ten years because the Roman emperors had exiled him, and four under the dominion of the Moslem. And concerning the remaining history with the conclusion of the work.

CHAPTER CXXII. A second epilogue concluding this history.

IN THE NAME OF GOD MERCIFUL AND GRACIOUS

The holy father,[1] John bishop of Nikiu,[2] who put this work together, said: 'O thou that hast loved toil till thou hast acquired the love of goodness, till the love of toil, which is pain,[3] giveth increase to all the good qualities which every zealous man covets, and for the sake of all the good qualities which constitute the eternal wisdom belonging to the Omnipotent and Lord of all; for He hath reserved it for those who come after them, that they may accomplish what they have chosen.' For this task, moreover, I am wanting in eloquence beyond [4] all authors and feeble in discourse, though with many a testing I have tested the chosen portions. We will begin to compose this work from many ancient books, which deal with the (various) periods and the historical events, which we have witnessed also in the times to which we have come. And I have been honest (in this work) in order to recount and leave a noble memorial to the lovers of virtue in this present life. And we have left this narrative which is written in good order and in an exalted translation. Yea it is exalted beyond everything that has been by the interpretation of the translator, so that those who find it may not be without past and present gain, without portion or inheritance.

CHAPTER I. We will begin with the first beings that were created; for it is written concerning Adam and Eve, that it was God who named them, but as for his children and all created things it was Adam that named them all.

---

[1] Zotenberg does not attempt to translate this introduction, owing to certain obscurities and phrases the sense of which 'escapes' him 'completely'. I have only found it necessary to make one or two slight changes.

[2] This city was called Pshati by the Egyptians. Champollion (II. 164) identifies it with the ancient Prosopis. Next Pshati appeared in Arabic as Abshadi. This form is reproduced, somewhat slightly changed, as Absâi or Absâdi in our text. In Greek the form was Νικίου. Bury calls my attention to Strabo, xvii. 1. 14 Νικίου κώμη : Oxyrhynchus Papyri, ix, no. 1219, p. 262 εἰς τὴν Νεικίου (third cent. A.D.) : Hierocles, *Synecdemus* (ed. Burckhardt, p. 44), Νικίου (sixth cent. A.D.). In the *Itinerarium Antonini* 155 it appears as Nikiu (or Nicia or Nicium). In Arabic it was spelt Naqius or Niqius. For details on this important city see Champollion, *L'Égypte sous les Pharaons*, ii. 162–71 ; Quatremère, *Sur l'Égypte*, i. 423–30.

[3] I have omitted ወይእቲ:

[4] Text reads ማእከሳ: ፡ኵሎመ:, corrupt for እምኵሎመ: This idiom recurs eight lines later.

CHAPTER II. 1. And Seth, the son of Adam, who received wisdom from God, named five planets [1]: the first Cronus; the second Zeus; the third Ares; the fourth Aphrodite; the fifth Hermes. 2. And on a different ground he named the sun and the moon. And the number of the planets was seven. 3. And, moreover, he was the first to write letters in the language of the Hebrews; for he had received wisdom from God: and he composed history in it in the times of the giants. And, moreover, he said that Ovid a wise man of the heathen and Plutarch wrote about them after the deluge.[2]

CHAPTER III. The sons of Noah were great and strong, (and) they began to build ships [3] and to go upon the sea.

CHAPTER IV. 1. It is told regarding Cainan,[4] the son of Arphaxad, who was sprung from Shem, the son of Noah, that he was a wise man and a shepherd. 2. He was the first to compose †astrolabes† (read 'astronomy') after the deluge.

CHAPTER V. 1. And after him the Indians composed (it),[5] and there was a man from India, named Qantûrjûs,[6] an Ethiopian of the

---

[1] Cf. John of Antioch (Müller, *Fragmenta Historicorum Graec.* iv. 540): ὁ δὲ υἱὸς Σὴθ εἶχε σοφίαν ἀπὸ θεοῦ, καὶ ... ἔθηκεν ὀνόματα ... τοῖς πέντε πλανήταις ... καὶ τὸν πρῶτον πλανήτην ἐκάλεσε Κρόνον, τὸν (β′) Ζῆνα, τὸν γ′ Ἄρεα, τὸν δ′ Ἀφροδίτην, τὸν ε′ Ἑρμῆν· τοὺς δὲ β′ φωστῆρας τοὺς μεγάλους αὐτὸς ὁ θεὸς ἐκάλεσεν. Ὁ αὐτὸς δὲ Σὴθ εὖρε ... τὰ Ἑβραϊκὰ γράμματα. Cf. also Cramer, *Anec. Graec. Paris.* ii. 242 : *Kronos ... Zeus*, &c. These words are represented in the text by Zûḥal, Mashtarî, Marik, Zehrâ, 'Aṭard, which are Ethiopic transliterations of the Arabic names of these planets : زحل, مشتري, مريخ, زهرة, عطارد.

[2] *And he composed ... deluge.* Though Zotenberg abandons the attempt of translating these words as he fails to understand them, he very unwisely emends the text and wrongly. My translation follows the manuscripts and not the text here. አዊ.ደየስ: (so AB: wrongly emended in text) here is clearly = ᾽Οβίδιος and ብሉ.ደኅስ: = Πλούταρχος. Thus our text agrees closely with John of Antioch, *loc. cit.* : Οὕτω τὴν ἱστορίαν συνεγράψατο ᾽Οβίδιος, ἀληθέστερον δὲ εἶπεν ὁ Χαιρωνεὺς Πλούταρχος. After the word 'Plutarch' in the text the word ጸዐስ: (='weakened') occurs. This I have omitted in the translation. We are to follow B here, and read ደሐይሰው:, and not to follow A as in the text.

[3] *Began to build ships.* Cf. John of Antioch, iv. 541 πρῶτοι ἐποίησαν πλοῖα.

[4] *Cainan, &c.* Cf. John of Antioch, iv. 541 ; Syncellus, i. 150. For 'astrolabes' in the text we should read 'astronomy', as Zotenberg has already pointed out. Cf. John of Antioch's statement: Καϊνάν, ὅστις μετὰ τὸν κατακλυσμὸν συνεγράψατο τὴν ἀστρονομίαν.

[5] *And after ... composed it.* These words, which appear at the close of IV, I have placed here.

[6] *Qantûrjûs*, i.e. Gandubarius or Andubarius. Cf. Cramer, *op. cit.* ii. 234 ἐν δὲ τοῖς ἀνωτέρω χρόνοις ... ἀνεφύει τις Ἰνδὸς σοφὸς ἀνὴρ ἀστρονόμος, ὀνόματι Γανδουβάριος, ὅστις συνεγράψατο πρῶτος ἀστρονομίαν Ἰνδοῖς: also *Chron. Pasch.* 36, where

race of Ham, who was named Cush. 2. He begat Afrûd, i. e. Nimrod, the giant. He it was that built the city of Babylon. 3. And the Persians served him and worshipped him as a god, and named him after the name of the stars of heaven and called him Orion,[1] that is, Dabarâh. 4. And he was the first to hunt[2] and eat the flesh of animals.

CHAPTER VI. 1. Cronus, moreover, was a giant of the race of Shem,[3] the firstborn of Noah, who was thus named after the name of the first planet, which is Cronus. 2. †And his son, named Domjos,† [4] was a warrior, a redoubtable man and a slayer (of men). 3. He was the first to rule over Persia and Assyria : and he married an Assyrian woman, named Rhea, and she bare him two sons, Picus whom they named Zeus,[5] and Ninus, who built a royal city in Assyria, i. e. Nineveh. 4. And Cronus left his son in his kingdom and went to the west and ruled over the people (there) as they had no king. 5. And Picus his son, who was named Zeus, rebelled against Cronus his father and slew him, because he had devoured his children.

CHAPTER VII. 1. And he made pregnant the daughter of †Nîks† his mother, who was named Rhea. And Picus, moreover, that is,

---

the name is Ἀνδουβάριος. Ἀνήρ τις Ἰνδὸς ἀνεφάνη σοφὸς ἀστρονόμος, ὀνόματι Ἀνδου-βάριος, ὃς καὶ συνεγράψατο πρῶτος Ἰνδοῖς ἀστρονομίαν. Ἐγεννήθη δὲ καὶ ἄλλος ἐκ τῆς φυλῆς τοῦ Σήμ, Χοῦς ὀνόματι, ὁ Αἰθίοψ, ὅστις ἐγέννησεν τὸν Νεβρώδ. Andubarius and Cush are distinct persons, but have been fused together in the present work.

[1] *Called him Orion.* So John of Antioch, iv. 541 ; *Chron. Pasch.* 36. *Dabarâh* is an Ethiopic transcription of the Arabic word for Orion.

[2] *First to hunt, &c.* Cf. *Chron. Pasch.* 36 ; John of Ant. iv. 541.

[3] *Shem.* The manuscripts read ' Ham ', but the fact that the person spoken of is defined by the subsequent words ' the firstborn of Noah ', and that all the Greek chronographers, so far as I can discover, describe Cronus as a descendant of Shem, shows that the text is corrupt. The corruption, too, is clearly native to our text. Thus ሴም፥ was corrupted into ካም፥

[4] †*His son, named Domjos*†. As Domjòs was the father (?) of Cronus, the text is corrupt ; for even a few lines later the son of Cronus is Picus, and not Domnus (Δόμνος). Hence ወልዱ፥ ዘስሙ፥ may be a corruption of ስሙ፥ ወአቡሁ፥ = ' His father's name was Domnus '. The remaining words of this sentence would then belong to Cronus. In Cramer, *op. cit.*, iv. 234, Cronus and Domnus are identified according to the present text : ἀνεφάνη ἄνθρωπος . . . ὀνόματι Κρόνος, ἐπικληθεὶς ὑπὸ τοῦ ἰδίου πατρὸς Δόμνος.

[5] *Zeus.* In manuscripts ርእዪ፥, which is due to faulty transcription of the Arabic زُواس, as Zotenberg has shown. For the still stranger Ethiopic trans-literations of this name in the next ten lines I have accepted his explanation also.

Zeus, was the first to take his sister to wife. 2. And he begat by her a son named Belus, who resembled his grandfather Cronus. 3. And this Belus ruled in Assyria after the disappearance[1] of his father and his grandfather Cronus. 4. And him also after his death the Persians worshipped with the gods.

Chapter VIII. 1. And after the death of Belus, Ninus his father's brother reigned over Assyria. 2. He married Semiramis his mother and made her his wife, and established this impure custom and transmitted it to his successors: and they are † designated by this evil name †[2] till the present day. 3. This conduct does not create a scandal amongst the Persians; for they take to wife their mothers and sisters and daughters.

Chapter IX. 1. After the death of Picus, Faunus, called Hermes, ruled in the west for thirty-five years. 2. And he became a silversmith. He was the first to begin to work in gold[3] in the west, and to smelt it. 3. And when he learnt that his brothers were envious of him and wished to slay him, he became afraid and fled to Egypt, taking with him a great quantity of gold. 4. And he dwelt in Egypt and clothed himself in a beautiful robe of gold. 5. And furthermore he became a diviner, for he declared everything before it came to pass, and he gave to people money in abundance and he gave gifts in abundance to the people of Egypt. 6. And for this reason they received him with honour and called him 'the Lord of gold'. And he was honoured by them as a god. And the poor worshipped him.

Chapter X. 1. And there was a man named Hephaestus. He ruled over Egypt: and they made him a god. And he was warlike and full of fury.[4] 2. And men believed that he investigated hidden things and received weapons of war from the non-existent;[5]

[1] Text reads 'appearance': we must, therefore, add ኢ. before ረእየ፡ Cf. *Chron. Pasch.* 36 ἀφανὴς ἐκ τῆς Συρίας γενόμενος.

[2] Corrupt.

[3] *He was the first to begin to work in gold.* The other chronographers give the sense differently, and no doubt rightly. John of Antioch, *op. cit.*, iv. 542 ἐφεῦρε τὸ μέταλλον τὸ χρυσοῦν ἐν τῇ δύσει πρῶτος, καὶ τὸ χωνεύειν: *Chron. Pasch.* 44.

[4] *Warlike and full of fury.* Cf. John of Antioch, *op. cit.*, iv. 543 πολεμιστὴς καὶ μυστικός (μαντικός in Cramer, *op. cit.*, iv. 237).

[5] *He investigated hidden things and received weapons of war from the non-existent.* The original sense is, no doubt, that given in the *Chron. Pasch.* 45 ἀπὸ μυστικῆς τινος εὐχῆς τὴν ὀξυλάβην ἐδέξατο ἐκ τοῦ ἀέρος εἰς τὸ κατασκευάζειν ἐκ σιδήρου ὅπλα. Similarly John of Antioch.

for he was an ironsmith and was the first to make weapons of war
to fight with in time of war and stones wherewith men contended.[1]
3. Now he was lame; (for) when going to war he fell from (his)
horse and was injured and was lame all his days.

CHAPTER XI. 1. And Methuselah begat Lamech, and Lamech
married two wives. The name of the one was Ada and the
name of the other was Zillah. 2. And Ada bare Qâbêl and after
some time she bare Tôbêl who wielded the hammer in working
brass and iron. 3. And Tôbêl the son of Lamech was a brass and
iron smith before the deluge; for he had received wisdom from
God—Praise be to Him.

CHAPTER XII. 1. And after Hephaestus, who was named the Sun,
there reigned in Egypt his son who was named the Sun after his
father's name. 2. It was he who built the city of the Sun after
his own name, and in it there were temples of the supreme gods
and likewise the bodies of kings.

CHAPTER XIII. 1. And there was a man named Maṭûnâvîs who
succeeded Aiqâsbêrâ which name is by interpretation Dionysus.[2]
2. He built a city in upper Egypt, named Busir, and another Busir
in the north of Egypt.

CHAPTER XIV. Osiris, which is by interpretation Apollo, being
so named by the Greeks, built the city of Samnûd and (in it)
a temple of the supreme gods. And this is the city which is called
Bab'êl Fêgôr.

CHAPTER XV. 1. In the writings of the Egyptian sages 'Abrâṭûs [3]
is mentioned . . . at that time, (i. e.) he who was Hermes, a man of
extraordinary judgement, through whom they declared among the

---

[1] *In time of war . . . contended.* This clause is corrupt. The original sense is
that of John of Antioch : πρὸ γὰρ αὐτοῦ ῥοπάλοις καὶ λίθοις ἐπολέμουν. So also
Chron. Pasch., and Cramer, *op. cit.*

[2] Zotenberg conjectures that this chapter is an inaccurate resumé of a passage
in Diodorus Siculus (i. 17, 18) reproduced in Eusebius (*Praef. Evang.* ii. 1),
containing an Egyptian myth to the effect that Osiris, whom some identified
with Dionysus (καὶ τὸν μὲν Ὄσιριν εἶναι τὸν Διόνυσον), had, in his journeyings
through the world with his brother Apollo and his sons Anubis and Macedo
(i. e. the corrupt Maṭûnâvîs in our text), given the government of Phoenicia to
Busirus and that of Ethiopia and Libya to Antaeus.

[3] *'Abrâṭûs.* Who this is is difficult to determine, the word being so corrupt.
The passage in the *Chron. Pasch.* 47 runs : ἐν τοῖς χρόνοις . . . Σεσώστριος ἦν Ἑρμῆς
ὁ τρισμέγιστος, ὁ Αἰγύπτιος ἀνὴρ φοβερὸς ἐν σοφίᾳ. 'Abrâṭûs may thus be Sostris or
even a mutilated form of τρισμέγιστος. Zotenberg suggests that it is for
Herodotus.

heathen saying: 'There are three supreme powers that have created all things, (but only) one divinity.' 2. And this same Hermes, who was a great sage among the heathen, declared, saying: 'The Majesty of the holy coequal Trinity is the Giver of life and King over all things.'

CHAPTER XVI. 1. And there was a certain city that was the first to learn the use of the plough (and) the sowing of seeds and all kinds of grain. 2. It was the most elevated city in Egypt; for the land of Egypt is full of waters and lakes owing to the abundance of water in the river Gihon.

CHAPTER XVII. 1. And Sesostris, who ruled over all the land of Egypt and the adjoining countries, was the first to levy taxes and to measure the land. 2. And when he had gathered together much booty and many captives from all countries, thereupon [gathering them together] he brought them to the land of Egypt: and all the souls over whom authority was given to levy taxes he made to dig channels in the land and to fill up all the waters of Egypt with earth. 3. And owing to this measure the Egyptians were enabled to plant plantations and plough arable lands like those of Saïd, which was the first province to learn the art of ploughing. 4. And besides he commanded (the people) to pay taxes and a proportionate return of the products of the earth to the king. 5. And he dug the canal which is called Dîk unto this day.[1]

CHAPTER XVIII. 1. And after him Sabacon, king of India, reigned over the country of Egypt fifty years. 2. And he was a lover of his kind and was averse to shedding blood unjustly. And he established a law in Egypt to this effect, that no criminal should be put to death or torture; but should be permitted to live: and every criminal according to his crime he ordered to purify the earth and to collect soil together and cast it upon the morasses (lit. river or sea). 3. And when they had been long engaged in these forced labours, the waters of the river retired from the land, and (the inhabitants) made their towns higher through fear of being inundated by the waters. 4. And previously indeed in the days of Sesostris there had been inundations before that they had dug channels in the land for the river. And yet, notwithstanding all they did in casting earth into the marshes, they failed to realize their purpose because of the great quantity of water brought down

---

[1] Cf. Herod. ii. 108-9; Diodorus Siculus, i. 56-7.

by the river. 5. And Sabacon, king of India, in the vigilance of his affection had dwellings made for the people on the heights.[1]

CHAPTER XIX. 1. And there was a man named Rampsinitus,[2] the Pharaoh who reigned over Egypt. 2. He (i. e. Cheops) closed the temples of the gods and the other idols which the Egyptians worshipped: and they sacrificed to demons. And he built three temples (i. e. pyramids) in the city of Memphis and made the Egyptians worship the Sun. 3. And he paid the builders 16,000 talents of silver besides leeks and vegetables; for so it was found written in the inscriptions in the Egyptian language, which were engraved on a stone wall and made known these facts to such as read (them). 4. And he paid away all the taxes and exhausted the royal treasuries owing to the multitude of builders—and yet to no good purpose. 5. For when he fell into great poverty and want he was sore troubled: he had a daughter of beautiful form (who) was stirred up by the practices and foul seductions of Satan, and he placed her in the quarter of the debauchees: and she dwelt there in obscurity and sorrow and became a prostitute. 6. And such as wished to lie with her had to carry one of the great stones and add it to the structure. 7. And the stone so carried measured, it is said, not less than thirty feet, i. e. twenty cubits. (So they did) until they had built one of the three pyramids by means of the shameful lust of this wretched girl.

CHAPTER XX. 1. Heracles, a philosopher of the city of Tyre, discovered the art of making silk[3] and clothed himself (with it). 2. And Phoenix, king of Tyre, the Canaanite, and all the kings of all countries, as well as his successors, did likewise and so became conspicuously distinguished from the multitude. 3. Now the clothing of the ancients was of wool, but the kings and chief rulers abandoned such clothing and clad themselves in silk.

CHAPTER XXI. 1. And there was a man named Perseus.[4] He aspired to the throne of Assyria; but the sons of Ninus, the brother

---

[1] Cf. Herod. ii. 137; Diod. Sic. i. 65.

[2] Here ፈአው⁀ጓ፳ዩስ: is an internal corruption for ረአምስ፤ጦስ: i. e. ʽΡαμ-ψίνιτος, in Herod. ii. 121. The next verse, however, refers to Cheops: cf. Herod. ii. 124.

[3] The chronographers only speak of his discovery of the purple dye: cf. John Mal. 32 ʽΗρακλῆς ... ἐφεῦρε τὴν κογχύλην.

[4] Text reads Nirûs. The corruption has, as Zotenberg shows, arisen from a faulty transcription of an Arabic form which was itself corrupt.

of his father Zeus,[1] were his rivals. 2. And when he came to Qôrôntôs, there met him a young girl, walking alone. 3. And he seized her by her hair and cut off her head with (his) sword, and placed it on the shield which he had according to the magic which his father Zeus had taught him. 4. And he carried it with him in all his warlike expeditions. 5. And after he had journeyed and gone down into 'Elbâwnâ, he turned towards Assyria. And when the Lycaonians made war upon him, he took the head of the Gorgon the virgin magician and by displaying it before them vanquished them. 6. And he built the town of Iconium, which had previously been a small town named Amandra; ⟨and he called it Iconium⟩ because he had set up formerly his statue (εἰκών) near it together with the detestable Gorgon. 7. And when he came to Isauria, a city of Cilicia, and its people, moreover, warred against him, he vanquished them by the magical power residing in the head of the Gorgon. 8. And the village of Cilicia, named Andrasus, he made into a city and named it Tarsus. 9. And from Cilicia he went to the land of Assyria, and there moreover he slew Sardanapalus—now this is the name of a dignity. 10. And he disowned his claims of consanguinity and took possession of his kingdom as a spoil, and changed the name of the country, that is, Assyria, and named it Persia [2] after his own name and their kingdom by the second name. 11. And when he had taken away this name he planted trees there, called Persea, that is plums.[3] 12. These trees, moreover, are planted to the present day in memory of his name. And the Persians were Assyrians at that time, and he reigned over them all during fifty and three years. 13. And there was a great commotion and a hissing and much rain, and the river in Syria, named Orontes, was quickly filled. 14. (And) he urged the Ionians[4] to make prayers, and when they had

---

[1] Word corrupt here, as in vi.

[2] *Changed the name of the country, that is, Assyria, and named it Persia after his own name.* I get this excellent text by simply changing the order of three words. Thus instead of ⲱⲛ̈ⲥⲙⲣ: ⲥⲣⲣ: Ⲏⲱⲁ̈ⲧⲟⲙ: I read Ⲏⲱⲁ̈ⲧⲟⲙ: ⲥⲣⲣ: ⲱⲛ̈ⲥⲙⲣ: Cf. John Mal. 37 καὶ ἐπ’ ὀνόματι αὐτοῦ ἐκάλεσεν αὐτοὺς Πέρσας, ἀφελόμενος ἀπὸ Ἀσσυρίων τὴν βασιλείαν καὶ τὸ ὄνομα. The text as it stands is absurd: 'changed the name of the country and named it Assyria, that is, Persia after his own name.'

[3] *Plums*, or 'peaches'. The word Ⲁ̈ⲩ̈ⲃ: is transliterated from the Arabic (Zotenberg).

[4] *(And) he urged the Ionians to make prayers, and when they had offered supplications.* These words are found in the manuscripts after the clause 'And Perseus was

offered supplications there fell from heaven a globe of fire in the likeness of lightning. 15. And the people became still and ceased to be indignant, and the flowings of the river were stayed. 16. And as Perseus was surprised at what had befallen, forthwith from that fire he kindled a fire and preserved it.[1] 17. And this fire he took[2] and brought to Persia on his return and placed it in the kingdom of Assyria. 18. And the Persians made it a god and honoured it and built it a temple and named it 'The immortal fire'. 19. And they say that fire is a son of the Sun enveloped in crystal, and the form of the crystal resembles the cotton tree (?), the colour of which is like water; for it is born from water and its interior resembles water.

CHAPTER XXII. 1. Inachus of the race of Japhet, the son of Noah, who ruled in the west over the country of the Argives, was the first to rule over that country. 2. He paid honour to the Moon and made her a goddess. 3. And he built in the country of the Argives a city[3] named Iopolis after the name of the Moon; for the Argives in their secret mysteries name the moon Io unto this day. 4. And he built a temple, and set up an altar in it, and he

surprised at what had befallen' and before the clause 'forthwith from that fire he kindled a fire'. But since these two clauses form the protasis and apodosis of one and the same sentence, they must be taken together as in John Mal. and *Chron. Pasch.* (*καὶ θαυμάσας ἐπὶ τῷ γεγονότι ὁ Περσεὺς ἐξ ἐκείνου τοῦ πυρὸς εὐθέως ἀνῆψε πῦρ*), and the intruding words removed. From the same authorities we learn that the intruding clause should be read before the words 'there fell from heaven', &c. Hence I have restored them to their original context. In the next place, the words rendered 'And he urged . . . supplications' are in the manuscripts: **ይቤ፡ ከመ፡ እልፊናጥስ፡ ዘይገብርዎ፡ ሰብአ፡ ምትሐት፡ ጋኔናውያን፡** which = 'he said that the Ionians who did it were men of demoniacal apparitions'. As this is impossible I have emended and restored the text by means of John Mal.: *ᾔτησεν τοὺς Ἰωνίτας εὔξασθαι· καὶ ἐν τῷ εὔχεσθαι αὐτοὺς καὶ μυσταγωγεῖν κατηνέχθη σφαῖρα πυρὸς κεραυνοῦ ἐκ τοῦ οὐρανοῦ.* Hence I propose: **ይቤ፡ ከመ፡ እልፊናጥስ፡ ይግበሩ፡ ስእለተ፡ ወአመ፡ ተጋነዩ፡ ወረደ፡ እሳት፡ ክቡብ፡**

1 *Forthwith from that fire he kindled a fire and preserved it.* The text here is **ወበጊዜሃ፡ ነደ፡ እሳት፡ ወኮነ፡ የዐቅቦ፡ ለዝኩ፡ እሳት፡** = 'and forthwith a fire was kindled and he preserved that fire'. But this is corrupt, and the text of John Mal., *ἐξ ἐκείνου τοῦ πυρὸς εὐθέως ἀνῆψε πῦρ καὶ εἶχε φυλαττόμενον μεθ' ἑαυτοῦ*, shows that *ἀνῆψε* was wrongly taken by the Arabic translator as intransitive. Hence I restore as follows: **ወበጊዜሃ፡ እምዝኩ፡ እሳት፡ አንደደ፡ እሳተ፡ ወኮነ፡ የዐቅቦ፡**

2 *And this fire he took*, i.e. emending **ወበእንተ፡ ዝንቱ፡ ነሥአ፡** = 'and on this account he took' into **ወለእሳት፡ ዝንቱ፡ ነሥአ፡** Cf. John Mal. *ὅπερ πῦρ ἐβάσταζεν.*

3 **መዲና፡** a transliteration of an Arabic word for city.

represented the Moon by a brazen image, whereon he inscribed
'Ἰὼ μάκαιρα, which is by interpretation, 'full of light'.[1]

CHAPTER XXIII. 1. And Libya, who was the daughter of Picus
by her mother [2] Qalûnjâ,[3] became the wife of Poseidon, who ruled in
the south. 2. And he named the country over which he ruled after
the name of his wife Libya. And he begat by her Poseidon and
Belus and Agenor.[4] 3. And this (last), having gone to Canaan,[5]
took him a wife named Dîrô, and also built a city and named it
Dairûs, that is Tyre, after the name of his wife. 4. And during
his reign there he begat by her three sons, men of renown and
founders, i. e. Syrus and Cilix and Phoenix who was the first to
wear silk. 5. And when about to die he divided (his empire)
among his three sons and made the land subject to them. 6. And
Phoenix took Canaan and all the adjoining country and named it
Phoenicia after his own name. 7. And the second took Syria and
gave it his name. 8. And Cilix the third took his territory and
named it Cilicia after his own name.

CHAPTER XXIV. 1. And there was a man named Taurus, king
of Crete, and he made an expedition against Tyre about the hour
of sunset, and attacked it, and made himself master of it, and took
its riches and † led away captive many cities †.[6] 2. And in that way
he took Europa and made her his wife. For Taurus having made
a night expedition by sea [7] returned to his own country, Crete,[8]
and having taken Europa to be his wife, he named that country
after the name of his wife. 3. And he built a city there and

---

[1] Sense quite missed here. Cf. John Mal. 28 Ἰὼ μάκαιρα λαμπηδαφόρε.

[2] *By her mother.* The text gives 'with her mother'.

[3] *Qalûnjâ.* Should this be Ἰώ, or Μελία the mother of Ἰώ? Cf. John of Ant.
Ἴναχος . . . ἠγάγετο γυναῖκα Μελίαν.

[4] *Agenor.* The text gives አከበፉሩስ፡

[5] *And this (last), having gone to Canaan.* The text states that the sons of Poseidon
were born 'in Canaan'. But the phrase 'in Canaan' belongs to the next sentence. Hence with John Mal. 30 ὁ δὲ Ἀγήνωρ ἐπὶ τὴν Φοινίκην ἐλθὼν ἠγάγετο
τὴν Τυρὼ καὶ κτίζει πόλιν ἣν ἐκάλεσε Τύρον εἰς ὄνομα τῆς ἑαυτοῦ γαμετῆς, I have
emended በአከአን፡፡ ወዝንት፡ ሰበ፡ into ወዝንት፡ ሰበ፡ ሩሪ፡ በአከአን፡

[6] *Led away captive many cities.* The true text is probably that in John Mal. 30
ἔλαβεν αἰχμαλώτους ἐκ τῆς πόλεως πολλούς. Hence for ·በዘኃት፡ አህጉሪ፡ read
·በዘኃኑ፡ አምሀገር፡ 'led away many captives from the city'.

[7] *By sea.* The text አምበሐር፡ is a mistaken rendering of διὰ θαλάσσης.

[8] *His own country, Crete.* The text reads 'His own country Tarsus and Crete'.
Here Tarsus is corrupt for Taurus. Cf. John Mal. 31 ἀπήγαγε δὲ τὴν Εὐρώπην
εἰς τὴν ἰδίαν πατρίδα ὁ Ταῦρος.

named it Gortyna after the name of his mother. Now she was [1] of the race of Picus, i.e. Zeus.

CHAPTER XXV. And there was a certain man named Laius. †His father was Waikâ,†[2] who, seeing that his son would have commerce with his mother, commanded his soldiers to suspend him on a tree of which they had cloven the branches in order that the feet of him that was suspended might be made fast in it.

CHAPTER XXVI. 1. And there was a man named Seruch of the race of Japhet, the son of Noah. 2. He appears to have been the first of those who worshipped idols through the influence of Satan. And he set up altars to the idols and served them.

CHAPTER XXVII. 1. And Melchizedek was found to be [3] holy though of Gentile origin,[4] and he served God and was chaste (and) without sin. 2. And Holy Scripture declares him to be without father and mother because he was not of the family of Abraham. 3. And he hated his father's gods and made himself a priest of the living God. 4. He was descended from the race of Sidus, son of (Egyptus) the king of Egypt and Nubia, on whose account the Egyptians are (so) called. 5. Now Melchizedek signifies king of righteousness. 6. Now King Sidus, though a priest, ruled [5] over Canaan, being sprung of a powerful race, and the Egyptians so named him because of ⟨the land of⟩ the Canaanites, which is the land of Palestine until this day. 7. And when he warred with them, they submitted themselves to him, and as they were pleasing unto him, he dwelt in their country, and built a city and called it Sidon after his own name, which till the present day has been reckoned in

---

[1] *Now she was.* Text wrongly gives 'Now he was'. Cf. John Mal. ἣν ἐκάλεσε Γόρτυναν εἰς ὄνομα τῆς αὐτοῦ μητρὸς τῆς ἐκ γένους Πίκου Διός.

[2] *His father was Waikâ.* So text አቡ፡ ወይካ፡ But the manuscripts combine the two words. Hence the whole word may be a corrupt form of Labdacus, the father of Laius. Then read (ወለደ፤) ሰብይካስ፤ 'son of Labdacus'. Zotenberg finds Iokaste in ወይካ፡ The original text referred of course to the story of Oedipus.

[3] *Was found to be.* Read አስተርአየ፡ (for አስተርአየት፤) which = εὑρέθη. Cf. Chron. Pasch. i. 90 εὑρεθεὶς δὲ ἐν τῇ φυλῇ αὐτοῦ ἅγιον γέννημα : or three lines lower down ὢν δὲ ἅγιος ἐκεῖνος ὁ ἄνθρωπος καὶ δίκαιος.

[4] *Though of Gentile origin, and he served God.* Our text is closely connected with John Mal. 57 sq. Ὁ Μελχισεδέκ, ἀνὴρ θεοσεβής, ἐθνικός, καταγόμενος ἐκ τοῦ γένους Σίδου, υἱοῦ Αἰγύπτου, βασιλέως τῆς Λιβύης χώρας· ἐξ οὗ Αἰγύπτιοι κέκληνται. ὅστις Σίδος ἐκ τῆς Αἰγύπτου ἐπελθὼν παρέλαβε τὴν χώραν τῶν λεγομένων Χαναναίων ἐθνικῶν, τοῦτ᾽ ἐστί, τὴν νῦν λεγομένην Παλαιστίνην, κτλ.

[5] *Though a priest, ruled.* So the manuscripts.

Canaan. 8. Now as touching the father of Melchizedek who went forth from Sidon, we have learnt that such was his origin. But his father was an idolater and his mother likewise. And this holy man used to reprove his father and his mother for their idolatry. 9. And afterwards he fled away and became priest of the living God as has been recounted. And he ruled over the Canaanites and built on Golgotha a city named Zion, i.e. Salem, a name which being interpreted means in the language of the Hebrews 'the city of peace'. 10. And he ruled over it one hundred and thirteen years and died, having preserved his chastity and righteousness as the wise Josephus,[1] the historian, has written in the beginning of his work on the history of the Jews. 11. For he was the first ⟨to offer⟩ sacrifices to the God of heaven and bloodless oblations of bread and wine in the likeness of the holy mysteries of our Lord Jesus Christ[2]; as David has sung, saying : 'Thou art His priest for ever after the order of Melchizedek.'[3] 12. And again he said : 'God manifested Himself in Zion[4] and His name is great in Israel, and His place abideth in peace[5] and His dwelling is in Zion.' For the Jews learnt from Abraham the knowledge of God. 13. And Salem also, that is, Jerusalem, is named [Jerusalem][6] because peace abideth in Zion, that is, Melchizedek. 14. And the Jews were called[7] Hebrews from Heber, from whom Abraham, the chosen vessel, was descended. 15. And when the rebels against God built the tower and laboured in vain in their impious designs, Heber indeed refused to join with them : he alone preserved without wavering his loyalty to God. 16. And when the confusion of tongues took place, Heber alone was not deprived of his speech[8]

---

[1] The same reference with others is found in John Mal., *loc. cit.*

[2] *Sacrifices . . . Jesus Christ.* Cf. Syncellus i. 184 ἐν ἄρτῳ καὶ οἴνῳ τὴν ἀναίμακτον θυσίαν τοῦ . . . Χριστοῦ τοῦ ἀληθινοῦ θεοῦ καὶ Σωτῆρος ἡμῶν προτυπῶν. See also *Chron. Pasch.* 50.

[3] *Thou art His priest for ever, &c.* Ps. cx. 4. This particular form of the text is so far as I am aware peculiar to the Ethiopic version.

[4] *God manifested Himself in Zion, &c.* Ps. lxxvi. 1. 'Manifested' (አስተርአየ:), here instead of 'known' (ተዐወቀ:), appears to be due to the Arabic Version. 'In Zion' seems to be peculiar to our author for 'in Judah'.

[5] *His place abideth in peace.* So Eth. Version. The ungrammatical ብሔር: is found also in the manuscripts of the Pss. 'In peace' instead of 'in Salem' is found also in the LXX, Vulgate, and Arabic Versions.

[6] *Named [Jerusalem].* The manuscripts wrongly insert 'Jerusalem'.

[7] Emended.

[8] Lit. ' was left without being deprived of' (or 'divided in').

in its integrity and perfectness. 17. And his successors guarded
the language of angels which Adam spoke. And for this reason
they are called Hebrews and their language Hebrew.

CHAPTER XXVIII. 1. There was a man named Hesiod of the race
of Japhet, the son of Noah. 2. He invented Greek letters and was
the first[1] to teach them. 3. It is told[2] that there was in the times
of the kings of the country † in Lydia †[3] a certain philosopher
descended from the children of the giants who were of the race of
Japhet, named Endymion. 4. He, it is told, prayed in secret to
the Moon, and they say that he learnt from the Moon in a vision
the name of God. 5. And when he †went one day†,[4] he heard the
sacred name and thereupon he gave up the ghost and died and
rose not again. 6. And his body is preserved unto this day[5] in the
city of † Lydia †, and any one can see it once a year when they
open the coffin in which it is.

CHAPTER XXIX. 1. It is told that in the time of Joshua the son of
Nun, a king named Ogyges ruled over Attica, and that there was
a great deluge in that country only. And the king himself perished
and the inhabitants of that country. 2. And it became a desert
and no man dwelt therein for two hundred and six years,[6] as
Africanus has recorded in his chronicle.

CHAPTER XXX. 1. And in the days of Moses the lawgiver, the
servant of God who led the exodus of the children of Israel out of

---

[1] *Was the first to teach them.* In the manuscripts the word 'first' is wrongly
connected with the previous sentence. Cf. John Mal. 59 ἐξεῦρε τὰ Ἑλλήνων
γράμματα καὶ . . . ἐξέθετο τοῖς Ἕλλησι πρῶτος.

[2] *It is told that there was, &c.* The text in the manuscripts is very confused.
I have followed Zotenberg's restoration. The original was very closely related
to John Mal. 61 ἐν δὲ τοῖς χρόνοις τῶν βασιλέων τῶν προγεγραμμένων ἀνεφάνη τις
ἐν τῇ Καρίᾳ χώρᾳ γιγαντογενὴς φιλόσοφος ἐκ τῆς φυλῆς τοῦ Ἰάφεθ, ὀνόματι Ἐνδυμίων·
ὅστις μυστικὰς εὐχὰς λέγων εἰς σελήνην ᾔτει αὐτὴν μαθεῖν παρ' αὐτῆς τὸ θεϊκὸν ὄνομα
ἐν ὁράματι. καὶ ἐν τῷ εὔχεσθαι ἦλθεν εἰς ὕπνον καὶ ἤκουσε τὸ θεϊκὸν ὄνομα ἐν ὁράματι.
καὶ οὐκέτι ἀνέστη, ἀλλ' ἐστὶ τὸ λείψανον αὐτοῦ ἕως τῆς νῦν εἰς τὴν Καρίαν κτλ. Cf.
John of Antioch, *op. cit.*, iv. 547.

[3] This should be 'in Caria'. See Greek in preceding note.

[4] Since the Greek (see note 2) has here ἦλθεν εἰς ὕπνον, our text is apparently
corrupt.

[5] The words 'unto this day' are transposed in the manuscripts to the preceding clause. They are restored here in accordance with the Greek (see
note 2).

[6] Africanus does not give the number, but John of Antioch (iv. 547) and John
Mal. (62) give 270 years. Each author quotes Africanus as his authority.

Egypt, † in the days of Petissonius, that is, Pharaoh Amosius, king of Egypt, who ruled by the help of the book of the magicians Jannes and Jambres, who wrought shameful things before the mighty Moses, who talked with God—for this reason, they say, they were not willing to let the children of Israel go after the signs and the wonders which were wrought by his staff.†[1] 2. Now (Petissonius) went to the diviners who were in Memphis and to the celebrated oracle and offered sacrifice. 3. And when one of the Hebrews asked the diviner Taninus ⟨Who is first among you ? he answered :⟩[2] 'He who is in heaven, the Immortal, the First : before whom the heavens quake and likewise the earth and all the seas fear, and the Satans are affrighted and but a few angels stand ; for He is the creator of powers and measures.' 4. And Petissonius inscribed this oracle on a tablet and placed it in the temple of the gods near the water-measure whereby they learn the volume of the Nile. 5. We should recount that, when the temple was already destroyed : this tablet was the only one in Egypt that was still unbroken till the foundations of the idol temples were overthrown, and it was no longer possible for any one to maintain the temple of Memphis. 6. It was only through the power of our Lord Jesus Christ that all the temples were destroyed. 7. Now this mad Petissonius, that is, the Pharaoh Amosius, was overwhelmed in the Red Sea together with his horses and horsemen. 8. And when, after the children of Israel had gone forth from Egypt, he learnt that they had taken (with them) the riches of the Egyptians— a thing they had done with the approval of God and in accordance with His law ; for the children of Israel had taken the riches of the Egyptians in compensation for the heavy labours which had been imposed upon them without intermission—Pharaoh was filled with indignation. 9. Thereupon he went forth in pursuit of them with his army. And he was overwhelmed in the sea with his followers and there was not one left. 10. And the children of Israel marched in the sea as on dry land, and they came to the place where God willed : for He is the conqueror of all the elements of creation.—Glory be to Him. 11. And, after the Egyptians had been destroyed, those who remained worshipped demons and forsook God. Those unhappy ones destroyed themselves and became like

---

[1] Corrupt. Text translated as it stands.
[2] Supplied from Cramer, iv. 241 σαφήνισόν μοι τίς ἐστιν πρῶτος ὑμῶν.

unto the angels who rebelled against God, and they worshipped the
work of their own hands. 12. Some worshipped the cow, and some
the ox, and some the dog and also the mule : and some the ass, and
some the lion : and some fish, and some the crocodile : and some the
leek and many other like things. 13. And they named their cities
of Egypt after the name of their god. And they worshipped the
†buildings† of Bûsîr and Manûf and Samnûd and Sâhraisht and Esnâ
and of the Tree and of the Crocodile. And they gave divine honours
to † the building of many cities † [1] and likewise to the storm.

CHAPTER XXXI. 1. And during the time of him who first
reigned over the Egyptians, when they served idols and such
creatures as have already been mentioned and as regards the
celebrated city Absâi, that is, Nakius, and its king was named
Prosopis, a name which being interpreted means ' Lover of the
deities with three faces '—now he lived on the west bank of the
river and he was continually at war with the barbarians who were
named Mauritanians who came from the five countries.[2] 2. And
when these came in wrath, the inhabitants warred vigorously
against them and slew many of them. 3. And in consequence of
this happy victory, (the barbarians) did not for a long period come
again against the city, through the mercy of God who by the
mighty power of his Godhead hath made all things to come into
being out of nothingness. 4. And the great river of Egypt was
named Chrysorroas by the Greeks but it is named Gihon in the
book that is inspired by God. 5. Now this river flowed (anciently)
to the east of the city, but it changed its course from the east to
the west of the city, and the city became like an island in the
midst of the river like a plantation of trees named Akrejâs, that is,
the myrtle.

CHAPTER XXXII. 1. And as for Jerusalem which had been built
by Melchizedek its king under the sway of the Canaanites, that is,
the Philistines, Joshua the son of Nun subdued it and called it
Jebus. 2. And he dwelt in Shechem ; for he had subdued all the
adjoining country. And this (city) is named Nablus unto this
day. 3. And in the days of the wise kings David and Solomon,
David prepared all the building materials for the building of the
holy temple of God, and Solomon built it in Jerusalem. 4. And he

---

[1] Corrupt.   [2] This passage is corrupt.

called it the city of the sanctuary on account of the consecration and the sacrifices according to the law and the abundance of righteousness and because our Lord and Saviour Jesus Christ—praise be unto Him—underwent the passion there.

CHAPTER XXXIII. And in the days of the Judges, there was a judge of the Greeks named Πανόπτης, who was so named in regard to the hundred piercing eyes with which he beheld afar and saw better than all men. He was the first to devise in a city of the west all manner of handicrafts.

CHAPTER XXXIV. 1. Prometheus and Epimetheus discovered a stone tablet with an inscription which had been written and engraved in the days of the ancients. 2. And Elijah the prophet interpreted the verses. So the Greeks ⟨have recounted⟩ this saying that on account of this he ascended to heaven and that what had been in heaven was in his heart. 3. And Deucalion, moreover, wrote a detailed history [1] of what had happened in the days of the deluge and the strange events (of that time).

CHAPTER XXXV. 1. And after the deluge in Attica, the sovereignty passed into the hands of the Athenians. 2. And there ruled there a man named Elwâtes [2] and he established the (common) meal as a legal institution. 3. And he was also the first to ordain that all men should take as their wives young virgins and name them spouses: and that they should dig a fountain in a hidden place in order to cause milk to spring (from the earth) in abundance as a visible stream. 4. Now before his reign the women of Attica and the Athenians lived in unclean intercourse and male was joined to male. And they were like beasts: each lusted (after the other) and none had a woman to himself; but they ravished with wicked violence as we have already recounted. 5. And they knew not their own offspring, either their male or female. And who could have known, seeing that none of them had fathers and all whom they bare [3] were begotten by all. Owing to their promiscuous intercourse they could not know whether they had male or female offspring. And they were all pleased with this unclean mode of living. 6. As Cecrops the author of the prescript in his law has said: 'This country of Attica will be destroyed by a deluge from God.' 7. And after this time they became wise and

---

[1] = 'chapters and history'.   [2] = Cecrops (?).
[3] Slightly emended.

conformed to the law of marriage, the men and the women. 8. And Cecrops was highly honoured and esteemed all his days, and he brought it about that the children knew their fathers, as was befitting.

CHAPTER XXXVI. 1. And in these days lived Orpheus of Thrace, the lyric poet of the Odrysae,[1] called the great sage among the Greeks. 2. He expounded to them that which is called the Theogony, which being interpreted in their language means 'The combatant of God', which things are recounted by the chronicler Timothy. 3. He said: 'Before all time was the holy Trinity coequal in one Godhead, Creator of all things.'

CHAPTER XXXVII. 1. It is said that certain savants of the Athenians were the first to practise the art of medicine. 2. Indeed the philosophers were the first who made known the noble art of using medicines which agreed with the stomach. 3. And many people go to Athens for the sake of this art also, for it flourishes there until this day.

CHAPTER XXXVIII. 1. King Solomon the son of David was the first to build baths and places for reading and instruction in every place under his dominion; for he had the demons subject to him. 2. Now he enjoyed this privilege before he provoked God the Lord of all through the strange women who lived with him. These polluted Jerusalem with their gods.

CHAPTER XXXIX. 1. In the days of the Judges also there arose in Phrygia a philosopher named Marsyas. 2. He was the first to play upon the flute and the horn and the drum (?). And he deafened the ears of men and made himself out to be a god, saying: 'I have found food for man by means of a small member.' 3. And God was wroth with him and punished him and he became insane and cast himself into the river and perished.

CHAPTER XL. 1. And in those days also lived the hero Heracles and the Argonauts, the people that were with Jason.[2] And they

---

[1] The words አርፉስ፡ ብት፡ ረሕስ፡ እንሳሪኩኩ፡ ብትርሰስ፡ appear to be a transcription of 'Ορφεὺς ὁ Θρᾷξ ὁ λυρικὸς 'Οδρυσαῖος and to reproduce twice the Coptic article (Zotenberg). Cf. John Mal. 72.

[2] *The hero Heracles and the Argonauts, the people who were with Jason.* Here አያኑር፡ is probably corrupted from ὁ ἥρως, and ስኑይ a corruption of ያሱን፡ i.e. 'Ιάσων 'Jason'. So far Zotenberg. But another corruption lurks in the text. The words ትራረዮአዎሙ፡ ሰኖትያት፡ (= 'they helped the sailors') appear due to a misconception of 'Αργοναῦται, whereby this word was taken as

went to the Hellespont. 2. And the people (of the Hellespont) had a king named Cyzicus. And they attacked and slew the king Cyzicus without knowing it. 3. And when they learned (this), they were grieved; for they were all his kinsmen (and he was sprung) from their country. 4. And after they had attacked Cyzicus, who was called the lord of the seven images, and won the victory ⟨they built a temple in Cyzicum, and⟩ [1] named its name Rhea, which is by interpretation, mother of the gods. 5. It is told (further) that they went to the place of those who announced (oracles) and to the seat of the elders and asked one of them, saying: ' Prophesy to us, O prophet, servant of Apollo, of what nature this building will be and to whom shall it belong.' 6. And they presented gifts to him who spake to them and he said unto them : ' There are three (Persons) but one God only. And behold a virgin will conceive His word, and this house will be His and His name shall belong to thousands.' 7. And the idolaters wrote down this prophecy on a fragment of marble with a brazen pen, and they placed it in one of the temples. 8. After these times in the days of the Godloving emperor Zeno, this temple was converted into a church, dedicated to the holy Virgin Mary, the Mother of God. 9. This the emperor Zeno did at his own costs. And thus was accomplished the prophecy of the demons who proclaimed the coming of our Lord Jesus Christ.

Chapter XLI. 1. The Argonauts sailed to the Hellespont to an island named Principus. 2. Thence they went to Chalcedon and sought to pass into the sea of Pontus. 3. But the inhabitants brought with them a man of valour and fought with them. (And) he gained the mastery and overcame them. 4. And fearing the wrath of this man, they fled to a very desolate extremity of the coast. 5. And they saw a mighty portent from heaven which resembled a man with great wings on his shoulders after the likeness of a very terrible eagle. 6. And it said unto them : ' When ye fight with Amycus ye will overcome.' And when they heard these words from the apparition which they saw, they

---

a common noun compounded of ἀρήγω and ναῦται, and thus arose the rendering in our text 'helped the sailors'. This restoration is confirmed by John Mal. 77 ἐν δὲ τοῖς καιροῖς τοῦ Θῶλα Ἡρακλῆς ὁ ἥρως καὶ οἱ Ἀργοναῦται οἱ περὶ Ἰάσονα . . . οἵτινες ἀνίοντες τὸν Ἑλλησπόντον.

[1] Restored by Zotenberg.

took courage and fought and overcame him and slew him. 7. And they honoured that place where they had seen the mighty figure, and they built there a temple and they placed in it a statue resembling the apparition they had seen. 8. And they named this temple Sosthenium because they had sought refuge there and were saved. And so they name it unto this day. 9. And in the days of Constantine, the greatest and most illustrious of Christian emperors, the servant of Jesus Christ, when he first established the seat of empire in Byzantium, that is in Rome, he came to the Sosthenium to close the temple of the idols to be found there. 10. And when he saw the statue which was in it, he at once recognized that it was the statue of an angel. And as his thoughts were troubled with doubts he prayed and besought our Lord Jesus Christ in whom he trusted, saying: 'Make me to know, O Lord, whose image this is.' 11. And thereupon he fell asleep and heard in a vision that the image was the image of S. Michael the archangel. 12. Having learnt that it was he who had sent people to fight Amycus the emperor caused this temple to be adorned and commanded them to turn it to the east and [commanded them] to consecrate it in the name of the archangel Michael.

13. And numerous miracles were wrought in this (temple) through healings of the sick. And after that Christians began to build churches in the name of S. Michael the chief of the angels. And they offered in them holy offerings unto God.

CHAPTER XLII. 1. It is said touching the holy nails which were found in the cross of our Saviour Jesus Christ and with which his holy body was nailed, that the holy, Godloving Constantine took one of them and fixed it in the saddle[1] of his horse; and the second he made into a bit for his horse; and the third he cast into the pass of Chalcedon. 2. For they were in grievous danger till by means of this holy nail the waves of the sea, yea all the waves of the ocean, were quieted. 3. And the empire made itself strong in the city of Constantine. Now in the days of Zeno the empire had had its seat in Rome. Afterwards the (two) empires were united in one by a decree of the Senate.[2]

---

[1] An Arabic word. After 'horse' the translator adds the words 'which is a saddle'—the word being different from the former.

[2] Here ሡራፕት፡ should be written ሰራፕት፡ It is here a rendering of σύγκλητος, being elsewhere a rendering of στρατιά, ὄχλος, συναγωγή, &c.

4. For one (of these) had been established on account of the continual outbreaks of the barbarians, and the other in accordance with the counsel of the prefects in order that they might have another authority in Asia.

CHAPTER XLIII. 1. And in the days of Samson the last of the Judges, Lapathus ruled in the land [1] of Aegistheus.[2] And he had two sons, whose names were Achaius and Lacon.[3] 2. And he divided the provinces of his kingdom into two parts, one half for himself and the other half for his sons. 3. And when he died, one province was named Achaia after the name of his eldest son, and the other was named Laconia after the name of the younger son (and such are their names) unto this day.

CHAPTER XLIV. 1. And at that epoch there reigned in Hellas a king whose name was Pelops. 2. After this man the Hellenes called the kingdom Peloponnesian by his name unto this day.[4] 3. And he built a city and they named it Peloponnesus after his name. And the name of his kingdom is Hellas unto this day.

CHAPTER XLV. 1. And there was a man named Bîlâwôn. He built the city Farmâ after his own name. 2. And Priam built the city of Malkîbînûn (= Ilium ?), in Phrygia . . . in the city of Sparta in the country of Hellas, when he came there.

CHAPTER XLVI. And there was a wise and sagacious man named Palamedes. He was the first to teach the arts of playing on the harp and lyre [5] and the flute and all manner of musical instruments.

CHAPTER XLVII. 1. And Tros, also, who ruled over the country of Phrygia [6] . . . before that he had slain Priam and Hecuba, and he slew their young men and plundered their royal palaces that it might be a memorial unto him, and this city came under his power, and he named it Enderjân. 2. And Seṭâbarjâ of Panton he named Asia of the Ephesians.[7] It was named . . . which is now Saqîljâ

---

[1] Emended by Dillmann.

[2] This identification is most doubtful. The Ethiopic is አጊልዮስ፡

[3] Correct form, though transliterated from the acc.

[4] The original meaning is no doubt that in John Mal. 84 sq. ἐβασίλευσεν ὁ Πέλοψ . . . ἐξ οὗ καὶ Πελοποννήσιοι ἐκλήθησαν οἱ Ἑλλαδικοί . . . ἔκτοτε καὶ Πελοποννήσιον ἐκλήθη τὸ βασίλειον Ἑλλάδος. I have emended ገጉሡ፡ into መንገሡት፡

[5] According to Guidi's Amharic Lexicon this is a lyre of ten strings.

[6] After Phrygia there seems to be a lacuna. The text is full of confusion. Zotenberg does not attempt a rendering.

[7] Cf. John Mal. 108 ἐπιστάντες τῇ χώρᾳ τῶν Φρυγῶν ἐξεπόρθησαν τὰ αὐτῶν βασίλεια . . . παραλαβόντες Πρίαμον βασιλέα καὶ φονεύσαντες αὐτὸν καὶ Ἑκάβην

(= Sicily ?), and it became a great island and its earlier name was Qûbâbâ.

CHAPTER XLVIII. 1. And Solomon the son of David, king of Israel, built a great structure in †Bîlîmîktûn† [1] in the midst of the city to be a memorial unto him in order that his name and the name of his father should not be forgotten. 2. And he gave it to a man named Aiwanî, which is by interpretation in the language of Canaan 'light', but he named the structure Palmyra. 3. Indeed it was in that place that David his father, the strong and mighty one, was victorious when he slew and was victorious over Goliath the Philistine. 4. It is for this reason that he appointed its name to be Mêzâd in order that strange peoples (azmâd) might dwell therein. And a great number of Jewish soldiers dwelt there. 5. And Nebuchadnezzar king of Persia took this city, having to expend much toil and severe effort before he could take it and burn it with fire. And he caused the memorial of it to disappear till this day.

CHAPTER XLIX. 1. And (he took) the city Tyre also, which is an island surrounded by water. And he put forth many a mighty effort to take it. 2. And he commanded his soldiers, the cavalry and foot-soldiers, and all the Persians to cast earth into the arm of the sea which surrounded it. 3. And they filled it with earth till the water of the sea dried up and (the strait) became as land. And by these means Nebuchadnezzar the king of the Persians was able to take this city.

CHAPTER L. 1. And at the time of the Captivity which took place through Nebuchadnezzar—he was commanded to do so by God and a force of angels was given to him—before Nebuchadnezzar had come and burnt the sanctuary of God with fire, Jeremiah,[2] a prophet great among the prophets and a lover of that which is good, went into the second chamber which is called the Holy of Holies, and took the ark of God which was covered with gold, without and within,

---

βασιλίδα· τοὺς δὲ αὐτῶν παῖδας αἰχμαλώτους εἰληφότες καὶ πάντα τὰ βασίλεια διαρπασάμενοι ὑπέστρεψαν . . . κατέσχεν οὖν ἡ βασιλεία Ἐφέσου τῆς Ἀσίας πάσης καὶ Τροίης τῆς Φρυγίας. Also 200 B ὁ Τρῶος βασιλεὺς εἰς μνήμην αὐτοῦ . . . τὴν πρῴην λεγομένην Ἐπίτροπον ἣν μετεκάλεσεν Ἀσίαν.

1 Zotenberg conjectures that this word is a transliteration of ἐν τῷ λιμίτῳ = ' on the border '. He compares John Mal. 143 ἔκτισε δὲ καὶ ἐν τῷ λιμίτῳ πόλιν ἣν ἐκάλεσε Παλμοῖραν. Possibly it is a corruption of Παλμοῖρα.

2 The text is very confused.

and the glorious objects which were in it,[1] i. e. the tables of the law, and the golden box of manna, and Aaron's rod which bore almonds, and the stone from the hard rock, from which Moses had given the people to drink when they thirsted. 2. And, moreover, Moses the prophet carried this stone as he went before the people in their journey through the wilderness, according to the commandment of God. 3. And as often as the people thirsted, he cast it upon the earth and smote it with the rod, and water came forth and the people were satisfied and all the cattle. 4. And Jeremiah took those objects and the stone, and went hastily to the rock and hid them there until this day. 5. And on the second coming of our Lord and Saviour Jesus Christ, who will be preceded by the sign of the cross, this ark borne by angels will appear, and Moses also who made it will come and Jeremiah who hid it in the rock. 6. When the dead shall rise, the sign of the cross will appear and after it our Lord Jesus Christ who was crucified—glory be unto Him. 7. And these words are to be found in the teaching of S. Epiphanius, our light-giving father, bishop of Cyprus, who has written in his book a complete history of the prophets after the overthrow of Jerusalem and the disappearance of the kingdom of Judah.

CHAPTER LI. 1. Cyrus the Persian overcame Astyages and Cyrus became king [2] . . . that is, Cambyses. 2. And Croesus was stiffnecked and overweening. And all the kingdoms afar off and close at hand had submitted to him. 3. And the peoples that were subject to him paid him tribute and dwelt in peace. But those which resisted him, he led away captive, and spoiled their posses- sions and made himself master of their territories. For he was very great and formidable and victorious. 4. And Cyrus was disquieted in heart; for he had a wife named Bardane, who had previously been the wife of Darius the successor of Belshazzar. 5. She spake, saying: 'We have amongst us a prophet of the Hebrews named Daniel, in whom is the wisdom of God. He belongs to the captivity of the children of Israel. 6. Now Darius used to do nothing without his counsel, and every thing that he declared to him (beforehand) was accomplished.' 7. And when Cyrus heard these words he sent to Daniel the prophet and had

---

[1] Cf. 2 Macc. ii. 4–8 ; 2 Baruch vi–viii.
[2] Zotenberg rightly recognizes a lacuna here.

him brought with honour, and he asked him and said unto him :
' Shall I conquer Croesus or not ? '   8. But he was silent and did
not speak for the space of an hour.   And thereupon he spake,
saying : ' Who can know the wisdom of God ? '   And then Daniel
the prophet prayed and besought the Lord his God to reveal unto
him whether he (Cyrus) could resist this rapacious (and) overweening Croesus.   9. And God said unto him : ' If he sends back the
captivity of the children of Israel, he shall surely conquer and take
to himself the power of Croesus.'

10. And when he heard these words from God, he told Cyrus
that he should conquer Croesus if he sent back the children of
Israel.   11. And when Cyrus heard these words he cast himself at
Daniel's feet and sware, saying : ' As the Lord thy God liveth,
I will send Israel back to their city Jerusalem, and they shall serve
the Lord their God.'   12. And Cyrus, in accordance with his duty
to God, heaped benefits upon Israel and sent them back (to their
own country).

13. Now Croesus went out with a great army to war against the
provinces of Cyrus.   And having crossed the river of Cappadocia
in order to slay Cyrus, Cyrus put him to shame and [1] he was not
able to escape secretly because of the river confronting him.   14. Indeed when Croesus came to this river, a large multitude of his
soldiers were speedily overwhelmed (in it) ; but he himself was not
able to cross ; for God had delivered him into Cyrus's hands by this
means.   15. And Cyrus's soldiers pursued him and took him alive
and seized him and put him in chains, and slew of his army 40,000
men.   And Cyrus had his adversary Croesus suspended on a tree,
and the rest of his army he humiliated and shamed.   16. As for
the Jews and their king he sent them off that they might return
to their own country as he had promised to Daniel the prophet.
17. And when Cyrus returned into Persia, he settled [2] all the
affairs of his government and appointed his son Cambyses to be
king over Persia and Babylon.   And he was a bad man, and he
rejected the wisdom of his father and the worship of the Lord God.
18. And Apries moreover was king of Egypt and dwelt in the city
of Thebes and in Memphis and in two (other) cities, Mûhîl and

---

[1] There is no need for the addition of three words to the text by Zotenberg.
It is only necessary to excise the *ⲱ* before ⲕⲩⲛ̃ⲥ̃ⲥ; and place it before ⲓ.ⲕⲩⲗ;
[2] The text reads ⲱ̄ⲫ̄ⲧ̄ⲗ; which I have emended into ⲱ̄ⲧ̄ⲕⲗ;

Sûfîrû. 19. And in those days, in consequence of the intrigues of the neighbouring peoples Cambyses sent to Jerusalem and gave orders (to his officers) to restrain them (the Jews) from rebuilding the sanctuary of God. 20. And afterwards he made an expedition to Egypt with a great (and) innumerable army of horse and foot from Media. 21. And the inhabitants of Syria and Palestine got ready to oppose him (but in vain), and he destroyed not a few but many cities of the Jews, for he was supreme over all the world. 22. And in the pride of (his) heart he changed his name and named himself Nebu-chadnezzar. And his disposition resembled that of a barbarian, and in the evil counsel of his desire he hated mankind. 23. And his father Cyrus had been great and honoured before the living God, and had commanded that they should build the temple of God in Jerusalem with (all) vigilance and zeal, what time he had sent Joshua the high priest, the son of Jozadak and Zerubbabel, that is Ezra, and all the captivity of Judah that they might return to the land of the Hebrews and Palestine. 24. But Cambyses, that is, Nebuchadnezzar the second, and Belshazzar burnt the holy city Jerusalem and the sanctuary according to the prophecies of the holy prophets Jeremiah and Daniel. 25. And after they had burnt the city Cambyses came to Gaza and got together troops and all the materials of war, and he went down into Egypt to war against it. And in the war he gained the victory and he captured the Egyptian cities Farmâ and Sanhûr and Sân and Bastâ. And he captured Apries, the Pharaoh, alive in the city of Thebes and he slew him with his own hand.

26. Now there was in Egypt a warrior named Fûsid who practised righteousness and hated iniquity. When there was war between the Persians and Egyptians, he had gone and fought in Syria and Assyria and he had taken four sons of Cambyses prisoner as well as his wives—in all forty souls. 27. And he bound them and burnt their houses and took all that they had captive and brought them to the city of Memphis and he imprisoned them in the palace of the king. 28. And when a second war arose between the Assyrians and Egyptians, the Assyrians proved the stronger and gained the mastery over the Egyptians and took the palace which is in the city of Thebes. 29. And the Assyrian soldiers shot arrows, and, as they shot, an arrow smote the warrior Fûsid on the right side. But the Egyptian soldiers carried off the

warrior Fûsîd from the Assyrians, before he died. And he lived
but an hour more and after this died and left a memory to those
that came after. 30. But the Egyptians were moved with fear
because they had lost such a warrior as Fûsîd. And for this reason
they fled for refuge into the city Sais, because it was a strong city
and its fortifications stronger than those of the others. 31. And
Cambyses attacked this city a second time and carried [1] it by storm
and destroyed [1] it. And he captured all the other cities of lower
Egypt towards the north to the sea coast and plundered them of all
their possessions and destroyed their cities and neighbourhoods and
burnt their houses with fire and left neither man nor beast living.
32. And he cut down their trees and destroyed their plantations
and made the land of Egypt a desert. And returning in the
direction of Rîf he warred against the city of Memphis, and he
conquered the king who was in it. 33. And the city of Bûsîr also,
which lies below Memphis, he destroyed and annihilated and took
its possessions as a booty, and burnt it with fire and made it a
desert. 34. And the sons of the kings which survived fled for
refuge to another city, the nearest at hand, (even) into its citadel
and closed the gates of the fortress. 35. And the Assyrians
besieged this citadel and carried it by storm by night and destroyed
the city of Memphis the great. 36. And one of the kings of
Egypt, named Mûzab, had sent in secret to his son, named Elkâd,
bidding him to bring all his wealth and that of all his officers
and of the forty wives of Cambyses, that is, Nebuchadnezzar, even
those which had been brought by Fûsîd the captain. 37. And they
opened the gates of the fortress by night, and they took and led
them forth into the desert by another way which the people knew
not. And the four sons of Cambyses the inhabitants of the city
of Memphis led back, and they made them ascend to the summit of
the fortress and cut them in pieces and cast them to the base of the
fortress where Cambyses was. 38. And when the soldiers of Cambyses saw this evil thing which the inhabitants of the city of
Memphis had done, they were filled with wrath and warred against
the city without mercy. 39. And they set up engines against it
and destroyed the palaces of the kings, and they slew without
mercy the children of the kings Mûzab and Sûfîr and all the chiefs
of the army which were found in the city.

[1] I have transposed these words in the text.

40. And when (Elkâd) was informed of the death of his father, he fled into Nubia. And Cambyses also destroyed the city of On and upper Egypt as far as the city Eshmûn. And the inhabitants of this city on learning (of his approach) were seized with fear and fled into the city of Eshmûnîn. 41. And they sent to Nubia to Elkâd the son of Mûzab, asking him to come unto them that they might make him king in the room of his father. For he had formerly made war against the cities of Assyria. 42. And thereupon Elkâd gathered a large army of Ethiopians and Nubians and warred against the army of Cambyses on the eastern bank of the river Gihon. But the Ethiopians were not able to make the passage of the river. 43. And the Persians, full of stratagems, wheeled about as though intending to flee. Then in the early part of the night they crossed the river with vigilance and took possession of the city and destroyed it before the army of Elkâd were aware. 44. And when they had completed the destruction of the city Eshmûnîn they march into upper Egypt, and laid waste the city of Assuan. And they crossed to the opposite bank belonging to the city Ahîf, and they destroyed Phile as they had done the other cities. 45. And they turned back to the cities and provinces which still remained, and they ravaged them and burned them with fire till all the land of Egypt became a desert and there was no longer found in it a moving creature, neither a man nor even a bird of the air. 46. Then Elkâd king of Egypt devised another plan, he and all that had not been annihilated by the Persians. And they proceeded and came upon Cambyses at some distance off, and they took with them gifts and harps and drums and timbrels [1] and prostrated themselves before him and besought him that they might receive from him mercy and friendship. 47. And Cambyses showed mercy to the Egyptians that survived who had come to offer their submission, and he had compassion on them and led them away to Media and Babylon. And he appointed as their ruler one of their own number. 48. And as for Elkâd he did not take from him his royal crown but established him on the royal throne and did not lead him away with him.

49. And the number of the Egyptians whom Cambyses led away with him were 50,000, besides women and children. And they lived in captivity in Persia forty years, and Egypt became a desert. 50. And after devastating Egypt, Cambyses died in the city of Damascus.

---

[1] An Arabic word.

And the wise (and) great Artaxerxes reigned eight years, and he was not wanting in love either to God or man. 51. And he commanded Nehemiah the cupbearer[1] to build the walls of Jerusalem, and he dealt kindly with the Jews, because Cyrus and Darius had honoured the God of heaven, and served Him. And for this reason he supported all the enterprises of the Jews. 52. And as for the Egyptians he dealt kindly and well with them and made them[2] officers in order to take counsel with his prefects. And later he sent back the Egyptians to their own country in the one and fortieth year of their captivity and the devastation of their country. 53. And when they returned they began to build houses in their several cities: they did not construct great houses as formerly but small houses wherein to dwell. And they planted trees and vines in abundance. 54. And they set over themselves a king named Fîwâtûrôs in compliance with the command of Artaxerxes the humane.

55. And there was an Egyptian who comforted (his people), a man of indefatigable energy, wise and virtuous, named Shenûfî, which is by interpretation 'good news'. 56. And this man was very vigilant in rebuilding the cities and villages and restoring the tillage of the land so that in a short time he rebuilt all the villages of Egypt. And he restored Egypt and made it as it had been before. And there was great prosperity in his days, and the Egyptians increased very much, and their cattle increased also. 57. And he reigned over them forty and eight years in happiness and peace because of the return of the Egyptians from captivity. And he went to rest full of honour. But before he died he numbered the Egyptians, and their number was 500,000 men. 58. And after the death of Shenûfî the Egyptians remained for a long time without a king, but they paid taxes to the Persians and Assyrians at the same time. And they remained at peace till they appointed a second Pharaoh as king and paid the taxes to him.

59. Now the Persians did not approve that the Egyptians should pay the taxes to their own king. But the Persians also were without a king after the death of the great Artaxerxes who had had compassion on the Egyptians. 60. And he who reigned after Artaxerxes at first made war against the Jews and the Jews

---

[1] በዖዶ: in the text = potator, 'wine-bibber', whereas we require መኅበ: or ፕሕኢ: = pocillator or οἰνοχόος.

[2] We should expect 'some of them'.

submitted to him. And next he made war on the Egyptians and overcame them and took their possessions as a spoil ; for the land of Egypt is through the help of God a very goodly (land). 61. Now when Nectanabus, the last of the Pharaohs, was informed by the chief diviners—for he was himself also a magician and asked the impure demons whether he was to rule over the Egyptians or not— when (I repeat) he was surely informed by the demons that he should not rule over the Egyptians, he shore his head and changed his outward figure, and fled, and went to the city of Farmâ, and furthermore went to Macedonia and dwelt there. 62. And the Egyptians remained in subjection to Jûljânôs till the time of Alexander ὁ πάνταρχος [1], which is by interpretation ' the ruler of the world '. And he slew the last [2] king of the Persians.

63. And after some time Ochus reigned for twelve years over the Persians. And after him Artaxerxes reigned twenty-three years. And after him Darius, surnamed Akrejûs, reigned for six years. And then Alexander rose up against him and slew him and took his kingdom of Babylon from him ; for Alexander the son of Philip of Macedon was ruler of the world.

CHAPTER LII. And there was a man named Aeneas, who espoused the daughter of Latinus, named Lavinia. And he built a great city and named it after the name of Lavinia and established his kingdom in it.

CHAPTER LIII. 1. And there was in Italy a man named Pallas and he had a son. And he became a good and warlike man. And he stormed many cities belonging to Aeneas. 2. And when he warred against †Jûsten†, he took his city and built therein a great house, and he adorned it and there was no such house in any city. 3. And he built a palace also and named it Pallantium, which is by inter-pretation ' stronghold ', after his name Pallas.[3]

---

[1] The Greek is transliterated in the text.

[2] Text reads *hestâtes*, which Nöldeke has recognized as a transliteration of ὕστατος.

[3] The text is corrupt, as a comparison of John Mal. 168 shows καὶ ἀπῆλθεν ὁ Αἰνείας πρὸς τὸν Εὔανδρον καὶ τὸν υἱὸν αὐτοῦ Πάλλαντα, ἄνδρας πολεμικωτάτους· οἵτινες διῆγον εἰς τὴν ᾿Ιταλίαν, οἰκοῦντες κώμην λεγομένην Βαλεντίαν, ἰθύνοντες ἐπαρ-χίαν μίαν. ᾿Εν ᾗ κώμῃ καὶ ἔκτισεν ὁ Πάλλας οἶκον μέγαν πάνυ, οἷον οὐκ εἶχεν ἡ περί-χωρος ἐκείνη· ὅστις οἶκος ἐκλήθη τὸ Παλλάντ⟨ι⟩ον, κα ἰαπὸ τότε ἐκλήθη τὰ βασιλικὰ κατοικητήρια Παλλάντιον ἐκ τοῦ Πάλλαντος. In our text Jûsten is due to a faulty transcription of the Arabic for Βαλεντίαν, but the Arabic translator had already erred in taking Βαλεντίαν as the name of a king, as Zotenberg has already recognized.

CHAPTER LIV. And when †Creusa became king, he built a city named Alba. Then leaving Elbânjâ he came to Elwânjâ†,[1] that is, Alba, which by interpretation means 'light'.

CHAPTER LV. 1. And there was a Canaanitish woman named Dido, the wife of a man named Sichaeus. 2. And she came originally from a small city Kardîmâs,[2] situated on the sea-coast between Tyre and Sidon. 3. And she was very rich. And she had a brother named Pygmalion, who rose against her husband and slew him from the covetous desire to get hold of her wealth and treasures. 4. Then this woman arose in haste and collected together all the wealth and treasures in her house, and embarked on a ship and fled and went from Canaan to the country of Libya[3] in Africa, and built a great city in that province, which she named Carthage, but in the language of the Barbarians it is called 'New city'. And she reigned there wisely until her death.

CHAPTER LVI. 1. And in the days of Hezekiah king of Judah there were two brothers whose names were Romulus and Remus.[4] 2. And these built a great city near a small city Valentia in Italy, a city of Latinus where previously there had been a royal palace named Pallantium. And this they rebuilt. 3. Moreover they built a temple for their God named Zeus, and they named it in their own language the Capitol.[5] And the appearance of one of the buildings, the royal palace, was very wonderful. And in the Latin language they named the Capitol 'Head of the city'. 4. And in those days they called themselves 'Romans' and the name of their city 'Rome'. And the two brothers ruled together in it. But afterwards a cause of enmity intervened, and Romulus slew Remus his brother and reserved the throne for himself alone.

---

[1] This chapter is very corrupt. First, as we see from John Mal. 168 sq., the text should deal with Ascanius, the son of Aeneas and Creusa ('Ασκάνιος . . . ὁ υἱὸς τοῦ Αἰνείου ἀπὸ τῆς Κρεούσης). According to some traditions and those that have influenced our text, Ascanius left Lavinium (Elbânjâ in our text) and built Alba Longa (Elwânjâ in our text). But the text of John Mal. is here very confused and erroneous. Thus we have καὶ ἔκτισε ('Ασκάνιος) τὴν Λαβινίαν πόλιν, καὶ τὸ βασίλειον τοῖς Λαβινησίοις ἐπέθηκε, μεταγωγὼν ὁ αὐτὸς 'Ασκάνιος ἐκ τῆς 'Αλβανίας πόλεως τὸ Παλλάδιον εἰς τὴν αὐτοῦ κτισθεῖσαν πόλιν Λαβινίαν. See also Cedrenus, i. 238.

[2] Cf. John Mal. 161 ἀπὸ πόλεως μικρᾶς . . . Χαρτίμας.

[3] Text reads Iônâ through a faulty transliteration of the Arabic.

[4] Text reads Romanos by a corruption.

[5] Cf. John Mal. 171 ναὸν μέγαν τῷ Διὶ κτίσαντες ἐκάλεσαν αὐτὸν Καπετώλιον 'Ρωμαϊστί, ὅ ἐστιν ἡ κεφαλὴ τῆς πόλεως.

5. And thereupon the city was shaken with earthquake and all the people were panic-stricken together because of the great quakings in their midst. And Romulus also was terrified and became heavy of heart by means of his great terror, and [1] he learnt from the diviners and the unclean spirits that his throne should not be established in Rome without his brother Remus. 6. Then he had recourse to many a device in order to raise his brother and he was not able. But a great quaking ensued and in the midst of that quaking he saw an image of his brother, a perfect likeness from his head to his breast. 7. And he made an image of his brother in the likeness of the apparition which he had before seen, a golden statue representing his brother from the head to the breast, and he placed it on his throne and he adorned it with all manner of ornaments. 8. And in his prescripts he wrote after this manner, saying : ' (In) the prescripts emanating from me and my brother so we declare, and so we command, so we execute ', and so on. 9. And this custom derived from the Romans has prevailed to the present. Their kings and their magistrates have preserved this formula in the courts which are called ' praetorian ', that is, in their places of justice.

10. And Romulus also was the first to ride on horseback in Rome and to rush to the encounter at full speed and to be ardent [2] to be victorious. And he devised these diabolical practices and source of evils and vices, in order that his horse soldiers should be the strongest in the world. 11. And he appointed also a place of conflict for women called Elmanṭâṭûm [3] that the soldiers might resort (thither) in order to be with them (the women). For previously they had violated all the women, whether married, virgin, or widowed.

12. And by reason of his fear and discouragement Romulus instituted this order of female cavalry and made them alone without the men into one force. 13. And he divided them moreover into two parts, the virgins on one side and the married women on the other. And he assembled from all the cities far and near a great assemblage of women cavalry without number. 14. And

---

[1] This 'and' occurs in the text before ' by means of '.

[2] Read †ꝟ꘎†꘎†꘎:

[3] Unintelligible. Cf. John Mal. 177 sq. : *Chron. Pasch.* 112. Zotenberg conjectures it to be a corruption of στρατόν.

they kept watch over the foreign women in their midst [1] who did not belong to Rome, in order to accomplish (their) desire. And (Romulus ordered them) to lay hands on all they found.[2] 15. Now the young girls of the city of the Sabines which is near to Rome were beautiful women. And he summoned and assembled them (masc.) to him. And when Romulus had ended assembling the women, he gave them to the soldiers who had no wives. And he named those soldiers στρατιώτας,[3] that is, warriors. 16. And the rest he ordered to carry them (the women) off as best they could. And subsequently to this ordinance they chose their wives according to their individual tastes without violence.

17. And moreover he instituted [4] priests of the idols and named them priests of Apollo. 18. And next Romulus commanded his most illustrious officers and soldiers to entertain [5] in the winter season. And he invited (in order) from alpha to omega [6] the most illustrious of his officers, each in turn, and the commanders and magistrates of the people and all the soldiers whom he wished. And this ordinance existed in Rome. 19. And next he established a custom in Rome, called Abrâstûs . . . [7] this is the place, to wit, of the officers in which they keep guard of the citadel at all times. 20. And next he built the walls of the city of Rome and completed them. 21. And next he built a temple in the city of Ares, in the month

---

[1] In the text the words ' in their (masc.) midst ' occur after ' desire '.

[2] Read ᎄᎎᎎᎎ: ᎎᎎᎎᎎᎎ:

[3] ᎎᎎᎎᎎ: (?).

[4] The text is not to be emended as in Zotenberg, but the manuscripts to be followed. ᎎᎎᎎ: in some instances as here = ' to institute '.

[5] Zotenberg resigns the attempt to translate verses 18-20. The text refers to the Brumalia. Cf. John Mal. 179 τούτου οὖν ἕνεκεν ὁ 'Ρῶμος ἐπενόησε τὰ λεγόμενα Βρουμάλια, εἰρηκώς, φησίν, ἀναγκαῖον εἶναι τὸ τρέφειν τὸν κατὰ καιρὸν βασιλέα τὴν ἑαυτοῦ σύγκλητον πᾶσαν καὶ τοὺς ἐν ἀξίᾳ καὶ πάσας τὰς ἔνδον τοῦ παλατίου οὔσας στρατιάς, ὡς ἐντίμους ἐν τῷ καιρῷ τοῦ χειμῶνος, ὅτε τὰ πολεμικὰ ἔνδοσιν ἔχει. καὶ ἤρξατο πρώτους καλεῖν καὶ τρέφειν τοὺς ἀπὸ τοῦ ἄλφα ἔχοντας τὸ ὄνομα καὶ λοιπὸν ἀπολούθως ἕως τοῦ τελευταίου γράμματος, κελεύσας καὶ τὴν ἑαυτοῦ σύγκλητον θρέψαι τῷ αὐτῷ σχήματι. ᎎᎎᎎ: is to be emended into ᎎᎎᎎ: Cf. θρέψαι in last line of the preceding extract.

[6] The words ᎎᎎᎎ: ᎎᎎᎎ: ᎎᎎ: = ' to alpha and omega ' should be emended into ᎎᎎᎎᎎᎎ: ᎎᎎᎎᎎ: = ' from alpha to omega ', and should be transposed after ᎎᎎᎎᎎ:

[7] What this word refers to is doubtful. The words may, as Zotenberg suggests, form a fragment of a description of the four factions, and Abrâstûs in that case would represent πραίσεντον. Cf. Chron. Pasch. 112 ἐκάλεσε δὲ τὸ πράσινον μέρος πραίσεντον.

of March, that is Magâbît. Now March is the beginning of months. 22. And in the beginning of the month they celebrate a feast, and they named that feast 'Primus'. And after this feast he commanded the soldiers to fight. 23. And they named this month March [1] because of the custom of the heathen who are demon-worshippers according as the ancients had prescribed in their foolish ignorance. And the Romans have preserved this custom. 24. It is for this reason that the holy fathers, the Egyptian monks, who were clothed with God, offer at the beginning of every month an unbloody sacrifice to the holy consubstantial Trinity and receive the holy life-giving mysteries, while they chant the words of the 80th Psalm : ' Blow up the trumpet in the day of the new moon, on the notable day of our festival.' [2]

CHAPTER LVII. 1. And after Romulus Numa became king. He was a wise and very prudent man. 2. And he caused the government of the city of Rome to go along a good path by means of an excellent discipline. 3. And this illustrious man was the first to make money for selling and buying and for the exchange of silver. It is for this reason that stamped copper money is named felûs unto this day.[3] 4. And next he appointed two places : one for the officers and one for the judges that they might give orders to the officers and all the army. 5. And furthermore he established (them) outside that they might judge the peoples who were under their authority ; and not only those who judged but those with functions which are subordinate according to rank, and (others) which resemble this.[4] 6. And this law is ordained and established amongst the Romans unto this day.

CHAPTER LVIII. 1. And in the days of the high priest of Jerusalem who was named Judas, Philip was king of Macedonia. And when he became king he warred against Thessaly and came

---

[1] This passage is corrupt. The original sense can be inferred from the *Chron. Pasch.* 292 A ὁ δὲ αὐτὸς βασιλεὺς 'Ρῶμος . . . ἔκτισε καὶ τῷ ῎Αρει ναόν, καὶ ἐν αὐτῷ τῷ μηνὶ ἐποίησεν ἑορτὴν μεγάλην, θύσας τῷ ῎Αρει, καλέσας καὶ τὸν μῆνα Μάρτιον, πρώην λεγόμενον Πρῖμον, ὅπερ ἑρμηνεύεται ῎Αρεως, ἥνπερ ἑορτὴν κατ᾽ ἔτος οἱ 'Ρωμαῖοι πάντες ἐπιτελοῦσιν ἕως νῦν, καλοῦντες τὴν ἡμέραν τῆς πανηγύρεως Μάρτις ἐν Κάμπῳ.

[2] Ps. lxxxi. 3. The text agrees with the LXX ἐν εὐσήμῳ ἡμέρᾳ ἑορτῆς ἡμῶν.

[3] Cf. Cedrenus, i. 260 καὶ ἀσσάρια δὲ ἀπὸ ἀσήμου καὶ χαλκοῦ πεποιημένα πρῶτος 'Ρωμαίοις ἐχαρίσατο. Here ἀσήμου means ' silver ', but our author took it in its earlier meaning of ' unstamped ', and some scribe omitted the negative. Hence we have 'stamped'.

[4] The meaning of this verse is obscure. Zotenberg does not translate it.

off victorious over it. 2. And when he had won the victory, he built a city (in Macedonia) and named it Thessalonica.

CHAPTER LIX. 1. And when Alexander the son of Philip of Macedon became king he built in Egypt the great city Alexandria, and named it Alexandria after his own name. 2. Now its name formerly in the Egyptian language was Rakoustis.[1] And after this he warred against Persia. (And he came) to the confines of Europe, and he built there a place where his army and all his troops assembled. And he gave there gold in abundance to his chief generals and to all his officers and his numerous forces.

And he named that place Chrysopolis.[2] And so it is named by the inhabitants of Byzantium. 3. And in his war against Persia Alexander slew many of Darius's troops, (nor did he stop) till he had annihilated them. And he seized all the kingdom of Darius and made himself master of it. 4. And moreover he took captive his daughter, who was named Roxana. And she was a virgin and he made her his wife. And he did her no injury. 5. Nor yet did he offer any outrage to Candace the queen of Ethiopia, because of her great intelligence ; for she had heard tidings of the great deeds of Alexander and how it was his custom when he wished to war against the kings of the earth to join with spies (and so to visit their territories).

6. And queen Candace, being apprised of his arrival with the spies, had him arrested and said unto him : 'Thou art the king Alexander who hast seized upon all the world, and yet thou art to-day seized by a woman.' 7. And he said unto her: 'It is by means of thy knowledge and the subtility of thy intelligence and thy wisdom that thou hast seized me. Henceforth I will preserve thee unharmed, (even) thee and thy children, and I will make thee my wife.' 8. And when she heard these words she cast herself at his feet and made an alliance with him, and he made her his wife. And thereupon the Ethiopians submitted to him.

9. And when Alexander was dying he divided his kingdom among his four companions who had helped him in his campaigns. 10. And Philip, his elder brother, took Macedonia and reigned over

---

[1] In text Râkûdî. Cf. John Mal. 192 τὴν μεγάλην Ἀλεξάνδρειαν ἔκτισε τὴν πρῴην λεγομένην κώμην Ῥακοῦστιν.

[2] Cf. John Mal. 193.

it and all Europe. Furthermore he made Ptolemy, surnamed Lagus, king of Egypt.

CHAPTER LX. And in the days of Ptolemy Philadelphus, son of Lagus, whose name by interpretation means ' lover of the brethren ', a man of large thought and wisdom, the holy books of God were translated from the Hebrew into the Greek language by old men in the space of seventy-two days, for there were seventy-two translators, but two died before they had completed the translation.[1]

CHAPTER LXI. 1. And Antigonus reigned over Asia and Cilicia and the river which is named Draco in the province of Orontes. 2. And over Syria, Babylon and Palestine there reigned a king named Seleucus Nicanor. 3. And this (king) warred against Antigonus king of Asia and slew him, because he had built a city on the borders of the river Draco and had named it Antigonia. 4. And he seized all the property in the region of Iopolis and of the fortress which faces mount Silpion. . . . Now this city was formerly named Bottia.[2] 5. And he built there the great city of Antioch, and named it after the name of his son Antiochus. 6. And again he built another city [in the name of his daughter], and he named it Laodicea, for his daughter's name was Laodicea. Now this city had formerly been named Mazabdan. 7. And again he built a city and named it Apamea, which formerly had been named Pharnace.[3]

CHAPTER LXII. Seleucus, that is, Pausanias,[4] was the first to write Chronicles and annals and to name them.

CHAPTER LXIII. And Antiochus surnamed Epiphanes visited with punishment the Maccabees.

CHAPTER LXIV. 1. History of the Consuls of the early Romans. Julius Caesar the dictator seized the power and administration among the Romans before the incarnation of our Lord and Saviour Jesus Christ. 2. The birth of Julius was not like the birth of (ordinary) men whom women give birth to in the ninth month. For his mother died during her pregnancy, and after she died the babe stirred in her womb. And the wise men seeing that the babe stirred, cut open the womb of the mother and brought forth the

---

[1] Cf. John Mal. 196 ; *Chron. Pasch.* 173.
[2] Cf. John Mal. 199.   [3] Cf. John Mal. 203.
[4] The text is a corruption of the account in John Mal. 317 C ἔκτισε δὲ καὶ ἄλλας διαφόρους πόλεις . . . καθὼς ὁ σοφὸς Παυσανίας συνεγράψατο.

(babe) living and nursed it and called its name Caesar. Now Caesar means 'drawn forth', 'cut out', 'separated'. 3. And when he grew up they named him also Triumvir, and in accordance with a decree of the Senate of Rome he was appointed and became king. 4. And when his empire was consolidated, the Persians and barbarians were seized with fear. And this same Caesar made the month in which he became king the first month of the year. 5. And he issued prescripts for his commanders and prefects according to their various offices in every province of his empire. 6. And next he left the east and came to Alexandria the chief city of Egypt. And he met queen Cleopatra, the daughter of Ptolemy, surnamed Dionysus, king of Egypt. 7. And she was a very beautiful young girl. Caesar fell in love with her and married her and begat a son by her. And he gave her the kingdom of Egypt. And he named that son Julius Caesar. He was also named Caesarion. 8. He built a beautiful palace and also a beautiful and magnificent and comely house, and he named it after his own name and that of his son. 9. And when the great Constantine, the emperor of the Christians, took possession of the Roman empire he changed this (building) into a church and named it after the name of S. Michael. 10. And to this day it is named the church of Caesarion because it was built by Julius Caesar the younger and Caesar the elder.

CHAPTER LXV. 1. It is told regarding Archelaus the chief governor of Cappadocia and regarding Herod, who was full of wickedness (and) the murderer of his father, who was the first to eat raw meat with the blood, and not of the number of the faithful : now Herod was king of Judea : (it is told that) they submitted to Caesar the elder [1] and made him sovereign over their territories during all their life. 2. And Archelaus built in Cappadocia a city and named it Caesarea in Cappadocia to be a memorial of him (Caesar). And formerly it was named Mazaca.

CHAPTER LXVI. 1. And Herod also built a city in Palestine and named it Caesarea in honour of the emperor. And this is very beautiful and its name was formerly Straton's Tower (Στράτωνος πύργος). 2. And he constructed a way also which led into the city of Antioch, and he made the city more spacious and he covered the way with slabs of white stone at his own expense, and though

---

[1] i. e. Caesar Augustus.

previously impassable he made it a way fit for kings. 3. And
he sent also a Jewish army into Egypt and he made all the cities
submit to the emperor. And in like manner he caused the orientals
to pay tribute to Caesar.

CHAPTER LXVII. 1. And queen Cleopatra went down from
Palestine into Egypt in order to make her royal residence there.
And when she came to the city Farmâ she gave battle to the
Egyptians and overcame them. 2. And next she came to
Alexandria, and reigned there. And she was great in herself and
in her achievements (in) courage and strength. There was none
of the kings who preceded her who wrought such achievements
as she. 3. And she built in the confines of Alexandria a great
(and) magnificent palace, and all that saw it admired it; for there
was not the like in all the world. 4. And she built it on an island
in the quarter of the north to the west of the city of Alexandria,
outside the city and at a distance of four stadia. 5. And she raised
a dike against the waters of the sea with stones and earth, and
made the place of the waters over which they voyaged formerly
in ships into dry land, and she made it passable on foot.[1] 6. And
this stupendous and difficult achievement she wrought through the
advice of a wise man named Dexiphanes, who made the sea into
dry land that there might be a means of passage on foot. 7. And
next she constructed a canal to the sea, and she brought water
from the river Gihon and conducted it into the city. And by this
means she brought it about that ships could approach and enter
the city and by this means there was great abundance. 8. Now
the city was formerly without access to water, but she brought all
the water it required (lit. made it full of water) so that ships could
sail thereon, and by this means fish became abundant in the city.
9. And she executed all these works in vigilant care for the well-
being of the city. And before she died she executed many noble
works and (created) important institutions. And this woman, the
most illustrious and wise amongst women, died in the fourteenth
year of the reign of Caesar Augustus. 10. Thereupon the inhabitants of Alexandria and of (lower) and upper Egypt submitted
to the emperors of Rome, who set over them prefects and generals.
11. And Augustus reigned fifty-six years and six months. And in
the forty-second year of his reign our Lord and Saviour Jesus

[1] Cf. John Mal. 217 sq.

Christ was born in the flesh in Bethlehem Judah, very God alike in heaven and earth—to Him be praise. 12. (He was born) in the days when a decree went forth that all the world should be registered and every person numbered with a view to levying of taxes. And this measure was carried out through the advice of Eumenes and Attalus, illustrious and great men of Rome.

13. And Augustus moreover found the name of the month February inscribed in the middle of the year. Now if we start from the first, that is March, the earliest of the months of the Roman year, this month of February was the sixth in order of the Roman months. 14. Now Augustus decreed [1] that they should make this month the last of the months of the year; for Augustus blamed the chief of the army in those days, who was named Manlius of Cappadocia,[2] possessing as he had power and authority over them; for it was he who arranged the order of the months, and he was influential and powerful amongst the Romans. 15. And instead of this month of February which he had made the last month, because it was the shortest of all the months, they introduced in its stead the full month named August after his name; and it was the sixth month. 16. The month which preceded the sixth month, i. e. the fifth, he named Julius after the name of the emperor, the paternal uncle of Augustus. 17. And the Romans adopted and confirmed this regulation (and have observed it) till the present day. The sixth and fifth months are preceded by March.

CHAPTER LXVIII. 1. Now Christians complete in faith do not receive [3] any other rule than that ordained for them in accordance with the statement of Ezra the prophet,[4] the illuminator of under-

---

[1] Cf. John Mal. 187 Αὔγουστος . . . ἐπεμέμφετο τῷ Μαλλίωνι Καπιτωλίνῳ ὡς τάξαντι τὸν κακοιώνιστον Φεβρουάριον μῆνα μέσον, καὶ μεταγαγὼν εὐθέως . . . διὰ θείας αὐτοῦ κελεύσεως τὸ ὄνομα τοῦ Φεβρουαρίου μηνὸς ὕστερον πάντων τῶν μηνῶν ἔταξε, καὶ ἀντ' αὐτοῦ τὸ ἴδιον ἑαυτοῦ ὄνομα Αὔγουστον τὸν ἕκτον ἀπὸ τοῦ πρίμου, καὶ τὸν πρὸ τοῦ Αὐγούστου μηνὸς ἐκάλεσεν εἰς τὸ ὄνομα τοῦ θείου αὐτοῦ Ἰουλίου Καίσαρος.

[2] There is a dittograph and a disarrangement in the text. First ወሰሐራሰ: ዘሐመየ: is to be excised as a dittograph, and በመ: ማላየዋስ: ዘፀደፉየ: to be read immediately after መዋዕል:

[3] I have emended ይመስጡ: (= 'carry off', 'plunder') into ይፀመወ: = 'receive'. Our translator has already used this latter verb in the like connexion.

[4] In Fabricius, Cod. Apocr. Novi Test., p. 952, and in his Cod. Pseudepig. Vet. Test.,

standing †when the months come how on the sixth of Tûbâ, i.e. Ter, which is the first month amongst the Franks: 2. When the beginning of the month coincides with the first or second or third unto the end of the seven days.† 3. And they observe moreover the commencement of their months in seeking to know whether it will be lucky or unlucky. 4. And Socrates the sage and philosopher (and) astronomer established this custom in Rome. 5. And Socrates the ordainer and establisher of the practice had altered among the pagans the writings of Ezra the prophet and saint. He was deceived and he deceived those who read his book by his evil device.

CHAPTER LXIX. 1. And after the death of the emperor Augustus, his son Tiberius became emperor, who had brought Cappadocia into subjection to Rome after the death of Archelaus the governor of Cappadocia. 2. And he built also a city in the province of Thrace and named it Tiberia.[1] And in the days of Tiberius Caesar our Lord Jesus Christ was crucified in Jerusalem.

CHAPTER LXX. 1. And, after the death of Claudius, the abominable Nero became emperor in Rome. Now he was a pagan and an idolater. 2. And to his other vices he added the vice of sodomy, and he married as though he were a woman. And when the Romans heard of this detestable deed, they could no longer endure him. 3. And the idolatrous priests particularly inveighed against him, and the senators elders of the people) deposed him from the throne[2] and took counsel in common to put him to death. And when this impure wretch was informed of the purpose of the senators, he quitted his residence and hid himself. But he was not able to escape the mighty and powerful hand of God. 4. For when he fell into this disquietude of heart, owing to the debauchery which he had practised as a woman, owing to this cause (I repeat) his belly grew distended and became like that of a pregnant woman. 5. And he was greatly afflicted by the multitude of his loathsome pains. And therefore he ordered the wise men to visit him in the place where he was (hidden), and to administer remedies. 6. And

---

p. 1162, notices of this work of Ezra on the unlucky days of the twelve months will be found. See also Zotenberg *in loc.*

[1] Cf. John Mal. 236.

[2] The words 'deposed him from the throne' occur in the text at the close of ver. 4. I have restored to ver. 3.

when the wise men came to him thinking that he was with child [1] they opened his belly in order to deliver it. And he died by this evil death.

CHAPTER LXXI. 1. And after the death of Titus Domitian his brother became emperor in his stead. And he was a great philosopher among the heathen. 2. And he stirred up a persecution against the Christians and he brought many torments upon them by the hand of Decius and through the machinations of his officers. 3. And he had John the beloved evangelist brought to Rome, and he persecuted him and all the believers in God for their true and right faith. 4. And afterwards being struck with admiration at the greatness of his wisdom he set him free in secret and without the knowledge of his officers and the idolatrous priests he had him conducted to his residence. 5. But again Domitian, yielding to the persuasions of the wicked ministers of the demons, sent John the theologian into exile to the island called † Sun.[2] 6. And next Domitian built a city in the province of Isauria and he named it Domitianus after his own name. 7. And when the consummation of his sin was at hand, he had driven into exile the holy martyrs and he went to the temple of Titus and sought to offer a sacrifice to the demons; for he called a thing which could not speak a saviour. 8. Then his officers took counsel to put him to death; for he had always humiliated them through his stiffneckedness and pride of heart, and, philosopher though he was, he had wholly failed to do justice. And they rose against him and put him to death secretly. 9. But the people were not aware that they had put him to death. And they took his silk garments and suspended them on the chains of the temple lamps, in order to deceive all the people by a lying statement, saying: '(The emperor) had been carried up from earth into the air by the priests of the gods, because he was a philosopher.'[3] 10. Thus they misled the people for some time; but afterwards they were apprised of the death of this wicked man, and there arose a tumult because they had put him to death in the

---

[1] The words 'thinking he was with child' wrongly occur in the text after 'opened his belly'.

[2] ፀሐይ፡ = 'sun' is probably due, as Zotenberg conjectures, to a misreading on the part of the Ethiopic translator of the Arabic transcription of Πάτμον, i.e. شمس as فمن.

[3] Cf. John Mal. 267: *Chron. Pasch.* 250-1.

temple and by their mad act had profaned it, though they said :
' We are guiltless and our temple is not profaned.' 11. And after
this [there arose a tumult and] they agreed upon Nerva and made
him emperor. Now he was the commander-in-chief of the army, an
old man, very excellent, humane, and wise. 12. And forthwith he
sent to the sweet-tongued S. John and had him brought back from
his place of exile to the city of Ephesus, where he died in goodly
peace. And where his holy body is buried is not known save to our
Lord Jesus Christ—unto whom be praise. 13. Now this emperor was
a good man and he established good laws, and moreover he put an
end among men to the custom which prevailed of buffet for buffet
and blow for blow. And whilst he was engaged in this legislation
the emperor died aged † forty-four†[1] years after a reign of one.

CHAPTER LXXII. 1. And after the good emperor Nerva died,
Trajan became emperor, who was much addicted to the worship of
idols. 2. He was the third of those who persecuted the Christians.
And there were many martyrs in every place who were put to
severe tortures. 3. And furthermore the saint of God, Ignatius
the patriarch of Antioch, who was appointed after Peter, the chief
of the apostles, was brought by his orders in chains to Rome and
delivered to a lion. 4. And next he seized ⟨five Christian women
of Antioch⟩[2] and interrogated them and said unto them : ' Whom
do ye worship, and in whom do ye trust that ye run with such
haste to death ?' 5. They answered and said, ' We shall die for
the sake of Christ, who will give us eternal life and deliver us from
this body of corruption.' 6. And he was filled with wrath ; for he
was a heathen and was averse to the revelation of the doctrine
of the resurrection. And he commanded the bodies of the holy
women to be cast into the fire. 7. And he ordered the earth on
which the bodies of the holy women had fallen to be gathered and
† added to the brass which heated the public bath †[3] which he had
built in his own name. 8. And it came to pass afterwards that
when any one went to wash in that bath that a vapour arose, and

---

[1] This is corrupt. John Mal. 268 gives seventy-one years as his age. Nerva
died at the age of sixty-four.

[2] Restored from John Mal. 276.

[3] Text corrupt. Cf. John Mal. 276 τὸν χοῦν τῶν ὀστέων αὐτῶν συνέμιξε χαλκῷ,
καὶ ἐποίησε τὸν χαλκὸν εἰς ὃ ἐποίησε δημόσιον χαλκία τοῦ θερμοῦ. That is, he mingled
the ashes of their bones in the brass out of which the brazen vessels of the public
bath were made.

when he smelt that vapour he was overpowered by it and had to be borne out. And all who saw it marvelled thereat. Therefore the Christians mocked the heathen and gloried in Christ and praised Him together with his Saints. 9. And when Trajan was apprised of this phenomenon, he † changed those who heated the bath † [1] and removed the vessels of brass with which were mingled the ashes of the holy women, and he placed their ashes in five brazen pillars and set them up in that bath. 10. But he was on the watch to pour contempt on the martyrs, saying : † 'They belonged neither to me nor to their god, but they have died foolishly.' † [1] 11. And at that time his daughter Drusis and Junia the daughter of the patrician Fîlâsanrûn underwent martyrdom. And many other virgins likewise underwent martyrdom by fire through this unbeliever. 12. And during Trajan's stay in Antioch, the earth was troubled and quaked in the night owing to the wrath of God, for it had been polluted three times. 13. And not only (in) Antioch, but also on the island of Rhodes was there a similar earthquake after cockcrow.

14. And the Jews who were in the city of Alexandria and in the province of Cyrene assembled and chose a leader named Lucuas [2] to be their king. 15. And when Trajan was informed and apprised of this movement, he sent against them an officer named Marcus Turbo [2] with a numerous force, even a numerous army of horse and foot and also many troops in ships. 16. And Trajan came to Egypt and built a fortress with a strong impregnable tower, and he brought water into it in abundance and he named it Babylon in Egypt. 17. Nebuchadnezzar the king of the Magi and Persians was the first to build its foundations and to name it the fortress of Babylon. This was the epoch when he became its king by the ordinance of God, when he drove the Jews into exile after the destruction of Jerusalem, and also when they stoned to death a prophet of God at Thebes in Egypt, and added sin to sin. 18. And Nebuchadnezzar came to Egypt with a numerous army and made a conquest of Egypt, because the Jews had revolted against him, and he named ⟨the fortress⟩ Babylon after the name of his own city. 19. And Trajan moreover added some buildings to the fortress and other parts in it. And he dug also a small canal—sufficiently large to convey water from the Gihon to the city

---

[1] Probably corrupt. Cf. John Mal. 277.   [2] Cf. Euseb. *Hist.* iv. 2.

Clysma. And he put this water into connexion with the Red Sea,
and he named this canal Trajan after his own name. 20. And he
built also a citadel in Manûf. And after all these achievements
he fell ill and died in the twentieth year of his reign.

CHAPTER LXXIII. 1. And after Trajan [the first] Hadrian [1] his
cousin became emperor in Rome. 2. He built in upper Egypt a
beautiful city and its appearance was very pleasing, and he named it
Antinoe, that is, Ensînâ. 3. And afterwards misguided men made him
a god, for he was very rich. And he died by a distressing death.

CHAPTER LXXIV. 1. And after him Aelius Antoninus Pius
became emperor. He was kind, courteous, and virtuous. And the
Romans named him at first ' the servant of God '. He was a just
man throughout his reign. 2. The chroniclers report concerning him
that he was the first to do justice and to put an end to the unjust
practices which had prevailed among the Romans before his time.
3. Previously they used to commit the injustice of confiscating for
the benefit of the crown a moiety of the possessions of the rich on
their death on the ground of the covenant which the fathers had
made with their children.[2]   And his predecessors were not able to
abolish this regulation. 4. But he issued a prescript and put an
end to it in order that every man should have control over his own
property and should give it to whom he pleased. And he established
also many other equitable measures and laws in conformity with
justice. 5. And next he went down into Egypt even to Alexandria,
and he punished those who had wrought evil, and was gracious
to those who had wrought good ; for tenderness and graciousness
and forbearance were implanted in him. 6. And he built two gates
in Alexandria on the west and on the east (of the city), and he
named the eastern gate Ἡλιακή, and the western Σεληνιακή.[3]
7. And he built a place of pleasure with blocks of white stone
in the city of Antioch and named it Amûlûm.[4] And he transported the stone from upper Egypt. 8. And in all his cities he

---

[1] Text corrupt : = Trajan. Hence addition of the words ' the first '.
[2] Cf. John Mal. 281.   [3] Cf. John Mal. 280.
[4] The present form of the text misrepresents the facts, as we see from
John Mal. 280 ἐλθὼν δὲ καὶ ἐν Ἀντιοχείᾳ . . . ἐποίησε τὴν πλάκωσιν τῆς πλατείας
τῶν μεγάλων ἐμβόλων τῶν ὑπὸ Τιβερίου κτισθέντων, καὶ πάσης δὲ τῆς πόλεως, στρώσας
(αὐ)τὴν διὰ μυλίτου λίθου . . . ἀπὸ Θηβαΐδος. The facts shortly are : The emperor
constructed a great street between the two great porticoes (ἐμβόλων, transliterated
Amûlûm in our text) in Antioch, and had this and the city paved with stones
brought from the Thebaid.

built baths and academies. 9. And after this he returned with
a numerous army to Rome and remained there for some time and
died, aged seventy-seven years, in the twenty-third year of his
reign. 10. And he left his possessions to his son Marcus. And
Marcus his son resembled his father in graciousness and virtues.
And he did all that was lawful and just, and he died in the religion
of his father.

CHAPTER LXXV. 1. And after him the impious Decius, the enemy
of God, became emperor. 2. And he raised painful punishments
against the Christians and established the law of the polluted
heathen that search should be made for the Christians. And
accordingly he shed the blood of many saints[1] in every quarter,
even of those who worshipped the true God. 3. And this abominable Decius had many male and female lions brought from Africa,
and also from the desert had many serpents and venomous beasts
male and female and placed them † to the east of the city of
Fîlmûntî, of Arabia and Palestine †[2] to the fortress of Circesium
in order to form a source of strength against the barbarians and rebels.

CHAPTER LXXVI. 1. And after him a man named Aurelian
became emperor. And immediately on his accession to the throne
he rebuilt the walls of Rome, which had fallen into ruins, and finished
them in a short time. 2. And he made all the inhabitants of Rome
to work in order to accomplish the building, while he diligently
overlooked it himself without pride. 3. And at that time he
ordained a law that all the workmen should be registered and
* that they should be named chief citizens[3] of the empire in
honour of the emperor. 4. And all this was done in consequence

---

[1] Zotenberg inserts here in the text a word needlessly and without authority.

[2] The original form of the text can be reconstructed from *Chron. Pasch.* 271
ὁ αὐτὸς Δέκιος βασιλεὺς ἤγαγεν ἀπὸ τῆς Ἀφρικῆς λέοντας φοβεροὺς καὶ λεαίνας, καὶ
ἀπέλυσεν εἰς τὸ λίμιτον Ἀνατολῆς, ἀπὸ Ἀραβίας καὶ Παλαιστίνης ἕως τοῦ Κιρκησίου
κάστρου, πρὸς τὸ ποιῆσαι γενεάν, διὰ τοὺς βαρβάρους Σαρακηνούς. Ὁμοίως δὲ ἀπὸ τῆς
ξηρᾶς Λιβύης ἤγαγεν ἑρπετὰ ἰοβόλα καὶ φοβερὰ ἀρρενοθήλεα, καὶ ἀπέλυσεν εἰς τὸ τῆς
Αἰγύπτου λίμιτον διὰ τοὺς Νομάδας . . . βαρβάρους. In the obelized phrase
Fîlmûntî is due to the translator taking λίμιτον as a proper noun. Hence we
should restore here 'on the confines of the East, of Arabia and Palestine'. The
Circesian camp was on the Euphrates. The lions were placed in its neighbourhood, while the serpents were let loose on the confines of Egypt.

[3] The text is corrupt here; it runs: 'and that one should name them, and he
named them'. The sense is that all the artisans in the city were to be called
Aureliani after the name of the Emperor. Cf. John Mal. 300 ἐποίησε . . .
κέλευσιν ἵνα . . οἱ τῆς πόλεως πάσης ἐργαστηριακοὶ Αὐρηλιανοὶ χρηματίζωσιν.

of the labour he underwent in the building of the walls of the city. And this custom prevailed so among the Romans that it led to the registration of the peasants and artisans and sailors who sailed upon the sea. 5. And all the workmen Aurelian named ' Aurelians' after the emperor's name, and he had them registered in the register of dîwan, that is, dabdâbê. And this institution has prevailed to the present.

CHAPTER LXXVII. 1. And when Diocletian the Egyptian became emperor, the army turned to give its help to this impious man and persecutor of the faithful and the most wicked of all men. 2. But the city of Alexandria and Egypt declared against him and refused to submit to him. And he made himself strong to war against them with a numerous force and army and with his three colleagues in the empire, Maximian of a wicked stock, Constantius, and Maximian[1] (Galerius). 3. And he went down into Egypt and made it subject to him, and as for the city of Alexandria he destroyed it. 4. Now he built a fort on the east of the city and lay encamped there for a long time; for he was not able by these means to capture the city and bring it into his power. 5. And after a long time some people of the city came to him and showed him a means of ingress whereby he could enter. And so with much toil and trouble he stormed the city and he had with him an innumerable army. 6. And in the city also many thousand troops were assembled by reason of the war that was waged amongst them. And Diocletian set fire to the city and burnt it completely, and he established his authority over it. 7. And he was an idolater and offered sacrifices to impure demons and persecuted the Christians. He was indeed like a brute beast. 8. And he hated all good men and he resisted God; for all the power of Rome was in his hand. 9. And he put to death all the pastors, priests and monks, men, women and little children, and by the hands of his flesh-devouring agents whom he had appointed in every place, he shed without mercy or compassion the blood of innumerable saints. 10. And he destroyed churches and burnt with fire the Scriptures inspired by God. It was a persecution of all the Christians extending over nineteen years, beginning with the time of his accession to power and his conquest of the land of Egypt. 11. And at this time he sent men of

---

[1] Text wrongly reads Maximin here and in 77[25], but rightly on 77[75]. Text has to be corrected in 77[47, 48, 73, 74, 83, 88, 92].

Alexandria to cut off the head of the holy father Patriarch Peter, the last of the martyrs. 12. And he put to death all the bishops of Egypt whom he found attached to the orthodox faith and a pure course of life, till (at last) every one believed him to be the Antichrist, who had come to destroy all the world; for he was the home of evil and the lurking-place of wrong. 13. And his colleagues were like him in action and character, and these were Maximian, who had perpetrated many crimes, for his sovereignty was derived from him (i. e. Diocletian), and Maximian the second, whose empire was in the east. He resembled a treacherous beast, and was an enemy of God and the perpetrator of abominable crimes. 14. But Constantius, who was associated with him in the empire in Asia, had not committed any crimes, but he loved men and treated them kindly. 15. And he made also a proclamation by the voice of a herald to the Christians in all places under his sway that they should do the commands of the Lord, the one true God. 16. And furthermore he commanded that neither should violence be done to them nor persecution be stirred up against them, nor their property be plundered nor any evil inflicted upon them. 17. And he commanded likewise that no hindrance should be put to their worship in their holy churches in order that they might pray on behalf of him and his empire. 18. And in the third year after the close of the persecution which he had instituted against the Christians, the impious Diocletian in the midst of such enterprises fell sick of a grievous bodily disease and lost his mind and reason. 19. And in consequence thereof he was deposed and in accordance with a decree of the Roman senate sent in exile to the island named Wârôs, in which there were great forests, and it lay in the west. And he remained there alone. 20. And in that island there were some believers who had survived; these supplied him with daily food sufficient to sustain his body. And whilst he pursued this course of life in solitude, his reason returned to him, and he became ambitious (again) of empire, and besought the army and the Senate to come and take him from the fortress (where he was) and make him emperor as before. 21. But the officers, the army and senate refused, saying: 'This man, who has lost his reason and mind, whom also we have deposed, we will not receive back again. 22. And in consequence of this refusal this enemy of God and of the holy saints was deeply grieved and was not

able to accomplish his desire.   He wept and his eyes shed tears
in abundance now that misfortune surrounded him on every side.
And he lost his reason to a very great degree and became blind
and his vigour departed and he died.

23. And Maximian, persistent in evil deeds, wrought many
enchantments on Diocletian, and he was addicted to abominable
practices and to the invocations of demons; and he cut open the
wombs of pregnant women and sacrificed men and women to
impure demons.   24. And in the midst of such actions he was
strangled and died in the second year after his father's death, and
his end came about not by the hands of others but by his own.
25. And the impious Maximian (Galerius) also ceased not to
perpetrate the same crimes as Diocletian : yea he perpetrated (them)
in the east, in Africa, and in the great city of Alexandria and in
Egypt and in Pentapolis.   26. And he put to death without mercy
the holy martyrs : some he cast into the sea, others he gave to wild
beasts, others to the edge of the sword, and others to be burnt in
the fire.   And he destroyed churches, and burnt with fire the
holy Scriptures and restored the temples of the gods which were in
ruins.   27. And he had no compassion on the women with child,
but ripped open their wombs and drew forth the babes and sacrificed
them to impure demons.   And he compelled many to worship idols.
28. And no more did he escape the wrath of God; for by the
command of God a severe cough settled in his chest, he began
to fail in health, his intestines became ulcerated, deadly worms
were generated and the odour that emanated from him became
fetid, so that one could not come near him.   29. And when he
fell into this severe affliction and great tribulation, he despaired
of life and found no solace in his grievous disease.   And afterwards he recognized and learnt that his malady had befallen him
through Christ the true God because he had afflicted the Christians.
30. And when he had wisely collected his inner thoughts together,
he commanded his appointed officials to put an end to the persecution
of the Christians.   And when he had done this act of humanity,
the malady which God had inflicted on him departed from him,
and he was restored to health.   31. And he continued (to enjoy
health) for six months after his repentance for his sin, but again he
took thought to organize a persecution of the Christians, and he
forgat Him who had healed him of his grievous disease, (even)

Jesus Christ our Lord and Saviour.   32. And again he began to slay
the Christians, and he set up new gods in the great city of Antioch,
and he gave himself to dealings with demons and the enchantments which he used to practise.   33. But forthwith war stirred up
against him in Armenia and there arose likewise a severe famine in
every province of his empire.   And the fields yielded no produce
and nothing was to be found in the granaries, and the people fell
down and died through want of food.   34. And the rich became
poor; for the people of †Abrâkîs† had quickly plundered them.
And all men wept and lamented bitterly, and they died and
found none to bury them.   35. And the idolaters who lived in the
west were full of lamentation and grief because of their loss of
Diocletian and his son Maximian.

36. And (Maximian) sent to them his son Maxentius, who established a high reputation for himself in that place.   For this son of
the impious (Maximian) was on the watch to ruin them, but, being
treacherous, to begin with he sought to please all the inhabitants of
Rome.[1]   37. And he honoured our Faith, and he gave orders (to his
subjects) to cease from [2] persecuting the Christians, and he fashioned
himself after the likeness of the worshippers of Christ.   And he
began to exhibit a greater love for mankind than any of his predecessors that were like him.   38. But after a short time his treachery
discovered itself, and so, just as his fathers, he became like a wolf
in his lair.   And he wrought in its fullness the treachery of his
fathers and disclosed his secret vices, and committed every abomina-
tion and impurity.   And he became fierce and left no form of
impurity and licentiousness unaccomplished : and he perpetrated
every kind of debauchery and abused every man, and even legally
married women who had husbands he lay with [in public], not in
secret but openly, and thereupon sent them back to their husbands.
39. And further he was not willing to let them rest from the
oppression which they exercised upon them by his command.   And
he also seized under many pretexts the property of the rich and from
such as had nothing to give he took whatever he found in their
possession, and he put many thousands to death for the sake of

---

[1] Cf. Euseb., *Hist.* viii. 14, on which verses 36 sqq. appear to be based.

[2] The text has here 𝓛Ⲫ𝕬ⲛ: = 'to mitigate', 'relax', a possible meaning of
ἀνεῖναι, but not the right one in this context.   Cf. Euseb. *Hist.* viii. 14 ἀνεῖναι
προστάττει διωγμόν.

their property.   40. But one cannot give a complete account of the
deeds perpetrated by this impious man.   But the people of the city
of Rome were helpless in what they did; for he treated them
contrary to the customs of their city.

41. But Constantius was a servant of God, of good report, who
accomplished his course in wisdom and prudence, being beloved and
virtuous.   All manner of men made prayers and supplications on
his behalf, the nobles and people and army.   42. It was he that
built the city of Byzantium and he pursued the good path in
uprightness.   Then he fell asleep and went to God, leaving his
illustrious son, Constantine, the beloved of God, glorious and
resplendent in righteousness, whom he appointed emperor to bear
rule in his stead.   43. And this glorious (and) blessed worshipper
of the Trinity wrought the will of God always.   And he loved all
the subjects of his empire and he did good unto all, and he accomplished all the days of his sovereignty in modesty and firmness and
integrity, and he became great before God who liveth for ever.
44. And the army and all the people blessed him, for he was
zealous with a goodly zeal for God.   And there were revealed in
his days light and Christian wisdom, powerful and true, and
charity and tolerance.   45. And he rejected absolutely every charge
of the informer,[1] and yet he made, without exerting any violence,
all who were subject to his sway, servants of God.   Moreover he
could not endure to leave (as they were) the churches which had
been cast down, and so he rebuilt them.   Nor did he permit any
obstacle to withstand the holy Christian worship of God whereby
he had been consecrated to be emperor (endowed) with goodness
and modesty.   46. And he took Licinius his sister Constantia's
husband to be his colleague in the government of Rome, who
was wanting in none of the virtues of Constantine the upright
emperor; for he had made him swear a great and terrible oath
that he would do justice and transgress in no respect against
our Lord Jesus Christ or against His servants.   47. And at that
time there came from the east the impious Maximin, the adversary
of God and slave of Satan.   For he had usurped the empire of
the east as its sole ruler, and he plotted to put to death the

---

[1] So Zotenberg renders, and perhaps rightly, but this meaning is unknown
to classical Ethiopic, according to which it should be rendered—'apostate',
'heretic', &c.

upright emperor Constantine and refused to execute the sealed
rescript from [1] Constantine.   48. For he levied war on all the cities
and provinces under the sway ⟨of Licinius as far as⟩ the city of
Constantinople, but he was not able to make himself master of them.
And both the godly Constantine and Licinius his sister's husband
made preparations to war against these rebels.   Constantine
went to war against Maxentius who was in Rome, and Licinius
went to war against the impious Maximin in the east.   49. And
when Maxentius heard of the approach of Constantine the servant
of God, he proceeded by ship and entered the river of Italy
which flows by the city of Rome and built a bridge on a secure
structure for the passage of the combatants, and of his followers,
and of the augurs who announced to him the oracles of Satan.
50. He knew not indeed that the godly Constantine had the help
of Christ.   And when the impious Maxentius and all his people
had crossed the river of Italy, the cavalry that were posted on
the bridge came to meet him before the arrival of the Godloving
Constantine.   51. And when Constantine arrived, he took his
position at a distance and did not enter the battle but waited to
see the manifestation of the help of God.   And the enemy indeed
grew strong and powerful.   52. And while Constantine was so
engaged, he lay down and fell asleep, grieved and sad at heart.
And he saw a vision in the form of the holy cross in the heaven
and there was written thereon this inscription : ' By this sign of
the cross thou shalt conquer.'   53. And thereupon he arose hastily
and began the battle and fought and won the victory over his
adversaries ; and not one of them remained, and he exterminated
them all.   54. And those who were with Maxentius the commander-
in-chief wished to escape and reach the city of Rome.   But by the
command of God the bridge was broken and they were all drowned
in the depths.   And there was joy in Rome that the impious were
drowned.   55. And the senate of Maxentius, and his nobles and his
army and all the people and the peasants together with their babes
took waxen torches and clad themselves in clean and white garments
and went with musicians to meet the servant of God the emperor
Constantine.   56. And not only did the city of Rome rejoice but
also all the cities and provinces and the city of Constantinople
with them.   57. And Constantine was not uplifted in his heart

---

[1] I have emended **ㄱቤ:** = ' to ' or ' with ' into **አምㄱቤ:** = ' from '.

nor did he boast of his glory and his triumph as other kings
had done. He was, on the contrary, modest and humble of heart
and gave the praise to God and extolled his Lord, the Lord of
all, Jesus Christ, King of Kings, and Lord of Lords. 58. And
thereupon he entered the city of Rome in triumph, and all the
Romans prostrated themselves before him, and as many as had
survived the battle submitted themselves to his commands. And
Constantine thereupon entered the palace, crowned with the diadem
of victory. 59. And he made known to all men the miracle with
which he had been favoured and the victory which he had won
through the vision which he had seen in the heaven in the form
of the holy cross. And when they heard this recital all men
exclaimed : 'Great is the God of the Christians who has delivered
us and our city from the hands of the impious.' 60. And
Constantine thereupon ordered the temples to be closed and the
doors of the churches to be opened, not only in Rome but in every
city. And S. Sylvester the patriarch of Rome gave him many
excellent admonitions and instructed him in the pure faith.
61. And afterwards he went to war against the cities of Persia
and he conquered them. And when he had conquered them, he
†established them in peace and confirmed to them presents together
with a horn† [which they used to blow for the king].¹ 62. And
he received with kindness all the Christians who were there.
And he removed the city magistrates and all the officials and replaced
them with Christians. And he built beautiful churches in all the
cities and villages. 63. Furthermore he sent his mother the Godloving empress Helena to search in the holy Jerusalem for the wood
of the glorious cross on which was crucified our Lord and Saviour
Jesus Christ—Praise be unto Him. 64. It was in the days of the
blessed father † Ailîmûn†, bishop of Jerusalem. 65. And he built
also the holy edifice of the Resurrection in glorious fashion and
restored the buildings of Jerusalem so that they were finer than

---

¹ Our text here deals with the same subject as John Mal. 317 καὶ ἐπεστρά-
τευσε κατὰ Περσῶν καὶ ἐνίκησεν καὶ ἐποίησε πάκτα εἰρήνης μετὰ Σαραβάρου, βασιλέως
Περσῶν. Here the Arabic translator read μετὰ Σαραβάρου as μετὰ σαραβάρας, i.e.
'with a horn'. Σαράβαρος is otherwise known as Sapor. The words 'which
they used to blow for the king' is an explanatory gloss. Hence we should
probably read 'made peace with Sarabaros and confirmed it to them by
presents', i.e. እንበረ: ሰላሙ: ምስለ: ስረበርስ: ወአጽነዐ: ሎሰሆሙ:
እምአያሙ፦:

they had been at first, and so it has continued to the present.
66. And the emperor Constantine also built a church of great
magnificence and beauty in Byzantium. And its proportions were
not small but very lofty. 67. And when he had completed the
building of the city, he named it Constantinople after his own
name; for previously it had been named Byzantium. 68. And
he liked to reside therein, and he made it a habitation of Christ.
69. And he gathered also the sacred Scriptures and placed them in
the churches. 70. And next he assembled three hundred and eighteen
saints in the city of Nicaea and established the orthodox faith.
It is impossible to enumerate the good actions he accomplished.
71. Amongst the most notable officials (of the empire) there was
one named Ablâwîjûs, a Christian (who) laboured zealously to
discover the glorious cross on which our Lord and Saviour Jesus
Christ was crucified—Praise be to Him. 72. And the three hundred
and eighteen whom he assembled at Nicaea honoured the emperor
Constantine, the servant of God, and his mother the Godloving
empress Helena, and raised to them a worthy memorial and recounted
their glory from beginning to end.

73. And Licinius who took over the empire of the east [1] set out to
war against the impious Maximin. And this perverse wicked (man)
learnt that he was marching to war against him and (was apprised
of) the overthrow of Maxentius and his defeat by the godly emperor
Constantine, and he sought for peace from Licinius. 74. And
Licinius sent to Constantine saying : 'Maximin seeks for peace and
offers to accept the glorious and pure Christian faith and forsakes
his errors and concludes a treaty with me.' And Constantine sent
the reply that they should accept his proposals. 75. Then Maximin,
concealing in his heart his evil treachery, sent rescripts to all the
officials under his sway, forbidding them to disquiet the Christian.
76. And when the rescripts reached the officials they knew that this
policy was not in conformity with his wishes but only with the
faith of his superiors. And for this reason none accorded to him
honour, anywhere, because of the evil he had previously done to the
saints.

77. Now the emperor Constantine never prevented the chief
Christians from holding synods or building churches, but he

---

[1] The grammar of the verse is impossible. I have omitted በ: before
'set out'.

observed carefully the Christian faith and shunned the worship of idols. And thus he commanded and gave instruction to all that the churches should be left in peace, and he battled on behalf of the orthodox faith.

78. There was a man named Gelasinus of the village of Mariamme, which is near to Damascus, about one mile distant. And he lived in the midst of a large population who were devoted to the worship of idols and dwelt in the city of Heliopolis in Lebanon. 79. And at that time they were assembled in a theatre, and they had brought actors with them. They put cold water into a large brazen vessel and thus began to mock all who came to the holy baptism of the Christians. 80. And one of these actors went down into the water and was baptized, and when he came out of the water they clothed him in a white garment; for till this incident he had been an actor, but after he came forth from the water he refused to pursue the avocations of an actor or to play the mimic again, and said: 'I wish to die in the Christian religion on behalf of Christ'; and added: 'I saw a great miracle while I made a mock of holy baptism'. 81. And when he had gone but a little way from the place of that water, all who were there were filled with wrath and indignation; for they were worshippers of idols. 82. And they went down from the theatre and seized that holy man and stoned him. And he received the crown of martyrdom which fadeth not away, and he was enrolled with the holy martyrs. And his relatives came with many Christians and took his body and buried it in the village and built a church over the place where his body was buried. Now the man's name was Gelasinus.[1] May God have mercy on us through his intercessions.

83. Now the impure Maximin did not forsake his wicked errors and he was not possessed by the power of righteousness which had been acquired from God by the Godloving emperors, who pursued a good course through life in knowledge and in understanding. 84. But this perverse man resolved to make war on the Christ-loving emperors; for he was possessed by a demon that infuriated him. And as he had lost his former unlimited authority, he could no longer choose for himself those most agreeable or suitable to him. 85. And in his pride and stiffneckedness he began to violate the treaty he had made with Licinius. †And he exerted himself

---

[1] Cf. John Mal. 314 sq.; *Chron. Pasch.* 275 sq.

to execute deeds which should issue in his destruction through
fear †, and he changed his mind and stirred up all men and threw
all the cities into confusion and the officials under his sway.
86. And he mustered many thousands to war against the Godloving emperors and he trusted in the demons from whom he
received instruction.   87. But from the moment he began to war
the help of God was withdrawn from him, and Licinius conquered
him and slew all the soldiers in whom he trusted and the officers.
And all the remaining troops betook themselves to Licinius and
cast themselves at his feet. 88. And when Maximin saw this he
fled in fear; for he was dispirited, and he quitted shamefully the
field of battle and came to his own province.   And he was full of
wrath and indignation against the idolatrous priests and lying
prophets, and augurs, for they had persuaded him through favourable
counsels.   89. And for this reason he slew them in whom he had
(formerly) boasted himself, and whom he had made gods.   Then
it was that he learnt for himself that they were impostors and
powerless to give aid in war.   And he renounced the demons who
had instructed him with counsel, and he slew the magicians who
wrought evil.   But he had no zeal for the salvation of his soul : he
was feeble, and praised not the God of the Christians, and he refused
wholly to accept the law and its blessings.   90. And Licinius gave
orders to carry on the war against those who remained in the tenth
year after the persecution of the Christians, wherein Diocletian, the
father (of Maximin), the adversary of God, had persecuted them.
During all this length of days (Maximin) had not repented with
a genuine repentance nor truly hoped for salvation.   91. And after
his flight from the field of battle, he suffered from disease of the
heart, and grew weak from a grievous disease which came upon
him from God.   And his flesh was devoured through the fire of
the disease, and this fire burned in his belly, and his appearance was
altered and his limbs wasted away, and his intestines were consumed, and his bones became prominent and finally his eyes fell
out.   And in the midst of all this affliction, his soul left his body.
92. It is thus the three adversaries of God, Diocletian and his two
sons, perished.   But before he died the impious Maximin recognized
that all this had befallen him because of his rebellion against
Christ and the evils which he had inflicted on the Christian saints.
93. And in those days Licinius took possession of the east and

exercised authority over it and the adjoining provinces. And the church dwelt in tranquillity and peace, and he restored again its edifices and the church was lighted with the light of Christ. 94. But again thereafter Satan, the evil-doer, who is ever seeking to seduce all the faithful as a devouring lion, which is treacherous and cunning, seduced Licinius also and made him forget his honourable deeds of aforetime, and he inclined towards doing the actions of those whose eyes have been blinded, and he was zealous to follow their evil way, and his heart was not glad as before. 95. Formerly he had not been estranged from the emperor Constantine, but afterwards he forgot the covenant and the oath which had been made between them, and he took evil counsel against the great emperor Constantine to slay him. But Christ, the true God, foiled the plots of Licinius. 96. Formerly, indeed, he had honoured and praised Jesus Christ; but when he denied Him He delivered him over to a cruel death, refusing him forgiveness because of the shameful deeds that he had done. 97. And Licinius began to persecute the Christians and to levy war upon the God-loving Constantine as his impious predecessors had done, whose memorial had been blotted out by the Lord. 98. And he began also to demolish and close the churches and to put to death the holy believers. And as for the soldiers who were strong in the Christian faith, he degraded them, and subjected the rich to tortures.[1]   99. And he appointed agents in every city and village to put a stop to the holy, that is, the Christian worship of God, lest prayers should be offered up for the faithful emperor Constantine. And he turned them from the worship of God to that of demons. And he wrought very many evil acts. 100. But Constantine did not cease to praise and worship the one true Lord God. And together with Crispus, whom he had appointed Caesar, a strong man, kindly disposed to men and faithful to God, he assembled a strong army, and they went forth to war against the adversaries of God, under the guidance of our Lord and Saviour Jesus Christ, with invincible powers. 101. And though Licinius was his brother-in-law, Constantine had no mercy upon him, but he was firm on behalf of the holy faith which that rebel had forsaken, turning to demons. And for this reason he went against him

---

[1] Our author seems to have had Euseb. *Hist.* x. 8, or an equivalent source before him when writing this section regarding the apostasy of Licinius.

speedily armed with punishment, and he laid low him and all his army and exterminated them with a terrible and bitter death. 102. And all these happenings had come upon Licinius because he had denied Christ and had violated the oath and the covenant which he had made with Constantine. 103. And thereupon he took possession of the empire of Licinius and made it one with his own: yea, he took possession of the empires of the east and of the west and of the south and of the north. And they all came under his authority, and he established universal peace and was at one with all men and blessed by all men, and he duly made strong all the frontiers of the empire till his adversaries submitted to his authority through the might of our Lord Jesus Christ the son of the true Lord God. 104. And he made his two sons emperors, Constantius and Constans, with honour and majesty. Then he fell asleep without regret or trouble; for our Lord Jesus Christ, the true God, protected his empire to the third generation. 105. And the blessed Constans resembled his father, and he walked in the right way and accomplished all his days virtuously.

106. And after his death the people of Yemen received the knowledge of God, and were illuminated with the light of the praise of our Lord Jesus Christ—praise be unto Him—by means of a holy woman named Theognosta. 107. Now she was a Christian virgin who had been carried off captive from a convent on the borders of the Roman empire and had been conducted to the king of Yemen and presented to him as a gift. 108. And this Christian woman became very rich through the grace of God and wrought many healings. And she brought over the king of India to the faith, and he became a Christian through her agency as well as all the people of India. 109. Then the king of India and his subjects requested the Godloving emperor Honorius to appoint them a bishop. 110. And he rejoiced with great joy because they had embraced the faith and turned to God, and he appointed them a holy bishop, named Theonius, who admonished them and instructed them and strengthened them in the faith of Christ our God till they were worthy to receive baptism which is the second birth through the prayers of the holy virgin Theognosta. 111. Glory be unto our Lord Jesus Christ who alone worketh marvels and bestoweth goodly gifts on those who trust in Him. And so it was also in India, that is, the great India. For the men of that country

had formerly received a man named Afrûdît (i. e. Frumentius).[1] He was of noble birth of the country of India and they had made him their bishop, having been instituted and ordained by Athanasius the apostolic, the patriarch of Alexandria.   112. Now (Afrûdît) had told him concerning the grace which they had received through the Holy Spirit and the manner in which they had found the salvation of their souls through the grace of holy baptism and were made worthy of this gift.

113. As for the Christ-loving emperor Constantine, there was with him always a bright angel of God which at all times directed and instructed him in the will of God until the memorable day of his death.   And he waked him also from his bed for prayer every day.   And he was visible to him alone of the emperors.   114. And as he beheld visions in the heaven he fell asleep after a pure life : he was an oblation to God, and he went to his rest in heaven.

CHAPTER LXXVIII. 1. And these are the names of the sons of the great emperor Constantine, Constantius, Constans, and Constantine. And they divided the empire of their father into three parts which they assigned by lot.   2. And to Constantius there fell by lot the province of Asia and he became emperor over it.   And to Constantine (there fell) Constantinople, and he seated himself on the throne of his father.   And Constans became emperor over Rome, the great city of Rome.   3. But feuds arose between Constans and Constantine in regard to the empire and their subjects, and they warred against each other, and Constantine died in battle.   4. And thereafter Constans, the younger of the two, resided in Rome only, but Constantius reigned in Byzantium, that is, Constantinople.   5. And Arius appeared in his days and he attached himself to his doctrine and became an Arian.   And in consequence of this (heresy) Sapor-Arsekius,[2] king of Persia, attacked the Roman empire, and there was much bloodshed between them.   6. And afterwards they were reconciled and there was peace and tranquillity and love between Rome and Persia.   7. And on his way back to Byzantium Constantius built a bridge strongly constructed over the river named Pyramus in Cilicia.   8. And in his days, moreover, the city of Nicaea, the chief of cities of our three hundred and eighteen Fathers, was overthrown by a great earthquake.   And this fell out

---

[1] Cf. Socrates, *Hist. Eccles.* i. 19.

[2] Cf. John Mal. 325. The right designation is Σάπωρ ʼΑρσάκης.

through the will of God in order that the Arians should not assemble
therein to corrupt the holy orthodox faith established by our holy
Fathers, the three hundred and eighteen bishops, who assembled
formerly in the days of Constantine—a festival of happy memory.
And it was for this reason that the wrath of God prevented them.

9. And afterwards there appeared in heaven a sign, that is, the
holy cross standing at midday over the holy place where our
Saviour Jesus Christ was crucified, before the arrival of Cyril,
patriarch of Jerusalem, and other bishops who were with him.
10. And Cyril thereupon and the bishops who were with him wrote
a letter and sent it to the emperor Constans regarding the great
marvel and the great sign which had appeared.

11. Now the emperor Constans was zealous for the faith of his
father, and he was earnestly devoted to the religion of God.   And
he resembled his brother who died in battle (and) admired him, but
he hated his brother who ruled in Asia because he had not kept
the faith of the Godloving Constantine, and promulgated many
decrees against the apostolic Athanasius, the patriarch of Alexandria,
and chased him from his bishopric in order to please the heretics,
i. e. the Arians.   12. The hatreds and differences that divided the
two imperial brothers, Constantius and Constans, were very violent.
And this hatred had arisen not only on account of the death of
their brother, but also because of Athanasius the patriarch of
Constantinople, and of Constantius's declension from the faith
of his father and his unacceptableness to our Lord Jesus Christ.
13. And on these grounds he strengthened (his) hatred against
his brother.   And whilst so engaged Constans died, having pleased
God and cursed Constantius his brother because of his evil deeds.
14. And after the death of Constans, the emperor Constantius
sent an officer to slay Athanasius, the glorious Father, the head
of the church.   15. Heretofore Constans had protected him from
the evil designs of his brother, and Constantius feared his brother
and concealed his evil designs in his heart.   16. But after the death
of his brother Constans, he disclosed all that was in his heart
and sought to slay him.   But the right hand of the Most High
God protected him, and he took to flight and concealed himself
and was saved from his hands.   17. And the officer who was sent
to the apostolic Athanasius raised a tumult against the Christians ;
for he belonged to the sect of Manes.   And in those days it was

not only the Arians who disquieted the church : the Manichaeans also were roused on a different principle, and stirred up a persecution of the Christians, and there was much disquiet and shedding of blood.

18. And afterwards there arose against the city of Rome a powerful leader named Magnentius, and he usurped the imperial power †at the hour of sunset† [1] without the permission of Constantius.   And he marched into Europe and gave battle to Constantius, and many were slain on both sides, and finally the mighty Magnentius was slain also.   And Constantius won the day and made himself master of all the possessions of Magnentius. 19. And after Constantius won the victory he did not praise God as had the Christian emperors who preceded him.   In all his actions, on the contrary, he followed the guidance of the Arians.

20. And later he assembled a council of heretical bishops in Milan, that is in Italy, at the instigation of these heretics who had rejected the orthodox faith and denied the worship of the Holy Trinity.   21. And he made them write a sentence of excommunication against the apostolic Athanasius, the patriarch of Alexandria, and the bishops who followed him.   22. And these are the names of those who were exiled with the apostolic Athanasius : Liberius, patriarch of Rome, who was appointed after Julius ; Paulinus,[2] metropolitan of Gaul ; Dionysius, metropolitan of Italy ; and Lucifer,[2] metropolitan of the island of Sardinia.   And they made Auxentius the Arian bishop of the province of Italy. 23. And ⟨he sent into exile also⟩ the aged and illustrious confessor Hosius,[3] bishop of the west.   24. And he made also the holy (Fathers) who had assembled in Nicaea to go forth, and exiled them from their bishoprics.   And later, when the emperor Constantius was in Rome, illustrious women came in a body to him and besought him to recall Liberius the patriarch from exile. And the emperor brought him back to Rome.   25. Now Felix was the minister of Liberius the patriarch who had come to terms with the Arians, and they made him patriarch after the expulsion

---

[1] As Zotenberg suggests, this is a mistaken rendering : he compares Socrates, *Hist. Eccles.* ii. 25 Μαγνέντιος περὶ τὰ ἑσπέρια μέρη ἐπεφύη τύραννος. We expect ‘ imperial power of the west ’.

[2] Paulinus and Lucifer are very corrupt in the text, owing to faulty transliterations of the Arabic. Cf. Socrates, *Hist. Eccles.* ii. 36.

[3] So Zotenberg conjectures. Text corrupt.

of his master. But on the return of his master Liberius from exile,
he (Felix) treated him with hauteur and dislike on account of his
restoration.   Then he, too, was exiled from Rome to a city of the
west and obliged to reside there.

26. And in those days Constantius sent Gallus, his †sister's† son,
to the east by night. This (Gallus) had formerly fought against
Magnentius and slain him, and was a Christian in all his ways.
27. And after he had slain this powerful (rebel), he returned to
Constantinople.   Then Constantius appointed him emperor of
Rome and sent him to reside there. 28. And after Gallus arrived
in Rome, his brother Julian of evil name returned to Constantinople
from the province of Bithynia to the emperor Constantius; for he
had put to death many of his relations and feared lest they should
calumniate him to the emperor.   29. Now this Julian was a strong
and powerful man. Formerly he had resided as reader in the church
of Nicomedia, but he had been troubled with doubts regarding the
Christian faith.   30. And Gallus, who was emperor of Rome by
the will of the emperor Constantius because he was his †son-in-law†
and because he was attached to him, lived but a few days longer
and then died.   31. Thereupon Julian gave up reading the holy
Scriptures, and betook himself to the protection of the troops
and officers of Rome, and let the hair of his head grow long and
became a great captain.   32. And subsequently he was appointed
emperor in Europe, according to the Christian custom, by the
permission of the emperor Constantius.   But he did not wait till
they had placed on his head the imperial crown according to
custom ; but walked according to the misguidance of augurs and
the directions of magicians and became a servant of demons,
and aspired to the proud position (of sole emperor) and began to
make war on the emperor Constantius.   33. And when Constantius
became aware of this movement he mustered a numerous army from
the provinces of Syria, and he came into Cilicia in order to do battle
with Julian; for he thought he should slay him.   34. But when
Constantius was so purposing he fell ill and died, and so was unable
to carry out his purpose;[1] for God had brought evils upon him
that he might return to the earth from which he came. 35. And
when Julian was informed of the death of Constantius he took
possession of the empire. He was strong and powerful exceedingly,

---

[1] **ሀለዮት፡** is here emended into **ሀለየት፡** with Zotenberg.

and he restored the exiled bishops to their thrones. And he brought
the apostolic Athanasius from exile and sent him back to Alexandria :
Meletius to Antioch : Cyril, the author of the homilies, to Jerusalem :
Eusebius, Lucifer, and Hilary to the west : and others who were in
like plight to their several churches. 36. But after a short time he
discovered his unbelief and apostasy owing to the philosophers, of
whom one was named Libanius, of the city of Antioch, and the other
Maximus one of the augurs. 37. Supported and strengthened by
these, Julian closed the churches and opened the temples, and
plundered the precious vessels of the house of God and gave them
openly to impostors. 38. Next he attacked the worshippers of
Jesus Christ and proclaimed himself the restorer of temples, and
offered abominable sacrifices to idols and kindled fire before the
altars of demons, and polluted the earth with the blood of impure
sacrifices, and polluted the air with the smoke of fat. 39. And at
the instigation of the heathen he sent (agents) to slay the great
(and) apostolic Athanasius. But he quitted his bishopric and fled and
hid himself from him. 40. And this apostate emperor, like his
father Satan, destroyed the holy edifices that had been built by
the Godloving emperor Constantine, and made all these holy places
into dwellings of demons and temples of idols. 41. And they
lorded it over the inoffensive Christians and they began to mock
them and destroy them and slay them and evilly entreat them, not
only for a short time but for a lengthened period. And they
bellowed like ferocious beasts against them and terrified them.

42. It was at this period that evil and idolatrous men kindled
a fire in order to burn the body of S. John the Baptist. But the
power of our Lord Jesus Christ foiled their design, and all these
apostates seeing a terrible apparition took to flight. 43. And there
were there certain inhabitants of Alexandria who took the body of
S. John and conveyed it to Alexandria and gave it secretly to the
holy Athanasius the patriarch before his flight. 44. And he conveyed it and placed it secretly in the house of a magistrate, one of
the great people of the city. And this secret was known only to a
few priests and to Theophilus the third patriarch (after Athanasius).
45. Now the latter was reader and singer when they brought the
body of S. John. And after Athanasius Peter became patriarch,
and after Peter, his brother Timothy Aktemon, whose name is by
interpretation ' without possessions '; and after Timothy, Theophilus

who destroyed the temple named Serapis (?) and converted it into
a church. 46. Now (this church) was massive and its dimensions
lofty and it was very much decorated. And he made it with pomp
the abiding-place of the body of S. John the Baptist. And it is
also said that after many days Theophilus took the body of S. John
and his head and placed them in the tomb which had been constructed in the midst of the church. 47. And he made great
rejoicings and a glorious feast. And the inhabitants of the city
were uplifted because of him and made him notable with praise.

    CHAPTER LXXIX. 1. And it is said in regard to the holy Theo-
philus, the patriarch of Alexandria, that he was a citizen of Memphis,
the city of Pharaoh, formerly called Arcadia. And he was of Christian
origin. 2. And he had a little sister and an Ethiopian slave who
had belonged to his parents. Now they were orphans and he was
but a child in years and stature. 3. And one night about the time
of dawn this slave took the children by the hand and brought them
to a temple of abominable gods, namely of Artemis and Apollo, in
order to pray there according to the errors of their worship. 4. And
when the children entered, the gods fell to the earth and were
broken. And the slave was frightened thereby and she took the
children and went in flight to the city of Nikius; for she feared the
priests of the abominable idols. 5. And she feared also lest the
people of Nikius should deliver her up to the priests of the idols, and
so she carried off the children with her and came to Alexandria.
6. And, as the divine inspiration moved her, and the grace of God
rested upon her, she took the children and brought them to the
church in order to be rightly acquainted with the practice of
the Christian mysteries. 7. And at that time God revealed to the
Father Athanasius, the patriarch of Alexandria, the circumstances
of the children when they entered the church and their position
near the place of exhortation (i.e. pulpit). And he gave orders
that the three should be guarded till the celebration was over.
8. And thereafter they brought the children and the slave to the
holy Athanasius, and he interrogated the slave and said unto her:
'What hast thou done and why did not the gods who are without
understanding assist thee? Why rather, when they saw the
children of the Church, did they fall to the earth and were broken?
Henceforth these children will belong to me'. 9. And when the
slave heard these things, she was astonished at the words of the saint

in that he knew the secret things that had befallen in the temple. Then she could not deny all that she had done : nay more, she cast herself at his feet and begged to be baptized into the Holy Christian faith. 10. And he baptized them and made them Christians and they received the light of grace and were (born) anew. 11. And ⟨he sent⟩ the little girl to a convent of virgins to remain there till the time of her marriage. Then she was given in marriage to a man of Mahallê, in the north of Egypt, which was formerly called Didûsjâ. 12. It was there the holy Cyril was born, the great star which lighted up all places by his doctrine, being clothed with the Holy Spirit. It was he who became patriarch after Theophilus, his mother's brother. 13. And after the child, the holy Theophilus, was baptized, they shaved his head and numbered him amongst the readers and appointed him to be an *anagnostes*. 14. And he was reared with care in the manner that befitteth saints, and he grew up and became a youth well pleasing to God, and he learnt all the God-inspired Scriptures of the Church and observed their laws. 15. And next they ordained him deacon and he became very zealous for the faith of our Lord Jesus Christ, in purity and holiness. 16. And later he was clothed with the garments of the priesthood and he became the chief and sat on the throne of Mark the Evangelist in the city of Alexandria. 17. And when he became patriarch, he illuminated every city with the light of his holy faith, and delivered all the cities of Egypt from the worship of idols and he destroyed all the makers of images, even as the holy apostolic Athanasius had prophesied regarding him.

CHAPTER LXXX. 1. And the wretched Julian began to build the sanctuary of the Jews in Jerusalem which the Romans had destroyed, and he offered sacrifices there, for he was devoted to the shedding of blood. 2. But our Lord Jesus Christ—praise be unto Him—brought to nought his works and ordinances. 3. And Sapor Arsaces, king of Persia, who was of a pacific disposition and had paid tribute to the Godloving emperor Constantine, went forth to war with the Romans. 4. It was at that time that the holy martyr Domitius finished his course.[1] For the emperor Julian, the enemy of God, after having offered sacrifice to demons in the city named Casius,[2] in the neighbourhood of Antioch, about six miles distant,

---

[1] Cf. John Mal. 328 ; *Chron. Pasch.* 297.
[2] Κυρρηστικά in John Mal. and *Chron. Pasch.*

where there was the idol Apollo, arose and went forth to war with the Persians, he and the forces of Rome. 5. And he was accompanied by all the demon-possessed and deceitful augurs. And as he marched he came to a grassy spot, and he saw there many men, women, and children. 6. And many of the sick were healed through the prayer of the holy Domitius, the servant of God. 7. And he questioned (them) saying : ' What is this assemblage which I see ? ' And they replied : ' A monk is working miracles and healing the sick : and this assemblage which thou seest is composed of Christians ; they receive a blessing from him and are healed by him '. 8. And Julian was wroth and sent to him a soldier treacherously [1] in a menacing tone and said : ' If thou dwellest in this cave in order to please God, why dost thou desire to please men, and why hast thou not hidden thyself ? ' 9. And the holy Domitius answered and said : ' I have committed wholly my soul and my body into the hands of the God of heaven, the true God, Jesus Christ. And behold it is now many years since I have closed this cave upon myself. And as for the assemblage which have come to me in faith, I cannot drive them away '. 10. And when the emperor heàrd these words he commanded the soldiers to close the mouth of the cave on the righteous old man till he died. 11. And thus he accomplished his course in the twenty-third day of the month Hamlê, and received the martyr's crown which fadeth not away.

12. But the punishment of God was not slow in overtaking Julian the Apostate. 13. Now he marched against the Persians who were idolators like himself, and he marched with haste and never again saw Rome. 14. But he did not accomplish what the deceivers had promised to him saying : ' We the gods will unite to give thee aid the moment thou dost enter the river '. 15. And this unfortunate man was deceived by their words and was not able to open his mouth by reason of their flow of speech. 16. And they named that river the river of fire because there were wild beasts in it.[2] And for this reason it is named by this name.

---

[1] The text seems corrupt here. Better read 𝔏·𝕋ⁿ𝔷𝔦𝔓: = ἐδεήσατο for 𝔏·𝕋ⁿ𝔷𝔓𝔓:, and instead of ' treacherously ' render ' and requested '.

[2] The explanation of these words and ver. 14 is to be found in an oracle of Apollo given to Julian and recorded in Theodoret (*Graecarum Affectionum Curatio*, p. 382, ed. Gaisford): Παραπλήσιον δέ τι δέδρακε καὶ ἐπὶ Ἰουλιανοῦ τὴν ὁρμὴν ἔχοντος

17. And Julian was obstinately attached to error and called himself 'the despiser of the word of God'. For he trusted in idols and consulted demons who were not able to save him, but misled him with vain performances; for they destroyed his understanding and he became an adversary of God, the glorious Creator and our Saviour Jesus Christ, who shed His blood on behalf of many and became the true foundation for believers, who avenged His Christian servants. 18. Now Julian shed the blood of many Christians, and in his days many believers were put to death, and he visited with severe persecution those who called upon the name of Christ. 19. Now, while this apostate was proposing to war against the Persians, vengeance came upon him from our Lord Jesus Christ, and he was slain by the hand of His servant Mercury, the martyr. 20. And on the night on which this abominable transgressor was slain, the holy Basil, who was clothed with God, bishop of Caesarea in Cappadocia, saw a vision. 21. And he saw the heavens opened and our Lord Jesus Christ sitting on the throne of His glory (and) saying with a loud voice : 'Mercury, go and slay Julian the adversary of My anointed ones'. And the holy Mercury was standing before him clothed with a flashing corslet of steel.[1] 22. And on hearing the command of our Lord Jesus Christ he departed, disappearing for a short space, and after a short space he reappeared [2] and cried with a loud voice: 'I have slain the emperor Julian in accordance with Thy command, and he is dead, O Lord'. 23. The bishop awoke astonied and terrified. Now Julian used to honour the holy Basil greatly because they had been bound by ties of friendship from their youth. For they were versed in letters [3] and Basil also had written frequently to him in order to

κατὰ τῶν Ἀσσυρίων· Νῦν γάρ, ἔφη, πάντες ὡρμήθημεν θεοὶ παρὰ Θηρὶ ποταμῷ νικῆς τρόπαια κομίσασθαι.

[1] Cf. John Mal. 333 sq. Text has here 'a new and blooming corslet', which Zotenberg accepts. But 𝔛𐩣𐩴: = 'blooming' is only used of plant life. The wrong sense seems due to the confusion of the participles of two different conjugations of ﻰﺑﺯ by the translator. Here it should have been 'shining', 'flashing'. Again, ሐዲስ: = 'new' is corrupt for ሐዲድ = ferrum. Thus our text reproduces the same original as John Mal. 333 ἐφόρει θώρακα σιδηροῦν ἀποστίλβοντα. This corruption of the two manuscripts points to the fact that neither A nor B is an immediate copy of the original translation.

[2] Here text adds corruptly 'and appeared a third time'.

[3] We should not insert ዓቢረ: in the text as Zotenberg does. Cf. John Mal. 334 ἐτίμα γὰρ αὐτὸν . . . ὡς ἐλλόγιμον καὶ ὡς συμπράκτορα αὐτοῦ καὶ ἔγραφεν αὐτῷ συχνῶς.

prevail on him to forsake his errors, but he had refused. 24. And when the bishop Basil awaked from sleep, he called the venerable priests and the faithful to early morning prayers in the church. 25. And after the completion of the prayers, he recounted to them this vision which he had seen, saying : ' Can Julian really be dead ? ' And when they heard these words, the priests and the people feared and thereupon asked him to be silent till the matter was fully ascertained.   But the man of God was not willing to be silent, but spake out and feared not; for he trusted in God and in our Lord Jesus Christ.   26. And soon it fell out according to the vision of S. Basil, and the death of Julian the apostate was heard of throughout all the provinces, even his destruction which God had accomplished by the hand of his martyr S. Mercurius.   27. Now this apostate had brought destruction and disasters on the army. He had the noses of two Persians cut off who, as guides, had conducted the army into a mountainous and waterless desert whence there was no means of issue, when he wished to attack the Persians. 28. And the Roman soldiers perished in that region of hunger and thirst and many hardships; for these Persians had dealt subtly with the Romans and had destroyed them.   But this apostate Julian did not recognize (this) indubitable judgement of God. 29. And his crimes had continued all the days of his life, even forty and four years.[1]

30. After the death of Julian the Roman troops assembled in order to appoint an emperor, and through the help of God being all of one mind whilst they were in Persia, they chose Jovian to be their emperor.   31. Now he was an orthodox Christian (and) a faithful servant of God.   He, however, was unwilling to be emperor, but he was made emperor by force.   32. Previously indeed he had been commander-in-chief, and for this reason he received the imperial crown.   And after they had made him emperor, he ascended an eminence and addressed in a loud voice all the people and the troops as follows : ' If ye wish me to become your emperor, become Christians like me, and believe in Christ, and become the foes of idols '.   33. Thereupon all the people and the troops cried out with one voice, saying: ' We are Christians : Henceforth Christ is our emperor and His glorious Cross '.   And for

---

[1] Julian was only 32 when he died, according to Eutropius, 31 according to Ammian. xxv. 3, 23 ; Socrates, iii. 21 ; 33 according to John Mal. 333.

this reason they honoured the emperor and praised him with great praise.

34. And when the Persians had been apprised of the death of Julian they sent ambassadors to Jovian the Godloving emperor to negotiate terms of peace and friendship. And the emperor Jovian received them gladly, and peace and friendship were made between Rome and Persia. 35. And the Persians agreed to pay tribute, and he (Jovian) remitted the tribute of one year, because Julian the apostate had previously destroyed and made a wilderness of the city of Anderwân. 36. Nevertheless he commanded them to build outside the imperial frontiers a city for themselves, and he named this city Amîdes.[1] And he strengthened it with walls and fortifications, and filled it with a numerous population, and he made it like the first city which Julian the apostate had destroyed. And he that was set over this city besought greatly the emperor Jovian to name it after the name of Rome. But he refused on account of the peace and friendship subsisting between Rome and Persia.[2]

CHAPTER LXXXI. 1. And after the conclusion of the war the Christian emperor Jovian evacuated Persia and brought back safely all the remaining troops. 2. But such as he found holding the evil sentiments of Julian the apostate he destroyed and exterminated. 3. And forthwith he opened the churches of Constantinople and closed the temples. And he restored to the Christians the Christian cities which Julian the apostate had taken from them, and he appointed Christian (governors) in all the cities, and he destroyed all the temples to their foundations, and the worshippers of idols became few. 4. And he interdicted also the religion of the Arians who are adversaries of Christ; for he was an unwavering orthodox believer and a true worshipper of the Holy Trinity who give life to all. 5. And he became glorious as the light of the sun through all his actions and his true and upright faith. And he was full of virtues and did good unto all men of his time. 6. And he addressed also a decree to all the Roman provinces to this effect: 'I, the Godloving Jovian, commander-in-chief, true emperor (and) master

---

[1] The text is inaccurate. Cf. John Mal. 336 sq.; *Chron. Pasch.* 300.

[2] The true account is that Jovian surrendered five Mesopotamian provinces with the fortresses of Nisibis and Singara. Even John Mal. 336 sq. concedes most of this.

of the world, hereby write to all the Christians under my sway.
7. I am solicitous over you in the Lord and I rejoice with you in
regard to the holy church which is in the midst of the city, as
the navel in the midst of the belly. For it has triumphed greatly
over all who opposed it. 8. Now the anger of the emperor Julian
arose against it and he closed it; but I give orders to have it
reopened and restored to a condition of repose in order that there
may be given to it a pure and holy priesthood who may therein
offer prayers to heaven—which may God in His mercy vouchsafe
to receive. 9. And now let us exert ourselves to reopen the church
and let us perform its offices, and honour its ministers, in order that
all the people and army of Rome may assemble within it. For it
was given to them by God, merciful and gracious, in order that
prayer and supplications might always be offered therein with
befitting earnestness.'

10. And Jovian addressed a letter to this effect also to the
apostolic S. Athanasius, the patriarch of Alexandria, in order to
restore him to his city in great honour. 11. 'From the emperor
Jovian to the Godloving S. Athanasius. We admire thee and thy
wise manner of life and †thy near approaches to the kings† and
thy faithful virtues and thy noble earnestness to fulfil the work of
our Lord Jesus Christ—praise be unto Him. 12. We request thee,
honoured bishop; for thou hast undergone every labour and hast
not feared those who persecuted thee nor the tribulations that have
overtaken thee, but hast accounted wrath and indignation as a
thing of nought and reckoned them as no better than a worthless
straw. 13. And thou hast gone in the footsteps of the orthodox
faith and hast proceeded unto the end, and hast left (the example)
of thy life to those that come after thee and hast bound them with
perfect faith and virtuous deeds.†[1] 14. Return now to our imperial
domain and resume thy teaching which is full of salvation. And
preserve the churches and feed the people of Christ and zealously
address thy prayers to God on our behalf and on behalf of our
empire that we may be saved through thy prayers. 15. For we
think that we shall gain the help of the Most High God through
the supplications of thy pure and holy tongue; for it is inspired by

---

[1] Verses 11-13 are a faulty rendering. Cf. Athanasii Opera ; *Patrol. Graec.*
t. xxvi, col. 813.

the Holy Spirit. 16. And we have written[1] this letter to thee
that thou mayst enlighten the people with the light of Christ
and mayst put an end to idols, the adversaries of God, and likewise
to the heresy of the Arians who persecuted them [that we may be
saved by thy prayers].

17. And when the apostolic S. Athanasius, the light of the world,
had read this letter, he convoked all the holy bishops and the
honoured doctors and wrote two treatises : the first on the Word of
God, who is one of the Holy Trinity, and the second on the precepts
of Christ. 18. And he addressed a letter also to S. Basil, who
constantly thought upon and studied the works of God, and said :
'The Godloving emperor Jovian accepts absolutely and with joy
the orthodox faith of the Council of Nicaea : rejoice thou therefore ;
for he is orthodox and has established the pure faith of the Holy
Trinity.'

19. And the emperor Jovian finished his course in peace and
integrity, doing that which was well pleasing to God. 20. And
whilst he was so engaged he set out to go to the city of Byzantium,
and though attacked by an illness he passed through Cilicia and
Galatia and came to the city named Didastana,[2] and he went to his
rest there. 20. For the world was not worthy to receive such an
emperor, as he was good and pious and merciful and humble,
Christian and orthodox.

CHAPTER LXXXII. 1. And after the death of the Godloving
Jovian, Valentinian, being the foremost[3] amongst the officers, came
to mourn with them over the death of the emperor Jovian. 2. And
whilst they were so mourning and were anxiously deliberating on
the appointment of their emperor, then Sallust the prefect of the
praetorians came (forward) and enjoying a very illustrious position
amongst the officers advised them and said : 'It is most suitable
for us that Valentinian should be made emperor. At an earlier
date he was a general and was persecuted by Julian the apostate on
account of his orthodox faith.' 3. And when the officers and the
troops had heard the advice of Sallust they appointed him emperor
and had him proclaimed as follows by the voice of heralds in all the

---

[1] I have omitted the impossible **H** before Ꝗ𐊗ꝖꝔ𐊗:

[2] Cf. John Mal. 337.

[3] There is no reason for the insertion made here by Zotenberg either in this
line or the next. By these insertions a wrong sense is given to the text.

provinces: 'Valentinian, a just man (and) a Christian, whose words are just and whose utterance is true, has become emperor.' 4. And when he became emperor, he appointed Sallust vizier (*sic*) over all his officers; for he was no respecter of persons. And when Sallust became vizier and was empowered with authority, he strengthened the cause of justice and right in all the provinces, and was full of discernment and refused bribes and did not give his confidence rashly.[1] And the emperor was pleased with him because he was a doer of the right. 5. And next Valentinian made Valens his brother emperor in Constantinople, but he went himself to Rome and established his authority over all the empire of the west. 6. And he condemned many magistrates who were guilty of injustice and took bribes. 7. And there was an officer of the palace named Rhodanus who had committed an act of injustice on a widow and had taken possession of her property. 8. And she went and told the emperor, and the emperor commanded (him) to restore all her property.[2] And from that day he was honoured by the army and the senate, and by all peoples. 9. For this just and equitable emperor hated oppression and judged with the voice of justice and practised equity. 10. This great emperor did not spare (even) his wife, the empress Marina. Now she had bought a garden from a nurserywoman (lit. a female planter of plants) and had not paid her the price which it was equitably worth, because the valuers had valued (it) out of regard to the empress and so had inclined to do her a favour. 11. And when the pious Valentinian was apprised of what his wife had done, he sent Godfearing men to value that garden and he bound them by a solemn oath to value it justly and equitably. 12. And when the valuers came to that garden, they found that she had been guilty of a grave injustice and had given the woman but a small portion of the price. 13. And when the emperor heard, he was wroth with the empress (and) removed her from his presence and drove her from the palace and took to wife a woman named Justina, with whom he lived all the rest of his

[1] 'Refused bribes and did not give his confidence rashly.' I have emended ወኢአምን፡ into ወኢአምነ፡ Zotenberg emends it into ወኢአምኖ፡ and renders 'ne se laissait pas corrompre par des dons'. His translation omits his emendation, and also the word በከንቱ፡

[2] According to John Mal. 339 sq. Valentinian had Rhodanus burnt and his property given to the widow. Cf. *Chron. Pasch.* 302.

days.   14. As for his first wife, he drove and exiled her from the city, and gave back the garden to the woman who had sold it.

15. And the emperor Valentinian raised to the imperial throne his son Gratian, who was born to him by the wife he had driven into exile. 16. And after the emperor Valentinian had accomplished many noble deeds, he fell ill and died loyal to the faith of the Holy Trinity, in the castle named Wâtân.[1] 17. And after his death came his brother Valens, who had formerly been a Christian but afterwards had walked in the way of the Arians and had attached himself strongly to their abominable faith. 18. And he persecuted the orthodox, and their churches were openly given to the impious heretics. And he confiscated wrongfully the property of all the inhabitants of Byzantium and other cities.

19. And in the days of this abominable (prince) there was an earthquake in the city of Nicaea where the holy council had been held. For the sea rose against it and overwhelmed it. 20. And in those days also a man named Tatian was appointed prefect of Alexandria, which is the chief city of Egypt. And he built, in the place called Abrâkjûn, the two stone gates with enormous labour and he made these gates for the passage of the great river, and he fortified the country of Egypt.

21. And in those days there appeared a miracle through the intervention of the apostolic S. Athanasius, the father of the faith, patriarch of Alexandria. 22. When the sea rose against the city of Alexandria and, threatening an inundation, had already advanced to a place called Heptastadion, the venerable father accompanied by all the priests went forth to the borders of the sea, and holding in his hand the book of the holy Law he raised his hand to heaven and said : 'O Lord, Thou God who liest not, it is Thou that didst promise to Noah after the flood and say : " I will not again bring a flood of waters upon the earth ".' 23. And after these words of the saint the sea returned to its place and the wrath of God was appeased. Thus the city was saved through the intercession of the apostolic S. Athanasius, the great star.

CHAPTER LXXXIII. 1. Now these are the illustrious emperors, the servants of God, who were zealous workers of good—Gratian and Theodosius. 2. The one set free the holy believers from bonds

[1] Called Βιργιτίνων in John Mal. 341, and Βεργιτίων in Socrates, *Hist. Eccles.* iv. 31.

wherewith they had been bound by the emperor Valens, and put an end to the banishment of Christians. 3. As for the other he loved God ardently and restored to the faithful their churches, and destroyed idolatry. 4. And he prohibited also the teaching of the wicked Arians and established the pure and spotless faith. 5. And Gregory, the Theologian, appeared in the city of Constantinople and strengthened the churches. Previously indeed he had been obliged to find concealment in flight from house to house and from place to place. 6. And (Theodosius) built also a holy church as a noble memorial. And he drove from the city Eudoxius, the heretic, the blasphemer of the Holy Spirit. And after he had driven this miscreant from the city, he sent to Basil, bishop of Caesarea in Cappadocia, to Gregory of Nyssa, and to Amphilochius of Iconium, wise and godly divines, and he commanded them to construct a church in the truth and in the Holy Spirit. 7. And they disputed with the heretics and got the better of them and put them to shame, and they proclaimed the true orthodox faith in every place. 8. And again as regards the history of the Godloving emperor Theodosius, while he was on his way to Byzantium to meet the blessed emperor Gratian, he saw a vision in his sleep, in which Meletius the patriarch of Antioch placed the imperial crown on his head by the advice of the leaders.

9. And there was an Arian living outside the city.[1] And when Amphilochius came to the imperial court, he found seated on their thrones the emperor Theodosius and his two sons Arcadius and Honorius. For he had raised them to the imperial throne in his lifetime. 10. And when the bishop came before Theodosius and his sons, he saluted Theodosius but not his sons. 11. And Theodosius was wroth because he had not saluted his sons. And when the bishop saw that the emperor was wroth with him, he said unto him : 'Reflect, O king, that in like manner there are those who do not salute the Son and the Holy Spirit who are consubstantial with the Father, namely the blaspheming heretics. (And yet) thou hast not driven these from thy empire.' 12. And when the emperor heard these words of the bishop, the emperor perceived that the bishop was one of the highest types of the faithful, and thereupon

---

[1] It is not an individual but a community that is here referred to. The matter is referred to in Socrates, *Hist. Eccles.* v. 7, where it is recounted of Demophilus that ἔξω τῶν πυλῶν τῆς πόλεως τὰς συναγωγὰς τοῦ λοιποῦ ἐποιήσατο.

he held his peace. 13. And forthwith he became zealous for the orthodox faith, and he ordained a law in his days that no heretic should be permitted to live in any of the Roman cities, nor in the cultivated enclosures nor in the fields nor in the villages.

14. And during the stay of the emperor Theodosius in Asia there arose a usurper, named Maximus, of British descent, who slew the blessed emperor Gratian through treachery and seized his empire by force and made his residence in Rome. 15. And Valentinian, the younger brother of Gratian, fled to Thessalonica. And as for Maximus the heretic, he despised God; for he was an Arian. 16. And next there arose a man named Eugenius, who had previously been a teacher of the heathen and had persecuted the worshippers of Christ and loved to practise magic and made (*sic*). And by the advice of the officers who agreed with him, he seized the empire of Valentinian and slew him by treachery. 17. And when Theodosius the emperor heard of these events, he arose and mustered a numerous army and marched against them, and put to death both Maximus and Eugenius through the might of our Lord Jesus Christ whom he served. 18. And he avenged the two emperors Gratian and Valentinian and brought back under his own hand the entire empire of Rome and established his authority over it. 19. And he gave to the orthodox believers all the churches under his dominion, and he banished the blaspheming Arians. 20. And he assembled also in Constantinople a council of bishops, to the number of one hundred and fifty holy fathers. 21. And he drove out infidelity and heresy from all the provinces of his empire and he introduced the worship of the one God in three Persons, and he strengthened the orthodox faith. 22. And the Holy Spirit was (shed) abundantly upon the priests, and their hands and their tongues and all their thoughts were pure. And peace prevailed in the churches, because the bishops had assembled in peace and unity. 23. But afterwards when Satan saw (the prosperity of the church), he was jealous and began to divide and sunder the limbs of the one complete body, that is, the holy Church. 24. For Gregory, the Theologian, having come to the council of the chief clergy of the Church, comforted and adorned the city of Constantinople by his teaching. 25. And Timothy, patriarch of Alexandria, addressed Gregory like an angel and admonished him to leave the imperial city of Constantinople and return to the city of his bishopric and its ancient church, namely

Nazianzum (?),[1] in order to shepherd and protect it. 26. It was
unseemly for him to forsake a poor church and occupy a rich one;
for this was an act of [2] . . . fornication and contrary to the canons
of the Fathers. 27. But when the bishops of the east and the
other bishops present heard this address, they differed from him in
this matter. 28. A tumult, moreover, arose amongst them on this
question. For the patriarch Timothy took upon himself to nominate
Maximus to the patriarchate of Constantinople; for he was an
eminent man and had suffered many hardships from the Arians.
29. Now there was a feud between the Orientals and the Egyptians.
And S. Gregory mediated and made peace between them. And
Maximus who had been nominated to Constantinople without the
consent of the bishops remained there, but Gregory they banished
from the imperial city on the advice of all the bishops, and he
returned to his first church. 30. But the heart of Gregory was
firm as a stone and was not troubled by the troubles of this world.
And all the people were grieved on his behalf; for he had saved
the imperial city of Constantinople from the (spiritual) adulteries
of the Arians. 31. And they banished Maximus also from
Constantinople to the convent to which he had formerly been
appointed, and all the bishops which had been ordained by his hands.
32. Next they appointed a man named Nectarius [3] by the advice of
the one hundred and fifty bishops. Now he was a man of good
birth, of the city of Constantinople. He was also wise and prudent
and he led such a good and pure life that all the world admired
him for his conduct. And they forcibly appointed him to the
patriarchate. 33. And he kept up a continuous warfare against
the faith of the Arians, and he was zealous for the orthodox faith.
And peace was established in the council and all (the bishops) later
departed in joy to their cities. 34. But Satan the adversary of
our race did not suffer Nectarius the patriarch to remain untroubled.
For when the Godloving emperor Theodosius had set out with
a numerous army to war against Maximus, the Arian usurper,
and had reached a place named Milan, within which lay the Arian
usurper, and had thus come face to face with him but as yet no
engagement had ensued between them, certain Arians went and
announced through all the city of Byzantium a lying report to

---

[1] MSS. Atrâsjûs of Nîsîjûs.   [2] ⲌⲪⲦ: gives no intelligible sense.

[3] Cf. Socrates, *Hist. Eccles.* v. 8.

this effect: 'The emperor Theodosius has been defeated in battle and all his army destroyed.' 35. And by reason of this rumour fear and terror fell on all the Christians, and the orthodox out of fear inclined to the Arians. And the Arians arose in wrath and burnt the mansion of the patriarch Nectarius. 36. And after they had wrought these evil deeds, an account thereof was reported to the Godloving emperor Theodosius. And forthwith he arose and gave battle to Maximus the usurper and slew him.

37. And in those days the holy patriarch Timothy built a church of marvellous workmanship in the city of Alexandria and named it after the name of the emperor Theodosius. And he built also a second church and named it Arcadia after his son. 38. And there was a temple of Serapis[1] in the city, and he converted it into a church and named it after the name of his (Theodosius's) younger son Honorius. But this church was also named after the names of the martyrs Cosmas and Damian. It faced the church of S. Peter the patriarch and last of the martyrs.

39. Throughout the days of the emperor Theodosius the Christians enjoyed tranquillity and peace. 40. And Theodosius constructed also many buildings in the outskirts of the city of Antioch. And he built a new wall from the mountain to the old (lit. 'first') tower[2] constructed by the emperor Tiberius. And he built walls also round the neighbouring lands and enclosures which had been without a wall.

41. After this there arose many heresies and divisions in the city of Thessalonica owing to the Arians. And a disturbance took place between the inhabitants and the officers and the Arians began to stone the officers, insulting thereby the emperor. When the emperor was informed of what the Arians had done, pretending that he was on his way to Rome he marched into Thessalonica with all his officers and soldiers. 42. And using a ruse he sent armed men among the population of the city and destroyed the Arians. And the number of those that were put to the sword was 15,000.[3] 43. And the emperor being reprimanded by the patriarch Miletius[4] for his great slaughter of the Arians—for he

---

[1] The text has been restored, i. e. by reading አበራ‌በ‌ቡ: ቡ7ር:

[2] Contrast John Mal. 346 καὶ περιέλαβε τὸ ὅρος τὸ νέον τεῖχος ἕως τοῦ παλαιοῦ τείχους τοῦ κτισθέντος ὑπὸ Τιβερίου.

[3] John Mal. 347 gives 15,000 ; Cedrenus 7,000 or 15,000.

[4] This should be Ambrose.

had been troubled on behalf of the Christians—was full of wrath
and indignation : but (afterwards) the emperor repented of his
wrath against the patriarch, and repented and fasted and gave
alms and shed many tears, praying for mercy and forgiveness of
the transgression.

44. And in those days there were animosities and great trouble
and destruction in the city of Antioch.   45. And the emperor
indeed was sore pressed by the war that had been waged in (that)
province and in every other quarter, and when this pressure upon
him became severe, he commanded an extraordinary tax to be
levied in all the provinces of his empire.   46. And they seized and
illtreated the people.   And when the crowds and multitudes that
were in the city saw their brethren being hanged without mercy or
pity, the men of the city cast down [1] from the top of the palace the
bronze †coffin† [2] which contained the body of the blessed Flacilla,
the wife of the emperor Theodosius, and they dragged it through
the streets of the city.   47. And when the emperor heard of this
outrage, he was wroth exceedingly and removed the officers of the
city and banished them to Laodicea.   48. And as regards the
officials of Antioch who had perpetrated this great offence against
the emperor, he gave orders, in order to punish them, that the city
of Antioch should be burnt together with everything that was in it.
49. And those, who were commanded to burn the city, were Caesar
an officer and Ellebichus a general.   50. And subsequently there
came from the desert a monk, a saint of God, to the officers who
were commanded to burn the city, and addressed them as follows :
51. ' Write to the emperor Theodosius and say to him on my part
as follows : " Thou art not only an emperor but thou art also a man
like us, though thou art the chief.   And thou art subject to the
same afflictions as every creature which bears the likeness of God.
When thou condemnest the likeness of God, thou dost provoke
to anger the God who created man in His likeness.   For thou
art angry because of a dumb statue of brass: how much more
therefore will God be angry with thee and thy empire when His
image endowed with utterance and a soul is in question.   52. For
it is He and He alone who is Lord and King over all that has

---

[1] There is no need for Zotenberg's addition to the text.

[2] The word means 'casket' or ' coffin', but in ver. 52 it means 'statue', as it
should here.

given thee power. And as for thy wrath because a †coffin† [1] of bronze has been destroyed, we can make one like unto it, but thou canst not make a single hair of the head of a single person whom thou dost wish to put to death."' 53. And in those days there was a priest named John and surnamed Chrysostom [2] who taught in righteousness before he was chosen patriarch. And at that time he taught and admonished in every city. And fearing death at the hands of the Arians he had fled and left the city deprived of his lifegiving doctrine. 54. And when the emperor Theodosius heard these words he repented and calmed his anger. And the magistrates of the city, whom he had previously banished, he restored to their functions in Antioch, and those who were in prison he set free. 55. And the emperor wrote a letter in reply and sent (it) to his officers to the following effect: 'I have been angry on account of my late Godloving wife Flacilla, who has most undeservedly suffered outrage at their hands. 56. And I have been desirous to punish them. But for the sake of God and His love for mankind, (and) that He may accept me and aid me and give me victory over the heretics and barbarians and all those who rise up against me, I now accord pardon to them. Let there be peace upon the city of Antioch and let them dwell in undisturbed tranquillity.' 57. And after the emperor Theodosius had conquered the usurpers he resided in the city of Rome, and he put to death many heretics.

58. And in those days the bakers made underground cellars [3] and secret resorts in the earth, and built likewise structures in which they prepared dough: and they perpetrated in them many abominable deeds on people (generally) but specially on strangers and foreigners and on many who came to them to get food and drink and on others with lustful purposes. 59. And the wine sellers sent on secretly those who came to them to the bakers who

---

[1] See note on ver. 46. The true account is given in the extract from Cedrenus in the next note.

[2] Cf. Cedrenus, i. 570 sq. τῷ αὐτῷ ἔτει Πλακίλλα ἡ γαμετὴ Θεοδοσίου ἐκοιμήθη, εὐσεβὴς οὖσα καὶ φιλόπτωχος . . . Ταύτης τὸν ἀνδριάντα κατέαξαν οἱ Ἀντιοχεῖς διὰ τὰ ἐπιτεθέντα δημόσια παρὰ τοῦ βασιλέως τελεῖν αὐτούς. Τότε καὶ Ἰωάννης ὁ Χρυσόστομος, πρεσβύτερος ὢν Ἀντιοχείας, λόγους περὶ τούτου θαυμαστοὺς ἐξέθετο, οὓς ἀνδριάντας ἐπέγραψε. Τότε καὶ ἡ ἐν Θεσσαλονίκῃ σφαγὴ τῶν ιε' χιλιάδων τοῦ λαοῦ ὑπὸ Θεοδοσίου γίνεται, καὶ τὰ παρὰ τοῦ ἁγίου Ἀμβροσίου ἐπισκόπου Μεδιολάνων εἰς αὐτὸν βασιλέα πραχθέντα.

[3] On the correct account of two great abuses in Rome and their correction by the emperor, see Socrates, Hist. Eccles. v. 18.

seized them by force. And these (captives) could not escape, and though they cried out, there was none to hear them. 60. Some of these were made to turn a mill all their days : others were placed in a brothel till they were old and even then not permitted to depart.

61. Now there was a soldier of the emperor whom they introduced to the mill-house by a stratagem, and tortured there for a long time. And when he was very weary (of it) he made a vigorous effort (and) drawing his sword slew many that sought to prevent his egress; those that remained were terrified and let him escape, and so he went and told the emperor. 62. And the emperor commanded the bakers to be brought and punished them severely and destroyed their secret buildings. 63. And he compelled the female prostitutes to walk publicly through Rome to the sound of a bell that their crimes might be made known to all, and the bakers also to be publicly exposed.[1] 64. Thus (Theodosius) exterminated utterly all this evil.

65. And (Theodosius) ended his life virtuously and left an illustrious memory to his successors and went to his rest in peace. He ended his earthly life pure and blameless, and he passed from this transitory world to the life eternal.

CHAPTER LXXXIV. 1. After the death of the Godloving emperor Theodosius, his empire passed into the hands of his two sons Arcadius and Honorius who were borne to him by his wife the blessed Flacilla. 2. They had been created emperors during his (Theodosius's) lifetime : Arcadius he had appointed emperor in Constantinople and Honorius emperor in Rome. And they placed the body of the emperor Theodosius in the Church of the Holy Apostles in Constantinople.

3. Arcadius and Honorius were very devoted to the Christian religion. And the Godloving emperor Honorius fell ill, and when his brother Arcadius was apprised (of this) he set out for Rome to visit him. 4. Now Honorius was in purity and chastity an ascetic, and though living in the imperial palace, he observed the mode of life of a hermit. 5. And he pursued a virtuous course marked with severe discipline and many a hardship. And he wore a hair garment under silk clothing which forms the imperial dress, and he made his bed upon the ground, and fasted every day, and prayed,

---

[1] This is not an accurate account ; see note 3 on p. 90.

and sang psalms, and to his religious exercises added always virtuous
deeds, and despising exceedingly the earthly kingdom, he set his
hopes on the kingdom of heaven, and he was prompt to do that
which is pleasing to God. 6. And he completed all the good
measures which had not been carried into effect by his father, and
he put an end to all the evil practices which were displeasing to
God. 7. Now it was the custom amongst his contemporaries that
two men should fight in the arena, and that the victor should slay
the other, without incurring bloodguiltiness. 8. And in those days
there came to Rome a monk from the east named Telemachus,
whose life had been like that of the angels of heaven. 9. And
the monk finding them practise such abominable and bloody deeds,
adjured them and solemnly bade them in the name of Jesus Christ
to make peace and to abandon this satanical act of slaying a
brother. And when they heard these words, they laid aside their
weapons and stoned him with stones and shed the blood of the
man of God, the devoted monk, Telemachus. 10. And when the
holy emperor Honorius was apprised of this event, he put a stop to
this custom in the city of Rome and abolished it. And the peace
of the glorious and Most High God prevailed in the city. 11. And
he destroyed also the unclean temples and made them edifices
consecrated to the holy martyrs.

During the sojourn of the emperor Arcadius in Rome, an officer [1] of
the army, named Gainas, of barbaric descent, revolted, and gathered
forces and made war on the emperor. And he mustered a large
host of barbarians and he caused great disquiet. 12. But the
emperor Arcadius went forth hastily from Rome (and) arrived at
Byzantium, full of zeal for the orthodox faith of his father, and he
slew this usurper Gainas the apostate, who was of the abominable
sect of the Arians. And he abode (thenceforth) in peace. 13. And
afterwards the Godloving emperor Arcadius fell ill and died in the
days of the partriarchate of S. John Chrysostom. 14. Now his son
Theodosius the younger had been proclaimed emperor before the
death of his father.

15. And when Theodosius the younger became emperor a serious
sedition took place in the city of Rome. For the emperor Honorius

[1] Cf. John Mal. 348 Γαϊνὰς ἐτυράννησεν ὁ συγκλητικός, θέλων βασιλεῦσαι. In
Socrates, *Hist. Eccles.* vi. 6, he is called commander-in-chief : στρατηλάτης Ῥωμαίων
ἱππικῆς τε καὶ πεζικῆς ἀναδείκνυται.

had abandoned (the seat of) his empire and withdrawn in indignation to the city of Ravenna; for many of the senators hated the emperor Honorius the saint of God because of his good life; for he feared God and fulfilled all His commandments.[1] 16. And just then a chief of the province of Gaul, named Alaric, set out with a numerous force to seize the city of Rome. 17. And when he arrived he came to terms with the enemies of the emperor and they offered him tribute from the city; but he refused to receive it and marched to the palace and seized all the imperial possessions. 18. And he carried off the sister of the emperor Honorius, named Placidia, who was a virgin. Then this conqueror returned into Gaul. 19. And he had a certain official with him, named Constantius, and he carried off the young girl to her brother the emperor Honorius without the knowledge of the conqueror. And the emperor honoured him and made him a vizier, and later raised him to the imperial throne, and gave him his virgin sister in marriage. 20. And subsequently they two, the emperor Honorius and Constantius, set out from the city of Ravenna and made themselves masters of Rome, and put to death the men who had originated the sedition against their lord, the emperor Honorius, and these were four in number. And he confiscated their possessions and broke the power of that rebel. 21. And he gave his (Roman) empire to his sister's husband Constantius, and the God-loving emperor Honorius went to Constantinople, where he made the younger Theodosius, his nephew, his colleague in the empire. 22. But after a short time he returned to the city of Rome, for he had fallen grievously ill owing to his excessive devotion to the religious and ascetic life with fasting and prayer. And his limbs swelled and he died, and he departed from this perishable world in his virginity and without a son. 23. Now Constantius the emperor of Rome had by Placidia, the sister of the emperor Honorius, a son whom he named Valentinian. 24. But there arose a usurper named John who made himself master of his empire by force.[2]

25. And after the death of Honorius his uncle, Theodosius the younger reigned alone in Constantinople. And when he grew up to manhood, as he was still unmarried, he was urgently pressed by his sisters, Arcadia, Marina, and Pulcheria, to marry and have children. 26. But he replied to them: 'I will only marry a girl

---

[1] Contrast John Mal. 349-50.   [2] Cf. John Mal. 350.

who is a virgin, comely, beautiful, Godloving, and wise.'   27. And after this reply they sought for him in every city of the empire, but there was none such among the imperial princesses nor among families of noble descent.   And they traversed every region (in their search).   (At last) they found a woman who had come to Constantinople, who was very beautiful and surpassed all the women of the time.   28. She was at variance with her brothers on the question of her father's property, and she had come to complain to the emperor of the injustice she had undergone.

And the girl's name was Athenais †that is, by interpretation†,[1] Eudocia.   29. Now her father, whose name was Heraclitus,[2] had two sons, of whom one was named Valerian and the other Genesius,[3] and this daughter whom we have mentioned.   30. And their father on dying commanded them to give his daughter one hundred *mithqals*[4] of gold as her portion.   But she refused (to accept them), for she was displeased, and said : ' Do I not deserve to have an equal portion of the inheritance with my brothers ? '   But they refused, and drove her forth from her father's house.   31. Then her mother's sister received her and escorted her from the province of Hellas and brought her to the city of Awṭâmôn and placed her with her father's brother.[5]   32. Now there was there a sister of a man named Heraclitus[6] a philosopher, who resided in the city of Byzantium.   And she resorted to an artifice by means of which he conducted the girl into the presence of the emperor's sisters. 33. On learning that the girl was a virgin, they had her brought to them in the palace and informed the emperor regarding her. And he approached her and looked upon her †openly†[7] and she pleased him.   And he had her converted to Christianity and she was named Eudocia ; for previously she had been a pagan of the sect of

---

[1] A misrendering of ἡ καὶ Εὐδοκία μετακληθεῖσα.   Cf. John Mal. 353.   Hence render 'who was also called Eudocia'.   This latter name she received on becoming a Christian (*Chron. Pasch.* 312).

[2] So also *Chron. Pasch.* 311.   But according to Socrates, *Hist. Eccles.* vii. 21, John Mal. 353, Cedrenus i. 590, he was named Leontius.

[3] John Mal. 353 gives Gesius.

[4] An Arabic word.   The Greek in John Mal. is νομίσματα, but in Cedrenus i. 590 we have χρυσίου νομίσματα.

[5] In John Mal. 354 and *Chron. Pasch.* 312 there is nothing corresponding to the words 'Awṭâmôn . . . father's brother '.

[6] Text has the corrupt form Lafrels.   In ver. 29 it is also corruptly written Abrelakles.

[7] John Mal. has διὰ τοῦ βήλου, 'through a curtain '.

the philosophers.   34. (And) he married her according to the law
of the Christians and celebrated a nuptial feast in her honour and
also made her empress.   And when her brothers heard regarding
her that she had become the wife of the emperor Theodosius and
had been proclaimed empress, they were terrified and fled into the
province of Hellas.   35. She sent a letter to them and had them
brought from Athens to Constantinople, and she promoted them to
high positions near the emperor and set Genesius over the province
of Illyria, and Valerian she set over the army.   36. And later she
said unto them : ' If you had not done me wrong I should not have
come to the imperial city and become empress, but by the will of
God I have come hither.   I will not do unto you as you have done
to me.'   37. Thereupon they bowed to the earth and did her
homage.   And subsequently she bare a daughter and named her
Eudoxia after the name of the mother of Theodosius.

38. And in the days of this emperor Theodosius dissensions arose
in the church at Constantinople because of the banishment of the
blessed patriarch John Chrysostom, who had been banished in
the days of Arcadius the father of Theodosius because of the empress
Eudoxia's anger in regard to the vineyard of the widow.

39. There was likewise a great earthquake in the imperial city.
And the emperor was profoundly grieved—he and all the senators
and priests and people together, and for many days they walked
with bare feet.

40. And the Isaurians seized the city of Seleucia in Syria in
a marauding expedition unexpectedly, * and likewise the city of
Tiberias.[1]   And they pillaged all its possessions and they marched
by the mountain named Amanus and returned to their country
Isauria.   41. And all the people were ignorant as to the reason for
which S. John Chrysostom was banished for so long a period till
the death of the empress Eudoxia.   42. Now at this period there
was a patriarch in the city of Constantinople, named Atticus, who
had lived so wisely and after good counsels that he prevailed on the
emperor Theodosius to write to the holy and wise Cyril, patriarch
of Alexandria, who had been appointed after Timothy, that the
name of the holy John Chrysostom should be enrolled in the diptychs
of the church together with all the patriarchs who had died before.
43. The holy Cyril accepted this proposal with great joy ; for he

_____
[1] Not found in John Mal. 363.

loved the Godloving, holy, orthodox John Chrysostom, and honoured
him as a great teacher.   44. And owing to this circumstance there
was great joy in the churches.   And the emperor Theodosius gave
large sums to the churches and rebuilt in a befitting manner those
which had been destroyed.

45. And in those days the orthodox inhabitants of Alexandria
were filled with zeal and they collected a large quantity of wood
and burned the place of the heathen philosophers.[1]

46. But the emperor Theodosius did not forget nor forsake the
city of Rome, but he sent to it an officer named Aspar, with
a numerous army in order to war against John the usurper.   And
he warred against John the rebel and overcame him, and saved
Valentinian, the son of his aunt Placidia, whom she bare to
Constantius.   47. And he placed him near his person, and married
him to his daughter whom the empress Eudocia bare him.   And
(Valentinian) begat two daughters by her, and named the one
Eudoxia and the other Placidia.

48. And (Theodosius) chose a man from among the philosophers,
named Cyrus, and appointed him prefect.   And he was a wise man
and of severe integrity; and he was incorruptible and walked in
integrity and uprightness.   49. Moreover he loved to restore the
buildings (of the city).   The towers [2] which had long been in a
ruinous condition he rebuilt in a short time, and he was without
pride and was greatly loved by all the inhabitants of Constantinople.
50. And on the occasion of a famine,[3] the emperor Theodosius
saw all the people acclaiming and honouring Cyrus the prefect.
(And certain people) were jealous of him and accused him to the
emperor Theodosius, saying : ' It is his intention to rebel and usurp
thy power.'   51. And the emperor listened to their calumnies and
had the man arrested, subjected to many punishments, and deprived
of all his possessions [and had him conducted into the palace].[4]
It was not on the ground of these calumnies only that he did so,
but because of the acclamations of the people : ' He is a second

---

[1] This verse would apparently refer to the death of Hypatia recounted in
Socrates, *Hist. Eccles.* vii. 15, but that our author treats of this at length in
lxxxiv. 87 sqq.

[2] Cedrenus i. 599 has τεῖχος.

[3] In John Mal., *Chron. Pasch.*, and Cedrenus the event that follows is said to
have occurred in the circus.

[4] An interpolation.

emperor like the great Constantine.' 52. And for this reason the emperor was wroth against him (and) desired to put him to death. 53. And when he heard of this purpose (of the emperor) he fled into a church, and was there appointed metropolitan of the city of Smyrna in the province of Asia, for (there) the people had previously put their bishop to death. 54. And when he was ordained metropolitan of the city of Smyrna, he made a great and long prayer to the God of heaven because He had saved him from the death threatened by calumny. 55. And whilst he was so engaged, the festival of the Nativity of our Lord Jesus Christ arrived. The people and the priests placed him on the throne as was customary for the bishops, and requested him as follows : ' Speak to us regarding the greatness and the glory and the praise of the Omnipotent and regarding His holy Nativity.' 56. And he spoke first to them regarding his deliverance from death, and next he addressed them as follows : ' Know ye, my brethren, that this day is the day of the Nativity of our Lord and Saviour Jesus Christ. 57. Let us honour him as is befitting, for it was of his own will alone that He was conceived in the womb of the holy Virgin Mary ; for He is the primaeval Word the Creator—praise be unto Him—together with His Father (supremely) good and the Holy Lifegiving Spirit, Consubstantial Trinity for evermore.' 58. And all the inhabitants of the city honoured him and he continued discharging the ministry and the sacred services without intermission. He fulfilled his sacerdotal duty till he died in (all) honour.

59. And likewise in the days of the emperor Theodosius there died Atticus and Sisinnius, patriarchs of Constantinople. And after their death they brought from Antioch to Constantinople Nestorius, in order to teach there because he represented himself to be like the ascetics and those learned in the Scriptures : and they ordained him patriarch there, and he became the scourge of the Christians in every country. 60. For at once he set himself to teach and blaspheme God : and he refused to believe that the holy Virgin Mary was the mother of God, but called her the mother of Christ, saying that Christ had two natures ; and so there arose many dissensions and great tumults in the city of Constantinople on this subject. 61. They obliged the emperor Theodosius to summon a council of bishops in Ephesus from all the world. And those who assembled, being in number two hundred, excommunicated and

deposed Nestorius and his followers. Now these subsequently returned
to the holy faith together with John, patriarch of Antioch. 62. They
agreed with the two hundred bishops and with our holy Cyril, patriarch
of Alexandria, and they confirmed this faith and rejected Nestorius
because he taught the same false doctrine as Apollinaris. 63. And
there remained but a few of those who had created the tumult and
followed Nestorius, whereas the orthodox believers grew strong and
multiplied exceedingly during the days of the emperor Theodosius,
till Archelaus, who was set over the east, joined them and became
one with us in the right faith. 64. And there remained but a few
who persisted in the error of Nestorius. And so the churches
enjoyed tranquillity and peace all the days of the Godloving
emperor Theodosius.

65. These are the patriarchs who lived in Constantinople in the
days of Theodosius, i. e. the wise patriarchs Maximian and Proclus.
66. The wise Proclus had studied diligently as a child, and when he
grew up, he was fitted to remain in the city in the devout service of
God. And he attended continually on the patriarch Atticus and
wrote down and learnt all the teachings of God. 67. And
subsequently they ordained him deacon, and when he was older
they made him a priest. And Sisinnius, who was appointed patriarch
after Atticus, consecrated him bishop of Cyzicum and gave it this
great gift; but the inhabitants of this town refused it; for they
were not worthy to receive this chosen vessel of God. 68. And so
(Proclus) remained in solitude in Byzantium, while Nestorius as
patriarch was disturbing the churches, by creating hatred against
our Lady the holy Virgin Mary, the mother of God. 69. Now the
holy Proclus composed a treatise on our Lady, the holy Virgin
Mary, the mother of God, and read it in the church of Constantinople
before the people assembled there, and he strongly reproved Nestorius
in his treatise because his heart was set on destruction. 70. And in
the beginning of his treatise it was written as follows: ' Let us
celebrate the festival of the Virgin and proclaim with our tongue
these words: To-day let us praise Mary the mother of God.'[1]
And when all the people heard these words, they glorified our Lady
and gave thanks to her, and admired exceedingly. 71. And Proclus

---

[1] This homily is placed at the beginning of the Acts of the Council of
Ephesus: Πανθενικὴ πανήγυρις σήμερον τὴν γλῶτταν ἡμῶν, ἀδελφοί, πρὸς εὐφημίαν
καλεῖ (Zotenberg).

having thus touched the heart of the emperor Theodosius and of all the people, they were eager to raise him to the throne (of the patriarchate) in Constantinople after the exile and deposition of Nestorius. But certain of the chief people of the city arose and said out of envy: ' This man has been bishop of a small city: how can he be the shepherd of this great city?' 72. And for this reason they appointed Maximian[1] to the patriarchate of Constantinople. Now he was a Godfearing priest, but he was not equal to Proclus in wisdom and learning. And he occupied the throne of the patriarchate for two years and six months, leading a solitary life of devotion, and he died in peace. 73. Then the emperor Theodosius made Proclus come forward before the interment of Maximian, and commanded that he should be raised to the (patriarchal) throne of Constantinople. And accordingly Celestine, patriarch of Rome, wrote to the patriarch of Alexandria and to other bishops regarding Proclus. 74. And they sent him an answer as follows: ' The canon law of the church does not debar Proclus from occupying the patriarchal throne of Alexandria; for it is by the command of God.' 75. And so Proclus occupied (the patriarchal throne) with honour and distinction, and guided wisely the interests of his flock in the imperial city and strove against those who followed the errors of Nestorius. 76. And he wrote a letter and sent it to the illustrious †Armenius†[2] in which he combated Theodore of Mopsuestia and the heretic Nestorius and anathematized and excommunicated them in his letter. And already in the days of the blessed Maximian who went to his rest, the east had been cleansed from the pollutions of the heretic Nestorius and peace had been established in the Church.

77. And Proclus also brought back the body of the holy John Chrysostom to Constantinople. Five and forty years had passed since his banishment to the island named Thrace in the days of the Christ-loving emperor Theodosius the elder. 78. And he placed the body in the church of the holy Apostles where repose (also) the bodies of the holy Fathers the patriarchs who had fulfilled their course virtuously and in the orthodox faith in Constantinople.

---

[1] See Socrates, *Hist. Eccles.* vii. 35.

[2] In 436 the Armenian bishops consulted Proclus on certain doctrines attributed to Theodore of Mopsuestia. In the following year Proclus replied in his well-known letter περὶ πίστεως.

79. And as for the other bishops who had been wrongfully banished with him (S. Chrysostom), whom he [1] could not bring back in the days of the blessed Atticus, the severed members were united together, and he made them one,[2] and thus discord disappeared from the churches.[3]   80. And he composed a treatise worthy of the holy John Chrysostom in which he besought God to pardon the sins of the parents of the emperor Theodosius the younger—the sin they had committed against the holy John Chrysostom.

81. In the days of this emperor also the barbarians who had survived the defeat of John the usurper reunited and proceeded to invade the Roman territories.   82. And when the Godloving emperor was informed of this event, he meditated, as was his wont, and turned his thoughts to our Lord and God and Saviour Jesus Christ—praise be unto Him—and he fasted and prayed.

83. And he was merciful to the poor and compassionate to the destitute and he devoted himself to the works which are pleasing to God with integrity and that which is beyond (all) these works. 84. He commanded Proclus and all the priests and monks to pray to God on his behalf that victory should be given to him over his adversaries and that his efforts should not be exerted in vain. 85. And God heard his prayer and the barbaric chief named Roilas died.   Indeed God struck him with a thunderbolt (and) he was speedily destroyed, and many of them died by this death which was sent from God.   And fire likewise came down from heaven and destroyed those that remained.   86. And all the peoples of the earth recognized by this event that the God of the Christians is great, and the righteousness and faith of the Godloving emperor Theodosius were made known.

87. And in those days there appeared in Alexandria a female philosopher, a pagan named Hypatia, and she was devoted at all times to magic, astrolabes and instruments of music, and she beguiled many people through (her) Satanic wiles. 88. And the governor of the city honoured her exceedingly; for she had beguiled him through her magic. And he ceased attending church as had been his custom.   † But he went once under circumstances

---

[1] So MSS.

[2] Cf. Socrates, *Hist. Eccles.* vii. 45 οἱ δι' αὐτὸν χωριζόμενοι τῇ ἐκκλησίᾳ ἡνώθησαν. Zotenberg quite mistranslates the text.

[3] The clause 'and thus . . . from the churches' is transposed in the text before 'the severed members'.

of danger.† And he not only did this, but he drew many believers to her, and he himself received the unbelievers at his house. 89. And on a certain day when they were making merry over a theatrical exhibition connected with dancers,[1] the governor of the city[2] published (an edict) regarding[3] the public exhibitions in the city of Alexandria:[4] and all the inhabitants of the city had assembled there (in the theatre). 90. Now Cyril, who had been appointed patriarch after Theophilus, was eager to gain exact intelligence regarding this edict. 91. And there was a man named Hierax,[5] a Christian possessing understanding and intelligence, who used to mock the pagans but was a devoted adherent of the illustrious Father the patriarch and was obedient to his monitions. He was also well versed in the Christian faith. 92. (Now this man attended the theatre to learn the nature of this edict.) But when the Jews saw him in the theatre they cried out and said: 'This man has not come with any good purpose, but only to provoke an uproar.' 93. And Orestes the prefect was displeased with the children of the holy church, and had Hierax seized and subjected to punishment publicly in the theatre, although he was wholly guiltless. 94. And Cyril was wroth with the governor of the city for so doing, and likewise for his putting to death an illustrious monk of the convent of Pernôdj[6] named Ammonius, and other monks (also). And when the chief magistrate[7] of the city heard this, he sent word to the Jews as follows: 'Cease your hostilities against the Christians.' 95. But they refused to hearken to what they heard; for they gloried in the support of the prefect who was with them, and so they added outrage to outrage and plotted a massacre through a treacherous device. 96. And they posted beside them at night in all the streets of the city certain men, while others cried out and said: 'The church of the apostolic

---

[1] The text here reads ⲁⲥ̄ⲑⲙ̄ⲛ̄: which I take to be a corrupt transliteration of ὀρχηστάς. Cf. Socrates, *Hist. Eccles.* vii. 13, where he speaks of the fondness of the Alexandrians περὶ τὰς ὀρχηστάς.

[2] The text adds 'and he'.

[3] I have emended ⲛ̄ⲏⲱ: into ⲛ = 'regarding'.

[4] Cf. Socrates, *Hist. Eccles.* vii. 13 τοῦ . . . ἐπάρχου πολιτείαν (= δημοτικὴν διατύπωσιν) ἐν τῷ θεάτρῳ ποιοῦντος.

[5] Cf. Socrates, *Hist. Eccles.* vii. 13.

[6] The Coptic word for the desert of Nitria, according to Zotenberg. Cf. Socrates, *Hist. Eccles.* vii. 14.

[7] This is apparently wrong. It should be 'Cyril'.

Athanasius is on fire: come to its succour, all ye Christians.'
97. And the Christians on hearing their cry came forth quite
ignorant of the treachery of the Jews. And when the Christians
came forth, the Jews arose and wickedly massacred the Christians
and shed the blood of many, guiltless though they were. 98. And
in the morning, when the surviving Christians heard of the wicked
deed which the Jews had wrought, they betook themselves to the
patriarch. And the Christians mustered all together and went and
marched in wrath to the synagogues of the Jews and took possession
of them, and purified them and converted them into churches. And
one of them they named after the name of S. George. 99. And
as for the Jewish assassins they expelled them from the city, and
pillaged all their possessions and drove them forth wholly despoiled,
and Orestes the prefect was unable to render them any help. 100. And
thereafter a multitude of believers in God arose under the guidance
of Peter the magistrate—now this Peter was a perfect believer
in all respects in Jesus Christ—and they proceeded to seek for the
pagan woman who had beguiled the people of the city and the prefect
through her enchantments. 101. And when they learnt the place
where she was, they proceeded to her and found her seated on a
(lofty) chair; and having made her descend they dragged her along
till they brought her to the great church, named Caesarion. Now
this was in the days of the fast. 102. And they tare off her
clothing and dragged her [till they brought her] through the
streets of the city till she died. And they carried her to a place
named Cinaron, and they burned her body with fire. 103. And all
the people surrounded the patriarch Cyril and named him 'the new
Theophilus'; for he had destroyed the last remains of idolatry in
the city.

CHAPTER LXXXV. 1. And some time after this event the Jews in
a place named Kemterjâ[1] between Chalcedon and Antioch in Syria
were amusing themselves after their customary manner in drinking
and debauchery. 2. And they performed a play in which they
brought forward one amongst them and named him Christ and
bowed down to him in mockery. And they blasphemed the cross
and those who trusted in the Crucified. 3. And when they had
insolently perpetrated this sacrilege, they took a child and bound

---

[1] Socrates, *Hist. Eccles.* vii. 16, reads Ἰμεστάρ . . . μεταξὺ Χαλκίδος καὶ
Ἀντιοχείας.

him on the cross and mocked him, and as their feelings grew more vehement [1] they put the child to death. And the child died courageously. 4. And when the Christians heard of the atrocities committed by the Jews, they were exceedingly wroth because of the evil deeds and came and attacked them, and many of them died. 5. And when the emperor Theodosius was told of the atrocities committed by the Jews, he commanded the magistrates of the province to punish the criminals. 6. And they punished the Jews that were in the east and took vengeance on all the mockers who had mocked Christ and His faithful ones.

7. And in those days many of the Jews in Crete believed and became Christians in consequence of the greatness of the persecution that befell them.

CHAPTER LXXXVI. 1. And there was a Jew named Fìskìs who in his own person played the rôle of impostor, saying : ' I am Moses the chief of the prophets; for I have been sent from heaven by God. 2. I have come to conduct the Jews who dwell in this island through the sea, and I will establish you in the land of promise.' 3. And by these means he led them astray, saying unto them : ' I am he that delivered your fathers out of the hand of Pharaoh when they were in bondage to the Egyptians.' 4. And he spent an entire year in traversing Crete and proclaiming this event and leading them astray in all the cities and villages. 5. And he prevailed on them to abandon their industries and to despise their goods and possessions. And so they dissipated all that they had. 6. And when the day which he had fixed for leading them out drew near, he commanded them to come with their wives and children and follow him to the sea-shore, and cast themselves into the sea. And many perished, some through the fall and others from being engulfed in the depths of the sea. 7. But God who loves mankind had compassion on His creatures and saved them lest they should all perish by this hard fate. 8. And many Christians who were present on the spot at the time in order to see (what would happen) saved a large number from being drowned in the sea. The rest who had not cast themselves into the sea were saved by this means. 9. And when they saw that the false prophet had perished,[2] engulfed in the sea, they recognized thereupon that he

---

[1] I have emended ደለ፡ into ደሎ፡

[2] According to Socrates, *Hist. Eccles.* vii. 38, he escaped.

was an impostor, and forthwith abandoned their erroneous belief. 10. Through these means many Jews turned to our Lord Jesus Christ and received the light of holy life-giving baptism and believed in our Lord Jesus Christ. 11. (This event took place) in the days of the Godloving emperor Theodosius the younger and in those of Atticus, patriarch of the great city of Constantinople.

CHAPTER LXXXVII. 1. And during the childhood of the emperor Theodosius, when he was learning the holy Scriptures inspired by God, he had with him a child named Paulinus, the son of a vizier who learnt with him, and they grew up together. 2. And the emperor Theodosius loved him and appointed him an emperor in the third degree, a dignity that is called Master (of the imperial household).[1] 3. And he reclined frequently at table with the emperor and empress; for a strong friendship existed between them. 4. And after some time Paulinus fell ill, and when he was ill a certain officer highly honoured by the emperor brought[2] him an apple that was wholly out of season, and the emperor and all his court who saw it admired the appearance of the apple. 5. The emperor gave one hundred gold dinars to the man who had brought the apple. (And) he sent that apple to his wife. And she indeed sent it to Paulinus because of his illness and her affection for him. 6. Now Paulinus was not aware that the emperor had given it to the empress, and so as the emperor came just at that moment to pay Paulinus a visit, he saw that apple in his possession and forthwith proceeded to the palace and called for the empress, and said unto her: 'Where is the apple which I gave thee?' 7. And she fearing lest the emperor should be offended with her, was not willing to avow the truth, and said: 'I have eaten it as I was not aware that you would question me regarding it.' And the emperor further said unto her: 'Hast thou not sent it to some one?' And she denied again. 8. Then the emperor ordered the apple to be brought, and the empress Eudocia was greatly put to shame. And a sense of pain and offence existed between them for a long time. 9. And subsequently the empress told the emperor all that had happened, and confirmed her statement by a terrible oath,

---

[1] ደግⶂⶉⶅⶅ: corrupt, owing to corrupt transliteration of the Arabic of Μάγιστρος. Cf. John Mal. 356 προηγάγετο αὐτὸν μάγιστρον.

[2] There is no need of the additions made to the text by Zotenberg. The only change needed is to read the verb in the singular instead of in the plural.

and she persuaded the emperor that she had feared aforetime and had not told the truth because of the offence (she was likely to give) and the fear wherewith she feared him.

10. Now Paulinus feared greatly and said within himself : 'It is better for the ailing man to remain in his ailment; for when he recovers from his ailment he conceives evil designs in his heart. For he ill-treated Mar Basilius who belonged to the solitaries of the desert, who had been rejected by the heretics.' 11. Some days later it was told the emperor that Paulinus was forming rebellious designs and was revolting against the emperor and preparing a revolt. And accordingly he had him executed, as (Paulinus) had wished to deal similarly with the Godloving emperor. 12. And the empress Eudocia and the emperor Theodosius loved him greatly and honoured him exceedingly. 13. But lying historians who are heretics and abide not by the truth have recounted and said that Paulinus was put to death because of the empress Eudocia. But the empress Eudocia was wise and chaste, spotless and perfect in all her conduct.

14. And the emperor Theodosius sent a letter to the desert of Scete in Egypt in order to consult the saints because he had no male offspring to succeed him on the throne. 15. And the saints wrote as follows : 'When thou quittest this world, the faith of thy fathers will be changed; for God out of love to thee has not given thee a male offspring lest it should become wicked.' 16. And the emperor Theodosius and his wife were alike pained by this communication, and they abandoned all conjugal intercourse and lived, by mutual consent, in befitting chastity. 17. And after they had married their illustrious daughter Eudoxia to Valentinian the emperor of the west, as we have already recounted, and they had consummated the nuptials in Constantinople, the bridegroom and his consort set out for Rome.

18. Thereupon the empress Eudocia requested the Godloving emperor Theodosius to permit her to visit the holy places in Jerusalem and to worship there in righteousness. For she had vowed a vow as follows : 'When I have accomplished the nuptials of my daughter I will visit the holy places, and I will pay my vow to the Lord in the courts of the house of the Lord before all the people in the midst of Jerusalem.[1] And I will pray to God to

---

[1] Ps. cxvi. 18-19. The text differs from the Ethiopic version in respect of the verb.

preserve thy empire for a long period in peace.'   19. The emperor
having agreed to this request wrote to the governors of every
province to make preparations for a fitting reception of the empress.
20. And he arranged that Cyril, patriarch of Alexandria, should
accompany her to Jerusalem, and bless her and instruct her in the
doing of good works.   21. Thus all her prayers to God were accomplished for her : and she arrived in Jerusalem, and she restored
the churches and the courts [1] of the convent of the religious virgins
and the hospice for pilgrims, and she gave them great endowments.
22. And she rebuilt likewise the walls of Jerusalem which had been
in ruins from an early period.[2]   And she accomplished with vigour
all her undertakings.   Then the empress withdrew from the world
and lived in solitude.

23. And the emperor also gave himself to fasting and prayer
and to the singing of psalms and hymns, and he pursued a virtuous
course.   And his virgin sisters, who were older than he, the blessed
Arcadia and Marina, had died before the empress quitted the
palace, and gone to Christ whom they loved.

24. And during the sojourn of the empress in Jerusalem, the
holy Cyril, patriarch of Alexandria, and John, patriarch of Antioch,
died.   25. Then the Nestorian heretics reappeared, the twelve
bishops of the east, who had concealed themselves from the holy
patriarch Cyril, who denied the Holy Trinity and divided Christ
into two natures.   26. And also the heretical bishops of Constantinople and of the other provinces met together apart by
themselves without the knowledge of any one, and said : ' The
separation of the emperor and the empress has not been due to
a desire to serve God, but they have separated through mutual
hatred because of Paulinus.'   27. It was for this reason that the
emperor was indignant with the patriarch Flavian and his associates,
and said unto them : ' The fire (which had been lighted) by the
Nestorians, and was extinguished, ye have kindled anew.'   For
they had caused many troubles in the churches.   28. But Pulcheria,
the emperor Theodosius's sister, protected the patriarch Flavian, but
she was not able to protect him openly because she feared the
strength of the empire of the emperor Theodosius ; for he was

---

[1] No addition to the text is here necessary.   I have omitted **ധ** before
* סᖈᖋ.ድር:*

[2] The account is somewhat different in Socrates, *Hist. Eccles.* vii. 47.

wroth with those who said, There were two natures in Christ after there had been one. But those who devised this evil conception laboured in vain.

29. Now the emperor's sister, Pulcheria, pursuing an evil course, besought him to give her a garden. And the emperor accomplished the object of her desire. And she wrote a fraudulent document to this effect: ' The entire palace, courts, and gardens of the empress have been given to me by the emperor,' and she gave it to the emperor to sign in his own hand. 30. And when the document was read before the entire senate, Pulcheria arose, and taking her stand in the midst of the men without shame reproved the emperor in insolent terms and said unto him: ' Thou hast done with negligence the duties of imperial government.' 31. And when he took the document and wished to read it and sign it, he saw written therein the following words: ' The empress Eudocia has become my slave.' 32. And when the emperor saw this he was exceedingly wroth both because of Pulcheria's insolence and her lack of shame. 33. And he had her seized and transported to a certain place, and he commanded the patriarch to lay his hands upon her and ordain her a deaconess. And for this reason there was great enmity and hatred between the empress Eudocia and Pulcheria. And so the emperor was parted from his sister Pulcheria.

34. And subsequently the emperor ordered a second council to be convoked in Ephesus, and he likewise ordered Dioscorus, the patriarch of Alexandria, who was appointed after Cyril, to be present. 35. And Flavian, patriarch of Constantinople, and Eusebius, bishop of Dorylaeum, and Domnus, patriarch of Antioch, and Ibas and John and Theodoret, and †Mâdjûs †, bishops of the east, were deposed.[1] And after this event the excellent emperor Theodosius fell ill and departed from this life and went to God. 36. And while the empress Eudocia was living in solitude in the holy places of Jerusalem, Pulcheria audaciously promulgated an imperial decree without taking the advice of Valentinian the emperor of Rome or that of the chief officers and senate, and married Marcian, the commander-in-chief of the army, and placed the imperial crown on his head and made him emperor. And she became his wife and sacrificed her virginity. 37. During his life-

---

[1] Cf. Evagrius i. 10.

time the emperor had guarded her, without any desire on her part,
lest any stranger should come in to her and then proceed to seize his
imperial throne.

38. And on the day of Marcian's accession there was darkness
over all the earth from the first hour of the day till the evening.
And that darkness was like that which had been in the land of
Egypt in the days of Moses the chief of the prophets.   39. And
there was great fear and alarm among all the inhabitants of
Constantinople.   They wept and lamented and raised dirges and
cried aloud exceedingly, and imagined that the end of the world
was at hand.   40. And the senate, the officers, and the soldiers,
(even) all the army, small and great, that was in the city was filled
with agitation and cried aloud, saying : ' We have never heard nor
seen in all the previous reigns of the Roman empire such an event as
this.'   41. And they murmured very much, but they did not express
themselves openly.   And on the following day the Divine 1.ove had
compassion on mankind, and the sun rose and the light of day
reappeared.

42. And the emperor Marcian convoked a council of bishops in
Chalcedon composed of six hundred and † forty-five † bishops.
43. And they deposed Dioscorus, patriarch of Alexandria, and
ordained that Flavian, who had been deposed on a former occasion,
should be mentioned in the diptychs after his death ; for he had
already died in exile in the days of the blessed emperor Theodosius.
And so they enrolled his name in the diptychs of the church as an
orthodox patriarch.   44. And when disturbances arose in Constantinople and amongst all peoples Marcian fell grievously ill,
and his illness lasted five months, and his feet mortified and he
died.   And the length of his reign was six years.   And Pulcheria
also had died before Marcian.

45. And in those days the empress Eudocia went to her rest in
the holy Jerusalem, full of good works and a pure faith.   And she
refused to communicate with Juvenal, bishop of Jerusalem, and the
men who had assembled in Chalcedon ; for she knew that they had
changed the true faith of our holy Fathers and of the orthodox
emperors ; but she was blessed by priests (and) monks through her
friendship and communion with Theodosius,[1] patriarch of Alex-

---

[1] This Theodosius was a fanatical Monophysite monk who had been punished

andria. 46. And when she had thus accomplished these things, she went to her rest, and they placed her body in a tomb which she had built in her lifetime, with honour and panegyrics. And she went to God the Glorious and Most High.

CHAPTER LXXXVIII. 1. And after the death of Marcian, Leo the elder became emperor.[1] And in the days of his rule the city of Antioch was † polluted † owing to the earthquake that befell it. 2. And † lightning † [2] rained from heaven on Constantinople instead of rain. And it rose high upon the roofs. And all the people were terrified and offered up prayers and supplications to God; for that lightning had been burning fire; but God out of His love for man [3] had extinguished the fire and made it † lightning †.[2]

3. And again after this † lightning † [2] fire fell a second time from heaven on the city of Constantinople, such as had never fallen before. And it extended from sea to sea. 4. And the emperor left the palace, fearing lest he should be burned in the conflagration, and took up his abode in the church of S. Mamas for six months, offering prayers and supplications as had been done in the days of Marcian.

5. And the emperor Leo put a stop to all theatrical exhibitions, alike of those that played on the flute and on the lyre,[4] on the holy first day of the week in honour of the sabbath. 6. And he likewise banished the Arians from every province in his empire, and he gave orders to all his subjects not to admit them to the churches.

7. And also in the days of this emperor an accusation was brought against a philosopher named Isocasius, an exquaestor.[5] He was a man of great prudence and a just judge. He was a pagan, and helped the people of Cilicia when he was † interpreter † in Antioch.

---

in Alexandria for sedition, and had taken forcible possession of the see of Jerusalem for twenty months ; see Evagrius ii. 5.

[1] For **ᎿᎡ-᎞**: read **ᎌᎤᎤ**: and make no further addition.

[2] This should be 'dust'. Cf. John Mal. 372 ἔβρεξεν ἐν Κωνσταντινουπόλει κονίαν ἀντὶ βροχῆς.

[3] Read ᎄᎄ᎞ᎾᎢ: ᎈ᎐ᎈ: ᎄᎁᎱᎅᎈᎁᎨᎣ:

[4] Cf. John Mal. 371 Λέων . . . ἐκέλευσεν . . . ἵνα μήτε αὐλὸς ἢ κιθάρα ἢ ἄλλο τι μουσικόν.

[5] Cf. John Mal. 369 Ἰσοκάσιος ὁ Κοιαστώριος. The Arabic translator took the last word to mean 'the son of Quaestor', or 'of a quaestor'. See also *Chron. Pasch.* 322.

And the emperor delivered him into the hands of Pusaeus, the prefect, the chief officer, to send him into exile. 8. But he was torn from the hands of the prefect and carried naked and with his hands bound behind him to the gate named Zeuxippus, where a crowd of people was assembled. 9. And the prefect standing on the tribunal addressed him thus : ' Canst thou see in what a guise thou art in the midst of this assembly ? ' He answered and said unto him : ' I see, and I am not surprised ; for being a man I have fallen into troubles incident to the body. As I have judged other men, so I now judge myself.' 10. And when the people that stood by heard this stern reply, they tore him away from the prefect and bore him to the church, and, without the exercise of any constraint on their part, he expressed his belief in Christ, and said : ' My fathers were idolators but I have now become a Christian.' 11. And they instructed him in the Christian faith, and baptized him, and he became a Christian. Then he was set free and restored to his functions, and he returned to his province beloved by the emperor.

12. When the emperor Leo heard of the disturbances which had taken place in Alexandria formerly in the days of Marcian, and of the massacre that had been occasioned by the council of Chalcedon, and of the restoration of the true faith in the one nature of Christ, and of the slaughter of Proterius, bishop of the Chalcedonians, because of it—13. For this bishop, who had formerly been the ecclesiastical procurator in Alexandria, was consecrated bishop by the Chalcedonians, when he signed the imperial rescript, but the orthodox population rose against him and slew him, and burned his body [1]— 14. (Now having heard of all these circumstances) the emperor Leo appointed (to be patriarch) unto them Timothy, who had been assistant to the patriarch Dioscorus. Formerly he had been a strict monk belonging to the convent of Qalmôn, and he was a priest. 15. And his appointment was made after the death of Dioscorus, who had wrongfully been deposed by the emperor Marcian and his Council. 16. But Timothy refused to abide by the Council of the Chalcedonians ; for this Council had disturbed the entire world.

17. And the emperor Leo likewise wrote to all the bishops, adjuring them to declare accurately in what way matters had taken place in the Council of Chalcedon.[2] 18. But as they feared the emperor, they concealed (these things) from him, and told him

<hr>

[1] Cf. Evagrius, *H. E.* ii. 8.   [2] Cf. Evagrius, *H. E.* ii. 9 sq.

nothing of what had been done in the Council. 19. But there
were two bishops who did tell him : one of them named Eustathius
of Berytus, a man wise and prudent and well versed in the holy
Scriptures. And he told the emperor that through fear of Marcian
they had altered the faith so that all the world was troubled
(thereby), as well as all the churches. 20. And the second bishop
was named Amphilochius, of the city of Maflejûs.[1] 21. But the
other bishops who were his subjects had not declared openly to the
emperor regarding the oppression of the emperor Marcian : all
that had been done at Chalcedon they had done out of fear of the
imperial authority and power.

22. And in those days Eutyches [the Nestorian][2] made himself
known, who was eager for destruction. He was ignorant of the
holy Scriptures, as he had not been eager to study them.

23. And Timothy the patriarch on his arrival in Alexandria was
seized and conducted to a place called Gangra, and made to reside
there.[3] 24. And there were alarms and fightings in Alexandria.
And the governor of the city, who used violence to the holy
patriarch Timothy, was eaten of worms and died. 25. And the
inhabitants of the city said to one another : ' All this evil that has
overtaken him is due to the judgement of the Glorious and Most
High God because of what has been done to the patriarch Timothy,
the servant of God, in order that all men might learn that God
dwells amongst His chosen and renders justice to the oppressed.

26. And after the emperor Leo and the other emperors who
succeeded him, Basiliscus ascended the imperial throne. And he
raised his son Marcus to the imperial throne, and appointed him as
his colleague for a short time. 27. And as his sister Verina was
on friendly terms with him, she asked †Augustus for the master of
the offices, and she received the dignity, which was named
Patricius†.[4]

---

[1] In Evagrius, *H. E.* ii. 10, he is said to be of Side.

[2] Eutyches was an opponent of Nestorianism.

[3] Cf. Evagrius, *H. E.* ii. 11.

[4] The text is here hopelessly unintelligible. Verina, who was the sister of
Basiliscus, was carrying on an intrigue with Patricius, the master of the
imperial household. According to Procopius i. 6 she had taken part in driving
her son-in-law Zeno into exile in order that she might advance Patricius to the
throne. See also John Mal. 378, *Chron. Pasch.* 325. This Patricius was a son
of Asper (John Mal. 371). In Cedrenus i. 613 the proper name Patricius is
taken to mean a dignity.

28. And the emperor sent and had fetched from his place of exile whither the elder Leo had driven him the holy patriarch Timothy. And when he was brought to the city of Constantinople with the honour and dignity due to the priesthood, he was welcomed by all the court and people. 29. And a letter was dispatched to all the provinces and to all the bishops with orders to expel all who confessed the faith of the Chalcedonians, (and likewise) to excommunicate and reject them.

30. The holy Timothy and his companions made the following prophecy in regard to the emperor Basiliscus : ' From the day thou deniest the faith set forth in this writing, thy empire will cease to exist and thy days will rapidly draw to a close.' 31. And he replied : ' I will never deny this profession of faith : on the contrary, I will assemble a Council in Jerusalem in order that the orthodox faith may be established and abide.' 32. And when the holy patriarch Timothy heard these words he went to the city of Alexandria, taking with him the profession of faith written out in the court of the emperor, and he seated himself on its (patriarchal) throne. 33. But the emperor Basiliscus took bribes and broke his word, and cast down that which he had previously built up, and did not assemble a Council in Jerusalem as he had promised the patriarch Timothy. 34. On the contrary, he wrote a second letter to this effect : ' Suffer the Chalcedonians to abide in their faith, and show them due regard.' And so the prophecy of the illustrious father Timothy and of his companions was accomplished. 35. And a terrible unlooked-for pestilence visited the city of Constantinople, and the bodies of the dead putrified, and there were not people enough to bury them. And the city of Gabala in Syria likewise was destroyed by an earthquake. 36. Then Zeno, the emperor of Rome, set out and stirred up the province of Isauria, and collected a numerous army and marched to Constantinople. And on arriving in the city of Antioch, he had the patriarch Peter seized in order that the latter might disclose to him all the designs which the emperor Basiliscus had designed against him. 37. And when Basiliscus heard of the march of Zeno, he sent the generals Armalis and Serbâtôs to war against Zeno, with a numerous army which he had had with him in the palace at Byzantium. 38. And when these officers came to him, he adjured them by holy baptism not to betray him or injure him. 39. But these officers abstained

from fighting with the emperor Zeno, and they sent a secret
message to him to the following effect : ' We will withdraw to
a certain locality, and do you make yourself master of the entire
country.' And these officers moreover treacherously tendered the
following advice to Basiliscus : ' Go by a different route and give
battle to Zeno at the gates of Constantinople.' 40. But the
moment Zeno drew nigh to the walls all the senators met him,
and he was greatly pleased by their reception of him. And Zeno's
mother-in-law, who was named Verina, had her brother Basiliscus
†seized and thrown into a pit†. 41. And as Basiliscus was sore
pressed, he and his wife Zenodia [1] and his children fled to the
baptistery of a church. And all the senators honoured the
emperor Zeno and proclaimed him their emperor. And he sent
to the church and took from him all the insignia of empire, and
induced him to come out by a treacherous promise, even him and
his children.[2] 42. Thereupon he drove the unfortunate wretches
from the palace and sent them in exile into the province of
Cappadocia, to a fortress named Lemnâs. And when they were
brought to the governor of the province, he put them in a tower
and barred them in, according to the orders of the emperor, and
mercilessly left them without food and drink till they died, and
buried them in the same place. 43. And as for the patriarch
Peter, he was brought in chains and transported to the town of
Euchaites in Pontus [3] ; for he had enjoyed the friendship of the
emperor Basiliscus, and had helped him, and placed the imperial
crown upon his head. It was on these grounds that (Basiliscus)
had appointed him patriarch. 44. Now this (Peter) had persecuted
the Nestorians. ⟨And next Stephen was appointed patriarch of
Antioch, and he belonged to the Nestorians⟩,[4] and for this reason

---

[1] So Cedrenus i. 616. Text corrupt : = Sûvânses.

[2] Accusatives, not nominatives, should here be read.

[3] Cf. John Mal. 380.

[4] I have supplied a clause which the text requires, and which has fallen out
through homoioteleuton. According to John Mal. 380 sq. and Theophanes this
was Stephen II, who was appointed patriarch by Zeno in 480, but according to
other authorities this was Stephen I, who was patriarch 478-80. Zotenberg by
a strange error supplies a like clause before the preceding sentence : '⟨On
nomma ensuite patriarche d'Antioche Étienne⟩, qui proscrivait la secte de
Nestorius '. But it was Peter the Fuller (intruding patriarch of Antioch 471-
488) who persecuted the Nestorians, and not Stephen, who according to all
authorities was put to death by a mob of Antioch on the ground that he was
a Nestorian.

all the inhabitants of the city hated him, and the people of Antioch and all the priests put him to a violent death in a place called Barlaams [1] on the day of the commemoration of the holy 'Forty Martyrs'. And after slaying him they cast his body into the river named the Orontes. And the emperor Zeno appointed in his stead another patriarch named Calandio, and paid him special honour.

45. And when the emperor returned to his city he distributed abundant alms amongst the poor, and he appointed †Armatus in his stead in that place commander, him and his father† [2] commander of the guard and his son to be Caesar as he had promised. But when this Armatus became master of the power of the empire he became very strong and powerful, and none could withstand him, and he formed evil designs in his heart. 46. And when the emperor was informed of his evil purposes, he sent and had him put to death in a gallery of the palace. And when the emperor wished to invade Persia, seeing that Basiliscus, the son of Armatus, the Caesar, was but a youth, he took from him the crown of investiture and gave orders for him to be consecrated metropolitan of Cyzicum, and dispersed his property amongst all the people.

47. And seeing these things, Theodoric, one of the consuls who was commander of the guard, began to fear lest he should suffer at the hands of the emperor Zeno as had Armatus his friend,[3] and so he led off the soldiers under his command, who were Goths from the province of Moesia. 48. Now Theodoric had been reared in the capital, and he was acquainted with profane wisdom. And he marched against the city of Selymbria and made its inhabitants subject to him, and he made himself master of the entire province of Thrace. 49. And next he went with a formidable force from the city of Sycene, and he lay there a long time, but was not able to inflict any injury on Byzantium, or on the emperor Zeno.

---

[1] This is the Church of S. Barlaam. Cf. John Mal. 381.

[2] Text hopelessly corrupt. The text was to the effect that Zeno appointed the son of Armatus, the commander of the praetorians, to be Caesar, as he had promised. Cf. John Mal. 381 προεχειρίσθη παρ' αὐτοῦ (Ζήνωνος) κατὰ συντάξεις καὶ ἐγένετο Καῖσαρ ὁ υἱὸς Ἀρμάτου τοῦ στρατηλάτου πραισέντου.

[3] The text is corrupt. The word ᎈᎉᎈ᎐ = 'his friend', I have transposed from before 'who was commander of the guard' (= στρατηλάτης ὢν πραισέντου, John Mal. 353).

50. Then he marched on Rome, and had the chief of the barbarians, named Odoacer, who bore the title of *rex*, brought before him through the treason of the senators, and he reduced the city of Rome and made himself master of it, and put all the barbarians to the sword, and resided there forty-seven years as its emperor. 51. And he refused to appoint a colleague, and made the emperor Zeno a friend,[1] and did everything in accordance with the advice of the emperor. And he possessed the respect of the magistrates and senate.

52. And there came to Theodoric the wife . . . ,[2] and she was of patrician rank in Rome, named Juvenalia, and spake unto him and said : ' Behold it is now three years since I have suffered wrong. My suit is with the patrician Firmus, and justice has not been done to me.' 53. And he called the judges and said unto them : ' Behold I give commandment and say unto you that unless in two days you bring to a conclusion the suit of this woman with her adversaries and render justice to the two parties equitably according to law, I will have your heads cut off with the sword.' 54. And thereupon they departed, and spent two days in bringing the suit of this woman to a conclusion equitably. And the woman lighted a waxen taper and went in to him (i.e. the king) to thank him, and she said unto him : ' My suit which lingered so long a time has now, thanks to thy orders, been brought to a conclusion.' 55. Thereupon he had the judges summoned before him, and said unto them ; ' Ye wicked men, ye have brought to a conclusion in two days a suit which ye were not able to conclude in three years.' And thereupon he gave orders to have their heads cut off with the sword. And great fear fell upon the city, and an end was put to all oppression on the part of the Roman officials.

56. And in those days after the death of Theodoric, Athalaric[3] came (to the throne), and he was an Arian.

57. And subsequently the emperor Zeno sent an officer named

---

[1] The text is unintelligible and corrupt. It reads, 'made the city to the emperor Zeno'. As John Mal. 383 has here : καὶ ἐφιλιώθη Ζήνωνι . . . τῷ βασιλεῖ καὶ πάντα ὅσα ἔπραττε κατὰ γνώμην αὐτοῦ, I have emended ᏃᏁᎨ: ᎀᎱᎸᎴ: (= ' made the city ') into ᏃᏁᎨ: ᎀᎧᏃᎸ: (= ' made a friend ').

[2] Text defective and corrupt. The event is recorded in John Mal. 384, *Chron. Pasch.* 327.

[3] 'Αλάριχος in John Mal. 385 ; Evagrius, *H. E.* iii. 27, iv. 19.

Quaestor[1] to Alexandria to bring back to him the patriarch
Timothy, the man of God. And when the quaestor came to the
patriarch Timothy, he said unto him : ' The emperor summons thee.'
And the patriarch answered and said unto him : ' The emperor will
not see my face.' And thereupon he fell ill and died, even as he
had said. 58. And the orthodox arose and appointed Peter, the
archdeacon, surnamed Mongus, to be patriarch. And the magistrates of the city sought to arrest him, but he escaped out of the
hands of the soldiers, and made his escape to the house of (one of)
the faithful, and there were alarms in the city. 59. And the
partisans of Proterius the Chalcedonian on their part elected
a patriarch, named Ajes,[2] but he died shortly after. 60. And the
faithful . . . ⟨Then the Chalcedonians elected a patriarch⟩ named
John Tabennesiotes. And he likewise got possession of the
(patriarchal) throne of Ajes by bribing the magistrates. And he
said : ' I have sworn a solemn oath to the emperor Zeno that I shall
take no measures regarding the ecclesiastical see (of Alexandria).'
61. And when the emperor Zeno heard of this event he was very
wroth, and he gave orders for his expulsion. And when John
heard that the emperor had given orders for his expulsion, he took
to flight and went to Rome. 62. And at that time Acacius,
patriarch of Constantinople, was on friendly terms with the
emperor Zeno. And so he prevailed on the emperor that they
should subscribe the Henoticon, that is to say, the confession of the
faith of the three Councils Nicaea, Constantinople, and Ephesus,
and should reject the other Councils.

63. And for this reason ⟨he had brought back⟩ Peter the
patriarch,[3] who had previously fled, to Antioch from the city of
Dînârûrjâ. And Calandio the patriarch of Antioch fled through
fear of being put to death, as he was a Chalcedonian. For (its
inhabitants) had previously put to death the patriarch Stephen, his

---

[1] Probably a transliteration of Κοιαίστωρ, the name of an office, which the
translator took to be a proper name.

[2] On the various names of Timothy, commonly called Salofaciolus, consecrated
patriarch of Alexandria 460 A. D., see Smith's *Dict. Christ. Biog.* iv. 1033.

[3] Peter the Fuller was banished by Zeno (Evagrius, *H. E.* iii. 8) to Petyus.
On the way thither he escaped his guards and took refuge in the church of
S. Theodore in Euchaites (Cedrenus i. 618). Thence he returned to Antioch,
and intrigued against the orthodox prelates, the two (?) Stephens and Calandio.
Finally, on the deposition of the last, Peter was restored by Zeno in 485 on
signing the Henoticon.

predecessor. And all the priests and people prayed to the emperor on behalf of him [1] (i. e. Peter). And the patriarch Peter accepted the Henoticon of the emperor. 64. And in his days there were tumults in the city because of the confession of the faith written by the emperor—for we anathematize the council of the bishops at Chalcedon and their impure creed which states that there are two natures in Christ, whereas the letter of Zeno says that there is (only) one nature in the Word of God which was made flesh, and that the bishops who had been expelled should be remembered (in the diptychs).

65. And the emperor Zeno made a compact with Illus and came to terms with him about the same time that he had received Armatus, the father of Caesar, into favour. But subsequently the army of Illus waged war on the emperor Zeno. For Illus, seeing that Armatus, though a friend of the emperor Zeno, had been executed, fled in fear (of a similar fate) to Isauria. [2] 66. Now Illus sent the empress Verina, the mother-in-law of the emperor, a message to this effect: ' Prevail on the emperor in his behalf.' But she could not prevail on the emperor. Now the emperor Zeno concealed his evil designs from his brother Longinus lest there should be a scandal and grounds for disturbances in Byzantium; for she had formerly been an empress. 67. And in this treacherous plot the emperor Zeno had arranged with Illus to banish her, and transport her to the province of Isauria and to keep her guarded [3] there. And when she arrived there, Illus came forth and shut her up in a fortress, and he appointed a large force to guard her. And he took with him Longinus the emperor's brother. 68. But when she (Verina) came to know these facts, she sent a message to her daughter (Ariadne) the emperor's wife. And her daughter requested the emperor to release her from the fortress where they had imprisoned her. [4]

---

[1] For ባእንት: I read ባእንቴ: ኃበ: ' on his behalf of him to '. Otherwise the text reads ' on behalf of the emperor Zeno '.

[2] With the confused text of this and the following verses cf. John Mal. 385-9.

[3] I have emended ይቀትሳ: ' have her put to death ' into ይዕቅባ:

[4] The text = ' to permit her to remain in the fortress of Isauria ', exactly the opposite of what she desired. Hence for ትንበር: ወ-ስት: ቅጽር: ዘኢሱራያ: I read እግመቅጽር: ወ-ስተዘ: አሰርዋ: Cf. John Mal. : ἵνα ἀπολυθῇ ἀπὸ καστελλίου ὅπου ἦν ἀποκεκλεισμένη.

And the emperor said unto her: 'I cannot incur the anger of Illus the patrician; but do thou ask him, and if he approves, I will set her free.' 69. And the empress sent to him and besought him with tears to set free her mother [1] and to pardon her wrong-doing.[2] 70. But he refused to have compassion on her and said unto her: 'Do you wish me to set up another emperor against thine own husband?' And she was very wroth with him, and she went to the emperor and said unto him: 'Am I and likewise Illus to live (at the same time) in the palace?' And the emperor said unto her: 'Do what you wish; for I love you more than Illus and many men.' 71. And when the empress heard these words of the emperor, her heart was strengthened, and she commanded †Adrian† to put him to death. And †Adrian† [3] who was chief of the eunuchs sent a man, named Scholarius, who being a captain of the guard could enter when he wished the palace of the emperor with his men. 72. And he went in and drew his sword in order to smite him (Illus) and cleave his head in a gallery of the palace. And one of the officers, seeing this, ran hastily and wrested his sword from him after he had cut off the right ear of Illus instead of his head. 73. And Scholarius [4] the eunuch was put to death, who had smitten Illus with the sword. And the followers of Illus transported him to his house. 74. And when the emperor Zeno heard of this event, he took an oath, saying: 'I know nothing of this outrage that the eunuch did to Illus.' And when Illus had recovered from his wound, he asked permission from the emperor Zeno to go to the east for change of air in order to avoid a return of his malady. 75. And he asked humbly that he would let him go, dissembling his treacherous designs. And, unaware of his treachery, (the emperor) let him go. And he appointed †in his stead another man named Jûlâljâ† with full powers.[5] And Illus wished to take Leontius and Pamprepius with him, apparently on the pretext that they would negotiate peace between Verina the emperor's mother and the emperor Zeno, and that (thus) she might return honourably to him.

---

[1] Zotenberg omits ' to set free her mother '.
[2] Text corruptly adds ' and to let her remain there '.
[3] Urbicius was the chief of the eunuchs.
[4] σχολάριος = an official of the palace guard. It is not a proper name.
[5] Utterly corrupt. We should read as in John Mal. 388: ἐποίησεν αὐτὸν στρατηλάτην Ἀνατολῆς δοὺς αὐτῷ πᾶσαν ἐξουσίαν.

76. And the emperor was pleased with this plan, and he sent these three persons and likewise (two) illustrious (senators) named Marsos and Vâljânôs, magistrates of Isauria, and many officials and troops. 77. And when they came to Antioch the Great, Illus stayed a year (there), and the inhabitants of that city paid him very high honours. 78. Then he marched into Isauria and brought Verina down from the fort, and they bound themselves by mutual oaths. And in agreement with Pamprepius, who was given to magic and the seductions of demons, he prevailed on the officers to create Leontius emperor. So they created him emperor in the oratory of S. Peter, outside the walls of Tarsus the capital of Cilicia. 79. And she (Verina) wrote and dispatched letters to all the cities and officials and troops of the east, and to the cities of Egypt, to gain their recognition of the imperial authority of Leontius without opposition. 80. And the empress Verina, Augusta, wrote likewise as follows: 'I make known unto you touching our imperial authority, that after the death of the emperor Leo, of happy memory, we appointed Trascalissaeus, that is Zeno, emperor, that he might be solicitous [1] as regards our commands and duly govern the army. 81. But now we have seen that he has abandoned integrity, while he is likewise devoid of understanding.[2] Accordingly we have accounted him as a rebel, a perverse man and a usurper. Behold, now, we have appointed another emperor, a Christian Godloving man, distinguished for righteousness and uprightness, that he may save the country by his virtuous conduct and put an end to the war: and may preserve his subjects according to law and order. 82. And we have crowned Leontius with the imperial crown that he may be emperor over the Roman empire, who will be solicitous after every good work.' 83. And when the letter was read in the city of Antioch, all the population cried aloud saying: 'Do unto us the good things, O Lord, which will be good for us.' And a letter also was sent to Alexandria. 84. Then Leontius came to Antioch and took up his residence in the palace, and he

---

[1] The text reads ኅፉይ፡ of which Zotenberg gives the impossible rendering 'l'exécuteur fidèle'. I have emended the above into ኅብይ፡ in accordance with the ይጎሊ፡ in ver. 82.

[2] This rendering follows the manuscripts, only omitting ወ. Otherwise read ወይጸግብ፡ ዘእንበለ፡ አእምር፡ 'and that he is unconscionably insatiable'. Zotenberg emends the text differently.

appointed Lilianus[1] prefect and judge. 85. And after fifteen days he marched to Chalcis, a city of Isauria, in order to attack the inhabitants of that city, because they refused to submit to him and called him a rebel against the emperor. 86. And for one and a half months he waged war on the inhabitants of that city but was not able to take it. And when the emperor Zeno heard of what had befallen, he sent a Scythian officer named John, a valiant man and a warrior, in command of a numerous army to wage war on the conspirators. 87. And when Illus who was in Cilicia discovered that he was not able to make head against the general John, he marched and joined Leontius and Verina, and they arranged to flee together and to take refuge in a castle in Isauria, named Papyris. 88. And Leontius went in precipitate flight from the province of the East, and these three personages, Leontius, Illus, and Pamprepius accompanied by Verina, withdrew into a castle. And when the troops of the emperor Zeno arrived they besieged that castle in which they were. And Verina died in the castle. 89. And the garrison of the castle, learning that Pamprepius was seeking to join the enemy against them, put him to death and cast his body from the top of the battlements. 90. And after many toilsome efforts, (the besiegers) captured the castle and brought forth the rebels, that is, Leontius who wrought his own destruction and Illus who was the cause of all the evil. 91. And they placed them on a tribunal in the midst of the assemblage and passed upon them the sentence of death, and they cut off their heads with the sword and carried them to the emperor Zeno in Constantinople.

92. And it is told also regarding the emperor Zeno that he was with Maurianus the astrologer : now the latter used to announce to him (beforehand) all that happened ; for they were friends. 93. And (the emperor) asked him saying : 'Who will succeed to the empire after me ? ' And he said unto him : 'A Silentiarius will take thine empire and likewise thy wife.' And owing to this (prediction) he thought (the person meant) was an illustrious man named Pelagius, who had become a patrician.[2] 94. Now they deposed him unjustly ; indeed the emperor committed Silentiarius to the charge of six trusty men and commanded them to strangle him in the night, though he was guiltless. After they had strangled him, they cast his body into the sea. 95. And when this wicked murder came to

[1] So Zotenberg restores the faulty name.   [2] The text adds 'first'.

be known, people could not keep silence on the matter—and
particularly Arcadius, an illustrious officer and a thorough observer
of justice. And he was one that judged uprightly and hated
oppression. And he blamed the emperor for the crime that in the
hardness of his heart he had committed in putting Silentiarius the
patrician to death. 96. And when Zeno the emperor heard (this)
he was wroth with Arcadius, and gave orders for him to be put to
death as he entered the palace. And (the guards) did as the
emperor commanded, but Arcadius escaped out of their hands, by
entering a church in order (as he pretended) to make prayer and
supplication to God.[1] 97. And the emperor fell sick of a dysentery
and died.

CHAPTER LXXXIX. 1. And after the death of the Godloving
emperor Zeno, the Christian and Godfearing emperor Anastasius
came to the throne. He was one of the emperor's chamberlains,
and became emperor through the grace of God and the prayers of
our Egyptian Fathers. 2. Now the emperor Zeno had banished
him to the island of S. Irâi, situated in the river of Memphis.
Now the inhabitants of Manûf had treated him with kindly
affection. 3. And Ammonius, who belonged to the city of Hezênâ
in the province of Alexandria, and ⟨the inhabitants of that city⟩
became his friends, and honoured him and showed him much
affection. 4. And one day the inhabitants of Manûf and of
Hezênâ agreed together respecting Anastasius, who was in disgrace
with the emperor Zeno, to ascend the mountain to the convent of
the God-clothed S. Abba Jeremiah of Alexandria. 5. And there
lived on their route a man who was endowed with the knowledge
of all the works of God. And they conversed regarding the holy
life of the man of God, and desired his blessing. And he prayed
for them to Christ whom he served. 6. And they proceeded and
entered into the dwelling of the man of God, the Abba Jeremiah.
And he blessed them all, but spake no word at all to Anastasius.
7. And when they came forth Anastasius was very deeply pained,
and he wept much, saying in his heart: 'It is by reason of the
multitude of my sins that the man of God did not bless me when
he blessed all the rest.' 8. And the inhabitants of Manûf and

---

[1] The words 'and the emperor' precede 'by entering a church . . . to God'
in the previous verse. John Mal. 390, Cedrenus i. 621 support this restoration
of the order of the text.

Ammonius of the city of Hezênâ went to the holy man of God and
told him of the grievous pain with which Anastasius was afflicted.
9. And he indeed called him apart, and likewise his trusty friends
and Ammonius, and said unto him : ' Grieve not so as to think and
say, " It is by reason of my sins that the old man blessed me not" :
the matter is not so ; on the contrary, as I have seen the hand of
God upon thee, I have on this ground refrained from blessing thee.
10. How should I who have been guilty of so many sins be worthy
to bless him whom God hath blessed and honoured.   And he hath
chosen thee from amongst many thousands to be His anointed ;
for it is written : " The hand of the Lord God is on the head of
kings."   11. And He hath set His trust in thee that thou mayest
become His representative on earth and strengthen His people.
Only when thou dost recall my words and hast accomplished the
prophecy, observe this command which I give thee this day, so that
God may save thee from thine adversaries : " Do no sin of any kind
and transgress not against the Christian faith of Christ, and reject
the Chalcedonian faith which hath provoked God to anger." '

12. And as for these commands which the Abba Jeremiah gave
to Anastasius, he indeed received them, (engraving them) on the
tables of his heart, even as Moses the prophet received the tables
of the Covenant from God whereon were engraved the commandments of the law.   13. And shortly after Anastasius was recalled
from the banishment into which the emperor of (this) world had
driven him by virtue of his power.   And subsequently Anastasius
was appointed emperor.   14. And thereupon he sent to the disciples
of the holy Abba Jeremiah ⟨and had them fetched⟩.   And the
Abba Wârjânôs, who was a relative of Abba Jeremiah, accompanied
them.   Now the emperor indeed besought them with many prayers
to accept money for their food on the way and for the convent ; but
⟨they refused⟩ because their father the holy Jeremiah had instructed
them not to accept anything save incense for the celebration of
the eucharist or for offering the sacrifice, and a few sacred utensils.
15. And he sent also to the island where he had formerly been
in banishment, and he had a great and massive church built (and)
named S. Irâi.   Formerly it was but a little church.   16. And he
sent to it many gold and silver vessels and beautiful vestments.
And he sent also much gold and silver to his friends in the city
of Manûf and Hezênâ.   And he conferred magistracies upon

them, and some of them he had ordained to the priesthood.
17. And this Godloving Anastasius sent to the city of Antioch
and to all the cities, and put a stop to the civil war which the
people waged on each other, and he made them submit to authority
as became Christians. And he wrote to all the magistrates that
were subject to him (bidding them) to execute this decree, and
they submitted to authority as became Christians.

18. And subsequently there arose disturbances in (the capital of)
his dominion through the enmity of Satan. For the people
demanded tumultuously that certain disorderly and factious persons
should not be cast into prison; for the prefect had delivered over
several of them to be stoned. But the emperor refused to let them
off, and he was wroth, and gave orders for them to be attacked by
the cavalry.[1] 19. And when these went down to make the attack
a slave audaciously rose up and approached the emperor's seat, and
hurled a stone with the intention of killing the emperor. Now
he stood up in his place, saying in his heart, 'No one will
recognize me'. 20. But the help of God shielded the emperor,
and the stone fell inside the enclosure that is within the imperial
seat and brake it. And when (the guards) saw that slave who
cast a stone at the emperor they marked him closely, and ran and
seized him, and dismembered him limb from limb. 21. And the
tumult waxed more serious, and they burnt the brazen circuit[2]
where stood the seats of the soldiers and the cavalry and all the

---

[1] The text misrepresents the facts, which were briefly as follows. On one
occasion the Green Faction in Constantinople besought the emperor during one
of the races to set free from bonds certain individuals who had been cast into
prison for throwing stones during an exhibition in the circus. But the
emperor refused, and ordered the soldiers to attack the people. Thereupon
the mob assailed the imperial guards, and a Moor among it hurled a stone at the
emperor. Cf. *Chron. Pasch.* 329 Ἱππικοῦ ἀγομένου παρεκάλουν οἱ τοῦ μέρους τῶν
Πρασίνων τὸν βασιλέα Ἀναστάσιον ἀπολυθῆναί τινας συσχεθέντας ἀπὸ τοῦ ἐπάρχου τῆς
πόλεως λιθοβόλους. καὶ οὐ παρεκλήθη ἀπὸ τοῦ δήμου ὁ αὐτὸς Ἀναστάσιος, ἀλλὰ ἀγανα-
κτήσας ἐκέλευσεν ἄρμα (? ἁρμάτους Ducange) κατ' αὐτῶν ἐξελθεῖν, καὶ ἐγένετο ἀταξία
μεγάλη, καὶ κατῆλθον οἱ δῆμοι κατὰ τῶν ἐξκουβιτώρων καὶ ἐλθόντες ἐπὶ τὸ κάθισμα
ἔρριψαν λίθους κατὰ τοῦ βασιλέως Ἀναστασίου, ἐν οἷς εἷς Μαῦρος ἔρριψεν ἐπάνω τοῦ
βασιλέως Ἀναστασίου. καὶ ἐξέφυγεν ὁ βασιλεὺς τὸν λίθον ... καὶ θεασάμενοι οἱ ἐξ-
κουβίτωρες τὴν τοῦ αὐτοῦ Μαύρου τόλμαν ὥρμησαν κατ' αὐτοῦ, καὶ ἔκοψαν αὐτὸν κατὰ
μέλος. .... ὁ δὲ δῆμος στενωθεὶς ἔβαλεν πῦρ ἐν τῇ λεγομένῃ Χαλκῇ τοῦ Ἱππικοῦ· καὶ
ὁ περίβολος ὅλος ἐκαύθη ἕως τοῦ βασιλικοῦ καθίσματος. καὶ ὁ δημόσιος ἔμβολος ἕως
τοῦ Ἐξαϊππίου καὶ ἕως τοῦ φόρου Κωνσταντίνου ὅλως καυθεὶς κατηνέχθη ... καὶ
πολλῶν ... τιμωρηθέντων γέγονεν ἡσυχία. See also John **Mal.** 394 sq.

[2] A misunderstanding of Χαλκῇ τοῦ Ἱππικοῦ. See above passage.

people all the way to the emperor's seat, and the portico of
Hexahippium which adjoins the seat[1] constructed by the holy
Constantine.

22. And after many great efforts they forcibly re-established the
(imperial) authority over the seditious, and punished many of them
till peace and tranquillity were restored throughout all the city.

23. And the inhabitants of Antioch also acted after the same
manner as those of Constantinople. They set fire to the synagogue
of the Jews, which is in Daphne, and set up within it the glorious
cross of our Lord Jesus Christ, and they transformed it (the synagogue) into a church, dedicated to S. Leontius, and they put many
of them (the Jews) to death. 24. And when the emperor was
informed of these events he sent Procopius, count of the east, in
order to subdue the seditious factions. 25. And when he and
Menas of Byzantium [2] arrived in Antioch the leaders of the factions
fled from the city and withdrew into the sacred dwelling of S. John.
26. And Menas the prefect at the head of a numerous force went
thither by night. And a great tumult arose, and he slew amongst
them a man named Eleutherius, whose head was carried to the
governor Procopius. 27. But the (Green) faction gained the day,
and burned the place of their assemblage [3] with fire, (and likewise)
the praetorium. Thereupon there was a terrible strife, and Menas
the prefect was slain and his body burned with fire.[4] 28. And
Procopius immediately took to flight and went to the confines of
Constantinople.[5] And when (the emperor) was apprised of the
flight of the governor Procopius he appointed in his stead a man
named Irenaeus, and ordered him to proceed to Antioch. 29. And
when he arrived there he punished many of them, and inspired
such great fear and terror that all the factions abandoned their
civil strife, and so he re-established peace among the inhabitants of
Antioch. 30. And the emperor rebuilt the edifices which had been
burnt, and he constructed many beautiful streets; for in his mercy
and compassion he loved to build edifices. 31. He built many

---

[1] It is the forum of Constantine that was affected. See above passage.

[2] The text has here አይሶም፡ በራኅትየ፡ The first word—a corruption of
በይሶም፡—ultimately goes back to Μηνᾶς. In transliterating from the Arabic
the confusion arose.

[3] This was the Basilica of Rufinus in Antioch.

[4] Cf. John Mal. 396 sqq.   [5] John Mal. says Alexandria.

edifices in Egypt, and likewise a fortress on the borders of the Red Sea. And he applied himself to completing all manner of beautiful works, that he might remain in tranquillity and peace. 32. And for the inhabitants of Doras[1] he had a wall built, and openings made in the walls like bridges to prevent the water of the river from spreading upon the fields.

33. And in the reign also of this Godloving emperor impious barbarians, who eat human flesh and drank blood, arose in the quarter of Arabia, and approaching the borders of the Red Sea they seized the monks of Arâitê,[2] and they put them to the sword or led them away captive and plundered their possessions; for they hated the saints, and were themselves like in their devices to the idolaters and pagans. And after they had taken a large booty they returned to their own country. 34. And when the emperor was informed of this event he had strong forts constructed as a defence to the dwellings of the monks, and he rendered many good services to them and all the monks of the Roman world.

35. And certain people in the city of Alexandria rose up and created a shameful disturbance, and slew the prefect of the city, who was named Theodosius, who had been brought up in the house of the patriarch of Antioch. And when the emperor was informed of this event he was wroth, and punished many of the inhabitants of that city.

36. And the good deeds alone of the emperor are beyond numbering; for he was an orthodox believer and trusted in our Lord and Saviour Jesus Christ, and prohibited the faith of the Chalcedonians because the holy Jeremiah, the servant of God, had (so) bidden him.

37. Now the people of Elwârîkôn[3] had refused to accept the letter of Leo which he dispatched to them from Rome. But when the oppression of Marcian and his magistrates became severe they began to fear lest they should experience the violence which befell Dioscorus the patriarch of Alexandria. 38. And the emperor Anastasius, the servant of God, agreed with the terms of the letter of the emperor Zeno. And subsequently he gave orders that the faith professed by the three Councils, Nicaea, Constantinople, and

---

[1] Cf. John Mal. 399 ἐτείχισε τὸ Δορὰς . . . καὶ κιστέρνας ὑδάτων. See Evagrius, H. E. iii. 37.

[2] Cf. Evagrius, H. E. iii. 36.   [3] Zotenberg takes this to be Illyria.

the first at Ephesus, should be established. 39. But Euphemius, the patriarch of Constantinople at that period, was a Chalcedonian, who divided the one nature of Christ into two distinct natures in its manifestations, saying that it was the Word of God that had wrought the miracles, but the weak human nature that had submitted to the passion. 40. And he changed likewise the trisagion which we recite thus : ' Holy God, holy Strong One, holy Immortal One, who hast been crucified for us, have mercy upon us.' But he did not recite it as we, but in the following terms : ' Holy God, holy Strong One, holy Immortal One, have mercy upon us.' 41. Indeed he declared, ' I do not recite it as ye do, to prevent the application of this formula to the Holy Trinity in three persons. Him who was crucified we adore together with the Father and the Holy Spirit. Now it was not the Father and the Son and the Holy Spirit who suffered. He that became incarnate without separating Himself (from the Trinity) and suffered is consubstantial with the Father and the Holy Spirit, but He did not suffer in His divinity. And there is none other than He—God forbid ! 42. Now whilst one of the Holy Trinity, He is capable of suffering in the body which is united with Him and the reasonable soul which are combined in (one) person, but He is not capable of suffering in His divinity which is consubstantial with the Father and the Holy Spirit, as our holy Fathers have taught us.' 43. The wise Proclus joined the Nestorians in saying : ' If Christ was in every respect incapable of suffering after His incarnation, He could no more suffer in body than could the divinity of the Son.' But in so saying he speaks falsely, for the Son of God could not then have suffered in reality. 44. These are the pestilent words of those who say there are four persons instead of three.

45. Of a similar character are the declarations of those impostors who say regarding the Son that it was another who was crucified ; for this wicked opinion was propounded by heretics. 46. And the emperor Anastasius deprived Euphemius of his dignities and banished him from Constantinople to Euchaites in Pontus. And he appointed Macedonius in his stead, who accepted from his hand the edict of the emperor Zeno, and refused to accept the Council of Chalcedon. 47. And he charmed the heart of the emperor Anastasius, though concealing the while treacherous devices in his thoughts regarding the faith. And (the emperor) obliged him to recite the

trisagion in these terms : ' Mayst Thou who wast crucified [1] for us have mercy upon us.'   And thus he ordained this rule.

48. Now the orthodox monks of Palestine had abandoned the study of the Scriptures, and a schism had arisen amongst them ; for they declared that they were unwilling to accept the edict of the emperor.   And they brought thereby persecution upon them- selves at the instigation of a monk named Nephalius, a promoter of dissension.   49. The monks of the desert sent certain aged anchor- ites to Constantinople, accompanied by Severus the chief of the Fathers—a wise man well versed in the Scriptures, and a perfect priest—to request the emperor Anastasius to issue orders to the monks to live peaceably in their dwellings and cloisters, and to pray on his behalf.   50. And when they came to speak to the emperor they were recognized by the officers and conducted to the patriarch Macedonius, and they conversed with him on the subject of the faith.   51. And thereupon he confessed openly what was hidden in his heart regarding the perverted faith which he followed ;   for he could not always conceal his views and prevent their coming to be known by some one.   52. Now there was an Alexandrian, named Doritheus, who possessed S. Cyril's treatise on the faith.   And he had conversed with Severus and had found him imbued with the doctrine of S. Cyril.   53. These two admonished Macedonius and the Chalcedonians, who † re- membered † two natures to Jesus Christ the Son of God, who is one.   And it was marvellous in their eyes, and they named this book *Philalethes*.

54. But Macedonius and his adherents, as well as the partisans of the Nestorians, were wroth, and said that after the manner of their (tris)agion the angels recite the trisagion.   But Severus answered: ' The angels recite as follows : " Holy God, holy Mighty One, holy Immortal One, have mercy upon us."   Indeed the angels have no necessity to say : " Who was crucified for us " ; for the crucifixion of our God was not on behalf of angels, but on behalf of us men was our Lord and Saviour Jesus Christ crucified.   55. And it was for our salvation that He came down from heaven and was in- carnate and became man, and was crucified for us in the days of Pontius Pilate, and rose from the dead on the third day, as it is written in the holy Scriptures which were set in due order by our

---

[1] For ሕትበፁበ: (= ' He who was crucified ') read ሕትበፉኡከ:

holy Fathers of Nicaea and Constantinople and Ephesus, who also
established a fitting definition of His divinity. 56. It is for this
reason that we Christians say of necessity: "O Thou who hast
been crucified for us, have mercy upon us." We believe also that the
holy, mighty and immortal God was crucified for us. In like
manner also we truly believe that the holy Virgin Mary brought
forth very God: and that they were not two different persons, but
one and the same whom the Virgin bare and the Jews crucified—
one and the same alike in birth, crucifixion, and resurrection.'
57. And many similar arguments were addressed to the emperor
and the magistrates, whereby the opinions of the heretical Nestorians were overthrown from their foundation. 58. And when
they had by their orthodox arguments reduced Macedonius to
silence, and his opinions had vanished because of the words of
truth, he thought out an evil device, and spake to the emperor and
the magistrates to this effect: 'I too believe the same facts as the
orientals, and I say in the church: "O Thou that wast crucified [1]
for us, have mercy upon us."' 59. But in secret he stirred up the
heretics against the emperor, saying unto them: 'They have introduced novelties into the faith of our Christian Fathers.' Then the
heretics assembled and proceeded to the court of the emperor in
order to stir up a tumult with a view to the banishment of Plato,
who administered all the affairs of his empire: he was very highly
and universally honoured. 60. And yielding to fear, he took to
flight and hid himself. And these heretics and the soldiers who
were with them cried aloud and proclaimed the name of another
emperor of the Romans. 61. And they proceeded with haste to the
house of Marinus the Syrian, an illustrious man.[2] And they burnt
his house and possessions. And they sought to slay him, but they
could not find him; for he had fled, and was saved through the
strong aid of our Lord Jesus Christ. 62. Now the lying patriarch
Macedonius had calumniated this Godloving man to the people,
and had said unto them: 'It is Marinus who turns the heart of
the emperor from the faith.' 63. And moved with evil zeal they
sought for him with a view to slaying him, though he was unaware
of it. And when they had plundered the house of this illustrious
man and carried out the silver vessels he possessed, they divided

---

[1] Reading as in ver. 56 ዘተሰቅልኽ፡

[2] In John Mal. 407 he is an ex-prefect.

them amongst themselves. 64. But indeed the moment the crowds entered the house of the magistrate they found (in it) a monk of the east, (and) they led him forth and put him to death, believing him to be the Godloving Severus. And they took his head and carried it about throughout all the city crying aloud these words: ' This is the enemy of the Holy Trinity.' 65. And they went also to the house of Juliana, who belonged to the family of the emperor Leo ⟨and proclaimed her husband⟩, who was named Ariobindus, ⟨emperor⟩. But when he was apprised of their coming he took to flight. 66. But the people kept shamelessly perpetrating these excesses. Then the Godloving emperor Anastasius, being guided by the true faith of Christ, arose and accompanied by all the senators ascended the imperial throne, clothed in the imperial robes. And when all the people saw him, they were pained and grieved and became repentant, and fearing the emperor they besought him to pardon their transgression, confessing their offences. 67. And the emperor said to them in a loud voice: ' Be not afraid: lo ! I have pardoned you.' [1] And thereupon all the people dispersed to their several dwellings, and tranquillity was restored. But after a few days, the same people stirred up fresh disturbances, and so the emperor Anastasius mustered a numerous force of soldiers and gave orders to them to seize the rioters, and when they were seized and brought to the emperor, some had their limbs broken, others were executed, and others sent into banishment. 68. And by these measures tranquillity was restored, and the fear of the emperor was inspired in the hearts of the citizens. It was then also that Macedonius was banished, who had brought about the destruction of many. He was stripped of his episcopal dignities and reckoned as a murderer, and expelled from the congregation (of the faithful).

69. And the bishops of the east arrived in Byzantium and made the following accusations to the emperor Anastasius against Flavian, patriarch of Antioch : that he was a Nestorian, though he had accepted the Henoticon of the emperor Zeno ; that he had again joined the Chalcedonians, and accepted the abominable letter of Leo, in which were mentioned the two natures and twofold operations of Him who is one only and indivisible, Jesus Christ, very God. 70. And the Godloving emperor Anastasius, moreover,

---

[1] Not so in John Mal. 407-8.

banished him to Petra in Palestine ; for he had cursed the orthodox
and had embraced the faith of the wicked heretics.

71. And Vitalian, moreover, who was commander of the troops
in the province of Thrace, being a man of perverse heart, hated
Severus the saint of God. Now the emperor Anastasius had
appointed Severus patriarch of Antioch in the room of the heretic
Flavian, whom he had banished, when the orthodox bishops of the
east testified in the favour of the former.

72. And Vitalian, whom we have just mentioned, raised a revolt
against the emperor Anastasius, and seized Thrace and Scythia [1]
and Mysia, and mustered a numerous army. 73. And the emperor
sent against him a general named Hypatius. And when they
fought together, he was vanquished by Vitalian and taken prisoner.
And on the payment of a large ransom he was set free. 74. But
immediately on his return to the emperor, the latter removed him
from his command, and appointed in his room another general,
named Cyril, of the province of Illyria. 75. And he also gave
battle to Vitalian, and there was great slaughter on both sides.
Cyril the general retired into the city named Odyssus, and stayed
there while Vitalian withdrew into the province of Bulgaria.
76. And he gave large sums of money to the guards who kept the
gates of Odyssus, and then, marching by night, he put Cyril the
general to death and captured the city. 77. And he attacked also
the province of Thrace, and plundered all its wealth, and likewise
the cities of Europe, and Sycae, and the region over against Constantinople and Sosthenium, and he established himself in the
church of the holy Archangel Michael, devising by what means he
could make himself master of the empire of Byzantium.

78. And the emperor Anastasius sent to the philosopher Proclus
in order that he might render help to Marinus. 79. And the
emperor informed him regarding the rebel Vitalian and the audacity
he had shown. But Marinus encouraged the emperor, saying :
' I will overcome this rebel by the might of God ; only give orders
that I may be accompanied by soldiers and the philosopher Proclus.
Procure for me also unpurged sulphur resembling powdered anti-
mony.' 80. And the emperor gave him the sulphur. And Marinus

---

[1] As Zotenberg shows, the **አስቈሪድ፡** is a transliteration of the Arabic words for
' Curds ', i. e. ' Scythians '.

ground it into a † hard powder †,[1] and said publicly : 'If you cast
(this) on a house or on a ship, it will take fire when the sun rises
and melt it like wax.' 81. And Marinus took with him many
ships, and he mustered all the soldiers he could find in Constantinople, and he proceeded to wage war against Vitalian as the
emperor had commanded. 82. And when the rebel saw Marinus
he took all the ships he could find and manned them with a large
force of Scythian and Gothic archers, and sailed in the direction of
Byzantium, believing that he should get the better of his opponents.
83. But Marinus and his companions, through the mighty help of
God, got the better of this enemy, and the design of this shameless
rebel failed of accomplishment, and thereupon Vitalian, the cause of
civil strife, took to flight.

84. And Marinus gave the unpurged sulphur to the sailors, and
commanded them to cast it on the ships of the rebel foe in order
that they might be burnt. And when the fleets of Marinus and of
this rebel encountered each other, they (the sailors) cast the sulphur
into the ships of Vitalian about the third hour of the day, and
immediately the ships burst into flames and sank in the depths.

85. And when Vitalian saw this he was stupefied, and his
remaining forces turned back and fled. And the general Marinus
put all the rebels he could find to the sword, and pursued them till
they came to the church of S. Mamas. And as night was approaching Marinus encamped there and guarded the route. 86. But
Vitalian after his defeat marched throughout the night and fled
with his followers in fear and terror to a place named Anchialus.
And he traversed that night a space of sixty miles, as he feared
lest Marinus should pursue him and make him a prisoner. On the
morrow every one forsook him and left him alone.

87. And the emperor Anastasius distributed many alms amongst
the poor and destitute in the district of Sosthenium. And he set
out from the imperial city and stayed in the church of S. Michael,
praying and giving thanks to God for all the benefits He had
bestowed upon him and for the victory which He had given him
over his adversaries, and displaying an irreproachable (and) orthodox
faith. 88. Next the emperor Anastasius ordered that a large sum
of gold should be given to the philosopher Proclus. But he refused

---

[1] This should be 'fine powder'. Cf. John Mal. 403 εἰπὼν τριβῆναι αὐτὸ ὡς εἰς
μῖγμα λεπτόν.

to take the money and, saluting the emperor, he requested him (to let him go back to Athens), saying: ' Whoever loves money is not worthy to be a philosopher, and the contempt of money likewise in those that cultivate philosophy is honourable.' And the emperor let him go, and held him in high honour.

89. And all the orthodox believers who had accepted the Henoticon of the righteous emperor Zeno were highly esteemed by the emperor. And at that time appeared from the city of Nikius[1] John priest and monk; for the patriarch had refused to accept him. 90. Now the priest John[2] was wise and Godloving and well versed in the Scriptures, and he lived in the convent of Fâr. 91. And the inhabitants of the city of Sa and those of the city of Akêlâ came to be at variance with each other. Thereupon the bishops of the two cities arose and went to the emperor Anastasius, and besought him to ordain for them suitable canons, to hold a Council, and expel the Chalcedonians and blot out their remembrance from the church and that of all bishops who agreed with the abominable Leo who proclaimed the two natures.

92. But the emperor in his goodness did not force them contrary to their inclinations, but (suffered) each (to) act according to his own inclination. And the emperor Anastasius paid great honour to those who agreed with him in the orthodox faith and distributed numerous alms and virtuously completed his work.

93. And subsequently the emperor fell ill. Now he was an old man, and at the age of ninety years he went to his rest in great honour, as saith the Scriptures: ' All the glory of man is but as grass: as soon as the sun ariseth, the grass withereth, the flower thereof fadeth, the beauty of the appearance thereof perisheth, but the word of the Lord abideth for ever.'[3]

CHAPTER XC. 1. And after the blessed Godloving orthodox emperor Anastasius went to his rest, Justin the terrible, the consort of the empress Euphemia, ascended the throne, and was crowned with the imperial crown in pursuance of the decision of the trusty councillors of the emperor. 2. Some say regarding him that he was †chief over the seventh assemblage in Byzantium †.[4] But all the officers

---

[1] Nakius on B.

[2] John Niciota, Monophysite patriarch of Alexandria 507–517.

[3] 1 Pet. i. 24.

[4] Hopelessly corrupt. John Mal. 410 has κόμης ἐξκουβιτόρων = ' Count of the imperial guard '. So also Chron. Pasch. 330.

did not approve of him ; for he was unlettered, but he was a soldier and a valiant man. 3. Now there was a man named Amantius whom the officers wished to make emperor over them after the emperor Anastasius, and the councillors had given large sums of money to Justin to distribute among the civilians and the soldiers, in order that they might proclaim his name and spread abroad the rumour that God had named him emperor. But these refused to do so. And so the councillors were thereupon obliged to make Justin emperor.[1]

4. And when Justin became emperor he put to death all the eunuchs, however guiltless they were, because they had not approved of his elevation to the throne ; for he thought they would plot evil against him.

5. And in the beginning of the reign of Justin there rose in the east a fearful and terrible comet.[2] And for this reason the emperor Justin sent and recalled Vitalian who had been the enemy of the emperor Anastasius, and appointed him a master of the forces.[3] 6. And he changed the orthodox faith of the emperor Anastasius, and the Henoticon of the emperor Zeno was rejected : communion with the Chalcedonians was restored, and the letter of Leo was accepted and enrolled amongst the writings of the Eastern Church.

7. In the first year of his reign the great Severus, the patriarch of the great city of Antioch, †appeared†. When he heard of the change of faith and the return of Vitalian and his reception at the court of the emperor Justin, he became afraid and fled into Egypt and abandoned his (patriarchal) throne. 8. Now Vitalian hated him and wished to cut out his tongue because he had written (and delivered) in the church long and short homilies, full of knowledge and invective directed against the †emperor†[4] Leo because of his corrupt faith. 9. And Paul was appointed patriarch of Antioch in the room of Severus, and this Paul was in communion with the Chalcedonians. And a schism then arose and none associated with him save the magistrates of the emperor only. 10. The people turned away from him because of his being a

---

[1] This account is incorrect. According to John Mal. 410 sq., *Chron. Pasch.* 331, Amantius gave large sums of money to Justin to distribute in order to secure the elevation of Theocritus, a Count of the palace guard, to the imperial throne.

[2] Here the text reads መኵናንት፡ = κόμης, corrupt for κομήτης (Zotenberg).

[3] John Mal. 411 στρατηλάτην πραισέντου.

[4] This should be the patriarch Leo referred to in ver. 6.

Nestorian and refused the sacerdotal benediction and baptism save
at the hands of the priests ordained in secret by the great Severus.
11. Now he who wished to cut out the tongue of the great Severus
soon died of a violent death. Now Vitalian's death was brought
about by his plotting, after his appointment by the emperor Justin,
to raise a revolt (against him) as he had done against the emperor
before him.   12. And thereupon (Justin) gave orders for his
execution. For God punished him speedily, even as Severus had
prophesied regarding him that he should die a violent death.

13. And the patriarch Severus ⟨composed⟩ a treatise full of
wisdom and the fear of God, and sent it to the patrician Godloving
Caesaria; for she was a chosen vessel, of the imperial family of
Rome, and she was strong in the orthodox faith in which she had
been instructed by the holy patriarch Severus. And this teaching
prevails to the present day among the Egyptian monks. 14. And
subsequently Paul the Chalcedonian, of Antioch, died, who had been
appointed after Severus, and another was appointed in his room,
named Euphrasius, of Jerusalem. This man hated the Christians
attached to the teaching of Severus. And many of the orthodox
were put to death on account of the faith which he taught.
15. And he stirred up civil war throughout all the Roman empire,
and there was much shedding of blood. And in the city of Antioch
there were great tumults during five years. And no one could
speak owing to fear of the emperor.

16. And there arose many men belonging to the people who in
Constantinople *and the cities of Hellas [1] loudly accused the patrician
Justinian his brother's son. Now Justinian helped the Blue Faction
to commit murder and pillage among the various nations. 17. And
(the emperor) appointed a prefect named Theodotus, (formerly
count) of the east to punish all who had been guilty of crime, and
he made him swear that he would show no partiality. 18. And
beginning with Constantinople he punished many guilty persons,
and subsequently had Theodosius arrested and put to death. And
he was very rich. And next he had Justinian the patrician arrested,
and wished to put him to death. But when he fell ill, he let him
go. 19. And the emperor on hearing these things was wroth with
the prefect and stripped him of his dignities and sent him in exile
from Constantinople into the east. And fearing lest he should be

---

[1] These words occur after 'patrician' in the text.

put to death there, he went to the holy places of Jerusalem and
lived there in seclusion.

20. And subsequently all the soldiers and people assembled
together in Byzantium and disowned their allegiance to the emperor.
And they besought God saying: 'Give us a good emperor like
Anastasius or else remove the emperor Justin whom Thou hast
given us.' 21. And there arose a man amongst them named Qâmôs,
who said unto them: 'Thus saith the Lord: see, I love you:
wherefore do ye supplicate Me. Behold him whom I have given
unto you—I will give you no other;—for if he did according to
that which is written, supplications would arise amongst the
adversaries of the emperor. For it is owing to the sins of this city
that I have appointed this emperor who is a hater of the virtuous.'
Thus saith the Lord: 'I will give you rulers according to your
own hearts.' 22. And the emperor was grieved when he heard
these words. However, he sought to gain the affection of the
people, as he feared lest the wise should admonish him according to
the laws of this world. 23. And so on his own initiative he chose
and appointed in the room of Theodotus and Theodore prefects of
the imperial city: and the names of those who were appointed
were Theodore and Ephraim of Amida. These, indeed, by great
efforts and severity, put an end to civil war amongst the citizens,
made feuds to cease, and established peace.

24. But these means were not yet sufficient to turn away the
wrath of God from the earth owing to the declension of the
emperor. For there came an earthquake from God and fire fell
from heaven on the city of Antioch, extending from the church of
S. Stephen to the house of the chief of the army, in breadth and
length, and as far as the bath called Tainâdônḫûs and the bath of
the Syrian nation. 25. And about the same time also fires burst
out in the countries of the east and along all the routes for six
months, and no one could pass in this direction or that. And there
were conflagrations in the city and many souls perished in the
flames, and the fire descended from above the houses and they were
destroyed to their foundations. 26. And likewise in the days of that
emperor, the great city of Antioch in Syria was sorely afflicted and
was devastated six times. The people who remained wasted away
in their houses and became as soulless bodies. 27. Burning coals of
fire like thunderbolts fell from the air and set fire to everything

they touched, and the city was overthrown to its foundations.
28. And the fire pursued those who wished to flee, whilst those who
remained in the houses were consumed by the fire. And the beauty
of the city of Antioch was destroyed, and none could escape the
fire. No more did the houses on the heights [1] escape this visitation.
And many edifices sacred to the martyrs were devastated, and some
of them were cloven in twain from the top to the bottom, and the
great church which had been built in the days of the emperor
Constantine was destroyed. 29. And weeping and lamentation
were multiplied throughout the city, and the number of men,
women, young people and babes that died was 250,000 souls.

30. And when the festival of the Ascension of our Lord and
Saviour Jesus Christ arrived, many people assembled in the church
called Kârâdâum, in order to make intercession because of this
terrible event. 31. And many who had survived the visitation
went out to bury their dead, and others drew forth (from the débris)
certain women with their babes which had escaped.[2] 32. Moreover,
the unfortunate Euphrasius, who had been unfitted for the
patriarchate, perished in the fire. And they appointed by lot as his
successor a man named ⟨Ephraim⟩, of Amida in Mesopotamia.
And he also was a Chalcedonian, and persecuted the orthodox as
his predecessors had done. 33. And the cities of Seleucia and
Daphne and all the towns within a radius of twenty miles ⟨were
destroyed⟩. And all who saw (these things) said: 'All these
calamities have taken place because the orthodox faith has been
forsaken, and also because of the unjust expulsion of the patriarch
Severus, and the evil deeds perpetrated by the emperor Justin and
his abandonment of the faith of the Godloving emperors that
preceded him. These are the causes alike of this affliction and this
tribulation.' 34. And when the emperor Justin heard these things,
⟨he put off⟩ his imperial crown and garments and wept and
lamented, and ceased to visit the theatre. And under the pressure
of strong necessity he went from the imperial court to the church

---

[1] John Mal. 419 contradicts this.

[2] This translation accepts Zotenberg's emendation of the text save that it
inserts ⲱ before ⳤⲫⲫⲥ·: Without it the text is untranslateable. Zotenberg's translation of his emended text is impossible. The original sense of this
passage is no doubt that in John Mal. 421 : πολλαὶ δὲ γεννήσασαι εἰς τὴν γῆν κάτω
ὑπὸ τὰ χώματα ἀνῆλθον σὺν νηπίοις ἀβλαβεῖς καὶ ἔζησαν μετὰ τῶν τεχθέντων ἐξ αὐτῶν.

on the fifth day of the Easter festival, walking on the ground with
bare feet. And all the people and the Senate wept and lamented
with abundant tears. And he gave much money in order to
rebuild the churches and towns which had been destroyed: no
emperor before him gave in the same measure.

35. And in his reign the Lazaeans, who had been under the sway
of the Persians, and had embraced the cult of their idols, came to him
and became Christians. 36. It was on the occasion of the death
of the king of the Persians that they received grace from heaven,
that is, faith in the Son of God, our Lord Jesus Christ. 37. And
thereupon they came to the city of Constantinople to the emperor
Justin, saying: 'We wish thee to make us Christians like thyself, and we shall then be subjects of the Roman empire.' And
he received them gladly, and had them baptized in the name of
the Father, and the Son, and the Holy Spirit, the consubstantial
Trinity. 38. And he honoured their chief exceedingly, and clothed
him after his baptism with a robe of honour, and rendered to him
imperial honours, and gave him for his spouse the daughter of
a great official, who was named Ionios,[1] and he sent him back to
his own country with great honours. 39. And when Cabades, the
king of the Persians, heard these things he was greatly grieved,
and sent ambassadors to the emperor Justin with the following
message: ' Heretofore there have been friendship and peace between
us: but behold now thou hast created enmity and hast †received† [2]
the king of the Lazaeans, who from the earliest times has been
subject to our sway, and not to that of Rome.' 40. And when
the emperor Justin heard this message, he wrote a reply in the
following terms: ' We have not taken from thee any of thy
subjects; but when a man named Tzathius came to us, humbly
begging us to deliver him from the error wherein he walked,
namely, the errors of demons and of pagans, and from impure
sacrifices, and besought us that he might be made a Christian, how
could I forbid one who desired to return to the true God, the
Creator of all things ? 41. And when he became a Christian, and
was deemed worthy to receive the holy mysteries, we permitted him

---

[1] *Chron. Pasch.* 332 Ὄνινος ; John Mal. 413 Νόμος.

[2] Corrupt. John Mal. and the *Chron. Pasch.* have προεχείρισω. In the latter,
some sentences earlier, this Cabades is stated to have been προχειρισθεὶς καὶ
στεφθεὶς βασιλεὺς Λαζῶν by Justin. Hence we should have here ' given investiture
to ', or the like.

to return to his own country.' And for this reason there was enmity between the Romans and the Persians.

42. And the emperor Justin ⟨requested⟩ Ziligdes, king of the Huns, to be his ally in the war, and he gave him numerous presents, and made him swear a solemn oath that he would deal truly and fairly with him. 43. But Ziligdes proved false to his oath, and set out to join Cabades, king of Persia, with 20,000 soldiers, and formed an alliance with him, and joined him. But the Christians had the help of God, who always wars against their enemies. 44. For when the Persians went forth to give battle the emperor Justin sent the following message to the king of Persia : ' Behold, it is fitting that we should be brothers in friendship, and not be mocked by our enemies. And behold we wish to inform thee that Ziligdes the Hun has received large sums from us with a view to helping us in the time of war, and behold now he has gone to thee with treacherous intent, and in the time of war he will come to our side and slay the Persians. And now, as thou sayest, let there be no enmity between us, but peace.' 45. And when Cabades, king of Persia, heard this, he asked Ziligdes and said unto him : ' Is it true that thou hast received moneys from the Romans to help them against the Persians ? ' And he answered, ' Yes '. And Cabades was enraged, and immediately commanded his head to be cut off; for he thought that he had done this with treacherous intent. 46. And he sent soldiers to fight against the 20,000 troops who had come with him, and he put them to the sword, and only a few escaped, who returned in great shame to their own country. And from that day friendship prevailed between Cabades, king of Persia, and Justin, the emperor of Rome.

47. But the reign of Justin did not last long after the conclusion of this friendship, and in the ninth year of his reign he fell into a grievous illness, for he had a wound in his head,[1] which had been struck by an arrow in battle. The wound reopened, and remained incurable for a long time. 48. And during his illness he appointed his brother's son emperor, and placed upon him the imperial crown, and put all the affairs of the empire in his hands. And thereupon he died.

49. And Justinian, after he had taken the empire into his hands, resided in Constantinople with his wife Theodora. And he

---

[1] According to other chroniclers the wound was in his foot.

practised every virtue, and all shameless persons concealed themselves from his notice. 50. And he built churches everywhere, and
hospices for strangers, and asylums for old men, and hospitals for
the sick, and orphanages, and many other like establishments.
51. And he restored many cities which had been destroyed, and
gave large sums of money to the people. None of the emperors
that preceded him had done as he did.

52. And Cabades, king of Persia, wished to make war upon ⟨the
king of⟩ the Lazaeans, because he had given aid to Rome, and had
become a Christian, and had embraced their faith. And (the
latter) wrote to the emperor Justinian (requesting him) to give him
aid because of his faith in Christ. And he sent thereupon to
him numerous forces under three commanders, whose names were
Belisarius,[1] Cerycus, and Irenaeus, in order to help him. 53. But
when they engaged in battle many of the Romans ⟨fell⟩;[2] for
(the generals) were at variance with each other. And when the
emperor heard (this news) he was very wroth, and sent Peter to be
commander with a large force of archers. And this Peter placed
himself at the head of the Roman generals,[3] and, forming a junction
with the Lazaeans, they attacked the Persians, and put a great
number of the Persians to the sword on that occasion.

54. And the emperor Justinian loved God with all his heart and
mind. Now there was a magician named Mâsîdês, who resided in
the city of Byzantium, and there dwelt with him a band of demons,
who served him. And all the faithful shunned him, and had no
intercourse at all with him. And this magician commanded the
demons to inflict evil plagues on men. 55. And those who lived
without using remedies for the soul and became remiss, attending
the theatre and the races, and particularly certain nobles in the
city, i.e. Addaeus and Aetherius, patricians, held this enemy of
God in high honour. 56. And these same patricians spoke of this
magician to the emperor, and said unto him : ' This man has caused
the destruction of the Persians, and will give victory to the Romans.
And he will be serviceable to the Roman empire by his practices,

---

[1] So *Chron. Pasch.* 335. But John Mal. 427 gives Gilderichus.

[2] Cf. *Chron. Pasch.* 335 πολλοὶ ἔπεσαν τοῦ 'Ρωμαίων στρατοῦ. Here John Mal.
427 has ἔπεσον ἐξ ἀμφοτέρων πολλοί.

[3] This is quite wrong. Peter removed these generals from their commands.
Cf. *Chron. Pasch.* ἀποκινήσαντος αὐτούς.

and he will see to the administration of the nations, and cause the
taxes to be collected excellently, and he will send demons against
the Persians, and make their stout warriors weak through manifold
plagues separate and distinct, and he will make them (the Romans)
victors without a battle.' 57. But being firm of purpose he mocked
the words of these servants of demons, and yet he wished to become
acquainted with their impure devices. And so Mâsîdês carried out
his evil practices as these patricians had told him. 58. And when
the emperor became acquainted (with these practices) he mocked
them (the patricians) and said unto them : ' I do not desire the
magic and sorcery which thou dost practise, thinking that thou
canst benefit the state. 59. Am I, Justinian, a Christian emperor,
to conquer by the help of demons ? Not so, my help cometh from
God and my Lord Jesus Christ, the Creator of the heavens and the
earth.' And accordingly he drove away this magician and his
assistants, for his hope was always in God.

60. And some time later the emperor received the victory from
God, and he commanded that the magician should be burnt.

61. And the Persians, renewing hostilities against Rome, requested the Huns to send 20,000 warriors to fight against Rome.
Now there was there a certain valiant woman amongst the †outer† [1]
Huns, named queen Boa, in the language of the barbarians.
62. And this woman, who was a widow, was wise. And she had
two young sons, and thousands of Hunnish warriors were under
her sway. And she exercised a vigorous rule since the death of her
husband, who was named Balach.[2] 63. And this woman arose and
went to the Christian emperor Justinian, and brought him a great
quantity of gold and silver and precious stones.[3] And the emperor
commanded her to attack the two chiefs who wished to make an
alliance with the Persians and to fight against the Romans. And
these are their names, Astêrâ and Aglânôs.[4] 64. And when this
woman had overtaken these chiefs, who were making terms with
the Persians, she gave them battle and defeated them, and slew
Aglânôs and his followers on the field of battle. 65. And Astêrâ

---

[1] John Mal. 430 has here ῥήγισσα ἐκ τῶν Σαβείρων Οὔννων.

[2] John Mal. has Βλάχ.

[3] It was Justinian made these presents to the queen of the Huns. Cf. John
Mal. 431.

[4] In John Mal. 431 these are named Τόραγξ and Γλώμ.

she took alive, and seized him, and sent him in chains to Constantinople. And they hanged him on a tree, and fixed him (thereto) with nails.

66. And subsequently there came a man of the Huns named Jârôks [1] to the emperor Justinian, and he was baptized and became a Christian. And the emperor Justinian was his sponsor at the baptism, and he gave him abundant honours, and sent him back to his own country. Now this man became a vassal of the Roman empire. 67. And when he returned home he told his brother regarding the gifts which the emperor had given him. And he also became a Christian. This Jârôks took all the idols which the Huns worshipped and brake them in pieces, and took the silver wherewith they were covered and burnt them with fire. And all the people of the country of the Huns who were barbarians were wroth, and they rose against him and slew him. 68. And when the emperor Justinian heard of this, he arose and went to war against them, and he sent many ships by the sea of Pontus and many warriors of the Scythians and Goths. And he set Tûlîlan, [2] a valiant general, over the ships. 69. But as for the cavalry he dispatched them by land, and there was a numerous army with Baduarius as commander. And when the inhabitants of the country of the Huns heard (of these forces) they took to flight, and concealed themselves. And the emperor seized their country and made peace with them anew.

70. And in those days there reigned in the country of the Huns a man named Grepes (text—Akraids), [3] and he went to the emperor Justinian and became a Christian, he and all his kindred and officers. And the emperor gave him large sums of money, and sent him back to his own country with honour as a vassal of the Roman empire.

71. And in the days of the emperor Justinian the Indians were at war with the Ethiopians. And the name of the king of the Indians was Endas. He worshipped the star called Saturn. Now the country of the Ethiopians was not far distant from Egypt: it comprised three Indian states and four Abyssinian states, and they were situated on the border of the Sea [of Salt] towards the east.

[1] John Mal. 431 calls him Γρώδ, and Cedrenus Γόρδας.
[2] In John Mal. 432 he is named 'John the ex-consul'.
[3] See John Mal. 427. In Cedrenus i. 643 Γρέτης.

72. Now the Christian merchants who travelled through the country of the star-worshippers and through the Homeritae,[1] whom we have mentioned and previously described, had to submit to seven trials. Damnus,[2] the king of the Homeritae,[1] used to slay the Christian merchants who came to him, and to take their goods, saying : ' The Romans used to oppress and slay the Jews, and on this account I also will slay all the Christians I find.' 73. And for this reason commerce ceased and came to an end in the interior of India. 74. And when the king of Nubia heard these tidings, he sent to the king of the Homeritae[1] the following message: ' Thou hast done an evil deed in that thou hast slain Christian merchants and inflicted injuries on my kingdom and on the kingdoms of other (kings) who live near at hand and far off from me.' 75. And when (Damnus) heard these words he went forth to fight. And when they encountered each other the king of Nubia[3] opened his mouth and said : ' If God give me the victory over this Jewish Damnus, I shall become a Christian.' 76. And then he gave battle to this Jew, and conquered him and slew him, and made himself master of his kingdom and of his cities. And at that time he sent messengers to Alexandria †in reference to the Jews and the pagans† requesting the Roman governors to send from the empire of Rome a bishop to baptize and instruct in the holy Christian mysteries all the inhabitants of Nubia and the survivors of the Jews. 77. And when the emperor Justinian was apprised of these facts, he gave orders that they should do for him all he requested, and should send to him some priests and a bishop †from amongst the clergy of the holy patriarch John†.[4] He was a chaste and pious man. 78. Such was the origin of the conversion of the Ethiopians in the days of the emperor Justinian.

79. In his days also the king of Hedjaz, named Alamundar, arose and invaded Persia and Syria, and committed great depredations

---

[1] Our text reads 'peoples' simply, but the error may have arisen, as Zotenberg points out, through the confusion of امير and امم. Cf. John Mal. 433, Cedrenus 656.

[2] In John Mal. Δίμνος, in Cedrenus i. 656 Δαμιάνος. Jewish proselytes held the throne of the Himyarites in the sixth century, and were conquered by the Axumitic king.

[3] This should be ' of Axum ' (?) ; cf. John Mal. 433.

[4] He was the παραμονάριος (= aedituus) of the church of S. John in Alexandria (John Mal. 430).

as far as Antioch, and put many people to the sword, and burned the city named Chalcis and other cities in the province of Sirmium and Cynegia. 80. Thereupon the army of the east went forth to meet them, but they did not await the attack, but seizing much booty retired into their own country.

81. In the days also of the emperor Justinian there was a great earthquake in the land of Egypt, and many cities and villages were swallowed in the abyss. And those who lived in the country made prayers and many intercessions with tears, being grieved on account of the destruction that had been wrought. 82. And after a year the wrath (of heaven) ceased and the earthquakes which had prevailed in every place were stayed. And the Egyptians celebrate the memorial of this day every year on the 17th of Teqemt.[1] 83. And the remembrance of this calamity has been preserved for us by our fathers, the divinely-influenced Egyptian monks. For these earthquakes were due to the change in the orthodox faith brought about by the emperor Justinian, who had hardened his heart more than his father's brother, who had preceded him.

84. And this Justinian commanded the Orientals to inscribe the names of the (bishops of the) Council of Chalcedon on the diptychs of the church, although they had sent the patriarch Severus into exile—a custom which had hitherto not existed and which is not mentioned in the Apostolic Canons nor in the Councils of the Fathers who came later : none of the Councils should be mentioned in public worship. 85. Now it was this emperor Justinian alone who established this custom throughout every province of his empire, and had the names of the (bishops of the) Council of Chalcedon inscribed. And Anthimus, patriarch of Constantinople, and Acacius who had been patriarch in the days of the emperor Zeno, and Peter, patriarch of Alexandria, were excommunicated. 86. And he caused their names to be removed from the diptychs, and abolished the Henoticon of the emperor Zeno : he proscribed the name of the patriarch Abba Severus throughout all the province of Antioch and the adjoining districts, enjoining that it should not be mentioned in the diptychs of the church, but

---

[1] Zotenberg points out that no such event is mentioned in the Egyptian Calendars, but that on this day the memory of the patriarch Dioscorus II was celebrated in the Monophysite Church.

cursed; and he caused the inhabitants of Alexandria to thirst after the waters of the doctrine of Dioscorus, who was succeeded by the patriarch Timothy. 87. Now the emperor Justinian had given the patriarchal chair to the Chalcedonians, but as the empress Theodora, his wife, besought him on behalf of Timothy, patriarch of Alexandria, he permitted him on her account. Now she called him ' spiritual father '.

88. And in the days of this father, the emperor Justinian sent numerous forces to Alexandria, and these encompassed the city and wished to shed much blood. But Timothy the patriarch sent many anchorites and ascetics to the emperor to intercede on behalf of the church, and avert a massacre in the city and the shedding of innocent blood, and to get permission (for its people) to abide by the faith of its fathers. 89. And when the emperor heard these petitions, he granted them on the intercession of the empress Theodora, who was near (?) to him, and he sent orders to the army to return to the province of Africa. 90. And the patriarch Timothy continued to reside in his palace, true to the orthodox faith. And again subsequently the emperor sent to Alexandria a chief eunuch, named Calotychius. In that year the Roman empire had reached its 1287th year.

And the city continued tranquil for a short period. And the illustrious father Timothy died full of honour.

CHAPTER XCI. 1. And likewise in the days of this patriarch Timothy there took place in the city of Alexandria an event, great and very terrible and strange exceedingly. 2. Now there was a house in the eastern quarter of the city, in a place called Arûtîjû, to the right of the church of the holy Athanasius. And in this house there dwelt a Jew, named Aubarûns, and he had a chest in which were the mandîl and towel of our Lord Jesus Christ, wherewith He girded Himself when He washed the feet of His disciples. 3. His kindred gave it (the chest) to this Jew. He indeed did not open it; for though he often wished to open it he could not. For when he touched it, ⟨fire⟩ descended threatening to consume him who wished to open it. 4. And he heard the voices of angels singing the praises of Him who was crucified on the cross, the Lord, the King of Glory. 5. And as this Jew was terrified, he, his mother, and wife, and children went to the patriarch Timothy and told him (regarding it). And forthwith he

proceeded with crosses, and gospels, censers and lighted waxen
candles, and he came to the place in which the chest was. 6. And
forthwith the lid of the coffer opened, and he took with great
veneration the notable mandil and towel and conveyed them to
the patriarchal palace, and placed them in the Church of the
Tabenniosites, in a holy place. 7. And an angel descended from
heaven and closed until this day the lid of the brazen coffer wherein
the mandîl and towel had been. 8. And all the inhabitants of
Alexandria were indignant, and went to the Persians (?) and
besought them to open the lid of the coffer, but they could not.
9. That Jew indeed and all his household became Christians then as
was befitting.

CHAPTER XCII. 1. And after the death of the venerable father
Timothy, the deacon Theodosius, who had been (his) secretary,
was appointed in his stead. Whilst he was going to occupy his
pontifical chair, an Ethiopian wished to kill him. He fled and
came to the city Kônûs and lived there in solitude. 2. Then the
foolish populace seized Gaïnas and made him patriarch in the room
of Theodosius, thus transgressing the holy canons. 3. And there
was strife in the city ; some said : ' We are Theodosians '; and others
said : ' We are Gaïnites ', even unto this day. 4. And when the
emperor heard of these events—now there was in the city a prefect
named Dioscorus, and Aristomachus, moreover, was commander of
the troops—the emperor Justinian ordered the military commander
to proceed to Alexandria and bring back the (holy) father Theodosius from his exile. 5. And (Aristomachus) established him in
his (patriarchal) chair and sent Gaïnas into exile . . .[1] And when
he had taken possession of the Church he gave it to Paul the
Chalcedonian, who had been a monk among the Tabenniosites, and
he made him patriarch. 6. And joining the Chalcedonian faith, he
furnished letters in his own hand (to this effect) and sent (them) to
all the churches. And forthwith there arose an uproar among the
Alexandrians, and they fought with one another; for there was
none who supported Paul, as he was an apostate and a Nestorian.
7. And it was not only Alexandria, but every city that disapproved
of him ; for he was a persecutor, and loved to shed blood. And
the emperor Justinian deposed this Paul from his office, as he was
found committing the abominable crime of sodomy with a deacon

---

[1] There appears to be a lacuna in the text.

in a bath, and he appointed in his room a monk, named Zoilus of the city of Aksenjâ. And him also the inhabitants of the city refused to receive. 8. And Zoilus, seeing that the inhabitants of the city were hostile to him, sent a letter to the emperor Justinian, resigning the patriarchal dignity. 9. Then the emperor appointed a reader, named Apollinaris, of the convent of Salâmâ, in the city of Alexandria. And he was of gentle disposition, and a member of the Theodosian party. 10. And they persuaded him to be patriarch in the place of Zoilus, and they promised him great gifts with a view to his re-establishing the faith of the Church. And Gaïnas died in exile before Theodosius.

11. And the emperor Theodosius assembled a great number of bishops from every country, and Vigilius, patriarch of Rome. And after painful exertions many accepted the orthodox faith, but others followed the wicked Nestorian and Chalcedonian creed, and of Theodore, bishop of Mopsuestia. 12. And (the Council) anathematized the blasphemer Nestorius, who spoke of the two natures. Now Theodoret[1] had opposed the words and teaching of our holy father Cyril. 13. And when the Nestorians had grown strong through the help of the new Marcian, i. e. Justinian, John of the city of Antioch (?)[2] helped our holy father Cyril. 14. And the emperor Justinian believed in the Chalcedonian creed which says Christ had two natures in one person—while they preach Him, as they say, according to Theodoret the Nestorian, who contended against John of the city of Antioch[3] in the Council of Chalcedon. 15. And Astûrâljûs the prefect wrote a letter establishing the one nature of Christ, the Word who became incarnate through union with the flesh, and submitted to the passion, and wrought true miracles : 16. And (showing) that the holy Virgin Mary bare God, Him who was crucified, one of the Holy Trinity, the Lord of glory. And this is the pure faith and the holy orthodox teaching. 17. And they wrongfully put to death the holy Dioscorus, the patriarch of Alexandria. 18. And Justinian believed in the Chalcedonian creed, and accepted the letter of Leo which declared that Christ had two natures, distinct in all His

---

[1] Bishop of Cyrrhus.

[2] Zotenberg does not attempt to translate verses 12-17, on the ground that the text is too corrupt to admit of translation. I render the text as it stands, saving for one or two changes.　　　　[3] Text reads Akâws.

actions, as the two Nestorian bishops, i. e. Theodoret, bishop of Cyrrhus, and Theodore, bishop of Mopsuestia taught.

19. And after the visitations which God had made to fall on the country, Justinian made peace with the Persians and conquered the Vandals. 20. And these great victories have been carefully recorded by Agathias, one of the renowned scholars [1] of the city of Constantinople, and likewise by a learned man named Procopius the patrician. He was a man of intelligence and a prefect, whose work is well known. 21. It was he (Justinian) that took all the imperial edicts of his predecessors, and duly arranged and re-edited them, and set them in the place of judgement, which went back to the ancient Romans, and they had left them as a memorial to those that came after.

CHAPTER XCIII. 1. There was a man named Romulus who had founded the great city of Rome; and likewise another who came after him named Numa, who adorned the city of Rome with institutions and laws, and subsequently established three orders in the empire. 2. And so also subsequently did the great Caesar and Augustus also after him. And it was through these that the virtues of the Romans were shown forth, and these institutions are maintained among them until this day. 3. And subsequently came the empress Theodora, the consort of the emperor Justinian, who put an end to the prostitution of women, and gave orders for their expulsion from every place.[2]

4. And there was a Samaritan brigand chief who assembled all the Samaritans, and raised a great war, and assumed the royal crown in the city of Nablus, and said: 'I am king.' 5. And he seduced many of his people by his lying statement when he declared: 'God hath sent me to re-establish the Samaritan kingdom'; just as (Je)roboam the son of Nebat who, reigning after the wise Solomon the son of David, seduced the people of Israel and made them serve idols.

6. And whilst he was at Nablus there were three horsemen who were leading in a race, a Christian, a Jew, and a Samaritan. And the Christian conquered in the race, and immediately dismounted and bowed his head to receive the prize. 7. And he asked saying: 'What is he who was first in the race?' And they replied: 'A

---

[1] I have here followed Zotenberg in rendering መትርጕም: as = σχολαστικός.
[2] John Mal. 441 sq.

Christian.' And thereupon they cut off his head with the sword.
8. And for this reason they named their troops troops of the
Philistines. And troops from Phoenicia, Canaan, and Arabia, and
many other Christian forces, mustered and made war on that
wretched Samaritan and slew him and his companions and his
officers. 9. And they cut off his head and sent it to Constantinople
to the emperor Justinian, in order to strengthen his empire.
And (the emperor) thereupon distributed alms to the poor and
wretched.

CHAPTER XCIV. 1. And there was discussion as to the body of our
Lord Jesus Christ, and much controversy in the city of Constantinople as to its being corruptible or incorruptible. 2. And they
were agitated [1] in the city of Alexandria regarding this controversy
which had arisen between the two factions, the Theodosians and
the Gaïnians. 3. And the emperor Justinian sent to Eutychius
the patriarch of the city of Constantinople at that time and asked
him regarding this matter. He agreed on doctrinal views with
Severus and Theodosius. 4. Accordingly, he answered and said
unto him : ' The body of our Lord which submitted to suffering on
behalf of our salvation is living, imperishable, incorruptible, and
unchangeable. We believe that He suffered voluntarily. And
after the resurrection He was incorruptible and unchangeable in
all aspects and ways.' 5. But the emperor did not accept this
pronouncement. Now the true solution of this question is to be
found in the letter sent by the holy Cyril to Successus.[2] 6. But
the emperor inclined to the views of Julian, a bishop of the Gaïnian
party who had the same doctrine; for they said : ' He was a man
like us, and the holy Scriptures say : " Christ suffered for us in the
body." ' 7. And the emperor Justinian was wroth with the patriarch Eutychius because he had not sent him a reply such as he
desired, but a pronouncement like that of Severus and Anthimus ;
' These ⟨he said⟩ had deceived the inhabitants of Constantinople,
and this (Eutychius) likewise had deceived them.' 8. And thereupon he sent a letter to Agathon the prefect of Alexandria, with
orders to appoint Apollinaris, count of the Monastery of Banton,[3] to
be patriarch of the Chalcedonians in the city of Alexandria and the

---

[1] I have here emended 𝔎𝔬𝔲·𝔜·: = 'turned about', 'went round', into
𝔈𝔱𝔘𝔬·𝔥·:   [2] Bishop of Diocaesarea in Isauria about 431.
[3] i. e. the Monastery of Ennaton (see Butler, *op. cit.* 51).

other cities of Egypt. 9. But the inhabitants of this city were strongly attached to the incorruptibility dogma, and followed the teaching of our fathers, written in books, which declares : ' The holy body of our Lord was incorruptible before the resurrection, and He submitted to suffering of His own will unto death, but since the resurrection it has become immortal and impassible.' Such was the declaration of Gregory the theologian. 10. Where-fore it behoves us, touching the proposition of the incorruptibility, to set aside the salutary suffering which He endured in the body of His own free will and power, and accomplished on behalf of our salvation.

11. And the emperor Justinian deposed and exiled Eutychius the patriarch of Constantinople, and appointed John of the city of † Jûdans †,[1] who promised to give the emperor an autograph letter signifying his agreement with him in the faith, and likewise to write a synodal letter. 12. But when he received the (patriarchal) dignity, he set at naught the command of the emperor and refused to write as he had promised him. He had indeed been formerly a layman, and was unacquainted with the Scriptures, and had no thorough knowledge of the holy faith ; but when he became a priest he studied unintermittingly [2] the holy Scriptures, and acquainted himself with the pains and troubles which our holy fathers sustained on behalf of Christ, and he learnt the orthodox doctrine, and forsook the perverse doctrine of the emperor. 13. Now it was this John the patriarch that wrote the *Mystagogia*, which set forth the one nature of Christ, the Word of God, which became flesh. And its testimony agrees with the testimony of the apostolic Athanasius who said : ' There is one hypostasis, divine and human.'

14. And a man, named Menas, who had previously been patriarch of Constantinople, wrote to Vigilius, patriarch of the city of Rome, to the following effect : ' There is only one will and one volition in our Lord and Saviour Jesus Christ. And we believe in God in perfect fear of heart, instructed as we are in the teaching of our fathers.' And all this discourse was in the hands of John, patriarch of Constantinople. 15. And so the emperor wished to depose John,

---

[1] According to Evagrius, *H. E.* iv. 38, John was a native of Seremis, in the district of Cynegica, belonging to Antioch.

[2] There is no need to emend the verb as Zotenberg does, but only to insert the negation before it and read ኢ·ተጸሮ፡

but, being troubled regarding this matter, because of Eutychius whom he had already driven forth without recourse to canonical judgement, he feared the outbreak of a tumult. Now while matters were in this train, the emperor Justinian died in an advanced old age in the thirty-ninth year of the reign. His consort, the empress Theodora, had died before him.

16. And the Romans deposed all the bishops. And subsequently the Romans abandoned their ancient institutions because of the heathen [1] who dwelt among them. Now the heathen concerted together and put the Romans to the sword at midday and seized the cities and a multitude of captives.

17. And the Samaritans dwelling in Palestine took up arms and rebelled. And the emperor Justinian [before he died] sent against them a monk of high rank named Photion and a numerous army under him. And he fought against them and conquered them, and put many of them to torture, and others he drove into exile, and he inspired them with a great fear.

18. And in those days there was a pestilence in all places, and a great famine. And when the emperor saw that all the nations were troubled when he published his edict on the faith in all the province of Alexandria, and stirred up a severe persecution in the land of Egypt, his mind was affected through the greatness of his grief, and he kept traversing the apartments of the palace in mental bewilderment. 19. And he longed for death but failed to find it; for God was wroth against him. And when he betrayed his madness before all the people they took from him the imperial crown, and placed it on Tiberius and made him emperor in his stead. And our Lord Jesus Christ gave power and strength to the latter. Now this Tiberius was a young man, very fair to look upon, virtuous, generous, and resolute. 20. And when he became emperor he put a stop to the persecution, and showed (due) honour to the priests and monks. And so they accused him of being a Nestorian; but their accusation was false. On the contrary, he was a very good man and never failed to show favour to the orthodox, and to those who believed in the one nature of Christ, perfect God and man of one essence, the Word that became flesh.

---

[1] The text may refer to the capture of Rome by the Goths and its recovery by Belisarius (John Mal. 480), its subsequent capture by the Goths and its recovery by Narses (*op. cit.* 483–5).

Let us worship and give praise to Him who gives help and power to kings. 21. Now this emperor never permitted any persecution throughout his reign. And he presented many gifts to all his subjects, and he built many edifices in honour of the martyrs and houses in which the monks could pursue their religious exercises, and †pulpits† and convents for the virgins. 22. And he presented many alms to the poor and destitute. And God caused peace to prevail throughout his days as a recompense for his good deeds, and preserved the imperial city through special mercies.

23. And John patriarch of Constantinople died in his reign at the close of a very prosperous career. And the emperor brought Eutychius back from exile and restored him to his (patriarchal) throne in the place of John who had died. 24. And Apollinaris bishop of the Chalcedonians died in Alexandria, and a man, named John, an ex-military man, was appointed in his stead. And he had a goodly presence and forced none to forsake his faith. But he glorified God in His Church in the midst of all the assembled people, and they gave thanks to the emperor for the noble acts he had done.

25. And Christ was with him (the emperor), and he conquered the Persians and the nations by force of arms, and he made peace with all the nations subject to him. And he died in peace in the third year of his reign. It was owing to the sins of men that his days were so few; for they were not worthy of such a Godloving emperor, and so they lost this gracious and good man. 26. Before he died he gave orders that his son-in-law, named Germanus, should be raised to the imperial throne. Now he had formerly been patrician. But owing to his humility of heart he refused to be emperor. Thereupon Maurice, who was of the province of Cappadocia, was made emperor.

CHAPTER XCV. 1. Now Maurice who became emperor in succession to the Godloving Tiberius was very avaricious. He had previously been in command in the province of the east, and had subsequently married †the daughter of Domentiolus†,[1] named Constantina, and made her his wife. 2. And straightway he gave orders to the city of Constantinople that all the cavalry should muster and proceed with Commentiolus[2] to the province of the east.[3] 3. And he sent also to Aristomachus in the province of Egypt. Now he was a

---

[1] The early part of this chapter is full of errors.
[2] Text reads Domentiolus.   [3] So restored by Zotenberg.

citizen of Nikiu, a son of the prefect Theodosius. And he was a proud and powerful man, and his father before he died had admonished him, saying: 'Be content with what thou hast and do not desire a different career: but be content with that which befits thee that thy soul may have peace; for thou hast wealth in abundance, sufficient for thee.' 4. But when the child grew up he sought after the (great) things of this world, and arrayed a numerous force with †rustic† arms which attended upon him, and so forgot the advice of his father. 5. Moreover he built vessels by means of which he could visit all the cities of Egypt with pleasure and delight. And so he became proud and forced[1] all the military officers to be subject to the emperor; for he had received the command in the reign of the emperor Tiberius. 6. And by reason of this command he became more and more presumptuous, and made all the troops submit to his orders, and led a fearless life. And he posted cavalry in the city of Nikiu without any authorization of the emperor. 7. And all the troops under his command were without means, and he seized all the houses of those who were richer than he, and he esteemed them of no account. And when men of high or low degree came to him from the emperor, he let them remain at the door and did not admit them for a long time. 8. And when the emperor Tiberius was informed, before he died, of the actions of Aristomachus, he sent to the city of Alexandria an officer named Andrew[2] to effect his arrest by wise measures, avoiding the shedding of blood, and to bring him back alive to him. 9. And the emperor Tiberius likewise sent orders to all the forces in Egypt to render him assistance in the war against the barbarians. And when the message of the emperor reached Aristomachus, he proceeded to the city of Alexandria with only a few attendants; for he was not aware of the treacherous device they had prepared against him. 10. And when the patriarch and Andrew saw him, they were delighted, and got ready a light ship on the sea close at hand to the Church of St. Mark the Evangelist. Then they celebrated divine service on the 30th of Mîjâzjâ,[3] the festival of St. Mark the Evangelist. 11. And at the close of the divine service, Andrew went forth accompanied by Aristomachus and

[1] So by a slight transposition of the text.

[2] Cf. Evagrius, *H. E.* vi. 10.

[3] Third Abyssinian month, beginning on April 8 according to the Gregorian Calendar.

walked towards the seashore. And thereupon Andrew made a signal to his attendants and to the soldiers to seize Aristomachus and to cast him into the vessel. And immediately they seized him, and, bearing him on their shoulders, cast him into the vessel, without his being aware (of the reason), and loosing thence they set sail to go to the emperor. 12. And when the gracious emperor saw him, he said : 'This face is not the face of a criminal : let us do him no injury of any kind.' And he gave orders for him to be kept in the city of Byzantium till he had examined into his conduct. And after a few days, finding no fault in him, he restored him to his command, and sent him back to the city of Alexandria. And he was beloved by all the people. 13. And he vanquished the barbarians in the province of Nubia and Africa, who are named Mauritanians, and others named Marîkôs. He destroyed them and laid waste their country, and took their possessions as a booty and brought them all in chains by the river Gihon into the land of Egypt; for the engagement had taken place on the banks of the river. 14. Now the chroniclers have recounted the victory he won. And there he reflected after this manner : 'Some envious person will go to the emperor and slander me, but I will forestall him and send a message to the emperor.' And forthwith he sent the following message : 'May I come to have interview with thee ?' And the emperor Maurice replied : 'Yes.' 15. And he arose at once with haste, and went to the emperor, and brought him many gifts. And the latter accepted all that he presented, and thereupon appointed him prefect of the imperial city. And the empress Constantina appointed him controller of all her house and loaded him with honours, until he was second only in rank to the emperor, and he became a very great personage in the city of Byzantium. 16. And he constructed aqueducts throughout all the city, for its inhabitants complained greatly of the want of water. And he had a reservoir of bronze made for them by a clever engineer, such as had never been made previously. And so the water flowed into the reservoir of bronze which had been appointed. 17. And the city was thus delivered from disquiet through the abundant supply of water ; and when a fire broke out in the city, they went to the reservoir and extinguished the fire. 18. And all the people loved and respected him. And he was fond of constructing public works, and his deeds were noble. And then there arose against him certain envious persons who were foolish and aimed at delivering him over to death through their devices. And whilst they were engaged in such designs a prefect who knew astrology came forward, and likewise another person named Leon, the logothete, and, observing a star which had appeared in the heaven, they said that this star which had appeared portended the assassination of the emperor. 19. And they went and made this announcement to the empress Constantina and said unto her: 'Learn what thou shouldst do and take measures that thou and thy children may escape destruction; for this star which has appeared is a presage of a revolt against the emperor.' 20. And they brought many accusations against Aristomachus, and they bound her by an oath not to tell the emperor. And she went at once and told the emperor. And he imagined that Aristomachus intended to slay him and take his wife. And the emperor became hostile forthwith to Aristomachus, and he robbed him of every hope, and exposed him to numerous humiliations, and sent him in exile to the island of Gaul where he had to remain till he died.

21. Now the emperor Maurice welcomed many false, turbulent persons, owing to his greed for money. And he sold all the grain of Egypt and converted it into gold, and likewise the grain for Byzantium he sold for gold. 22. And every one hated him and said: 'How is it that the city of Constantinople puts up with such a wicked emperor? And how is it that five sons and two daughters have been born to one who has wrought such wickedness to the end of his reign?'

23. And Hormisdas, named Chosroes, the king of Persia at that epoch, was the son of the great Cabades. It is said that his father had been a Christian, and believed in Christ our true God, but that through fear of the Persians had concealed his true faith. 24. But in his latter days he had gone into a bath with faithful attendants, and after he had been exhorted and admonished by a Christian bishop regarding the faith he was to believe in secret, he renounced Satan whom he had worshipped and was baptized in a font belonging to the bath in the name of the Holy Trinity. 25. And when he was baptized he gave orders for the destruction of the font in which he had been baptized. Then he took his son Hormisdas and made him king in his stead. 26. This unhappy man was addicted to the worship of demons; moreover he compelled the Christians to

worship fire and the sun. And the horses also that pastured on grass were objects of his worship.

CHAPTER XCVI. 1. And there was once a noble woman who was a Nestorian and she was called in the Persian language Golanduch.[1] And as she journeyed by sea, she was seized by the Persians and cast into prison. 2. And they put a chain[2] upon her neck after the manner of the Assyrians, and when a prisoner died, the (jailers) showed the king the chain still locked upon his neck. 3. Now while she was so situated an angel appeared to her and addressed her, and seized the chain that was upon her neck, and removed it without unlocking it, and placed it with the jailers in order that they might suffer no injury at the hands of their judges. 4. And she heard a mighty voice which said unto her : ' It is for the sake of the orthodox faith of our Lord Jesus Christ that thou hast been delivered.' And she arose and fled and she came to the territory of Rome, and abode in the city of Hierapolis on the river Euphrates. 5. And she went and recounted to the metropolitan Domitian all that had befallen her. Now he was the son ⟨of the paternal uncle⟩[3] of the emperor Maurice, and he went and told the emperor regarding this woman whom we have already mentioned. 6. And he gave orders that they should conduct her to him, and he prevailed on her to forsake the Nestorian faith and become a believer in the orthodox Christian faith. And she believed as he told her.

7. And our Lord Jesus Christ, though long-suffering and beneficent, did not remain indifferent and unmoved regarding the persecution which was brought upon His saints by Hormisdas the king of Persia. 8. And God was roused to anger against him and his house was destroyed from the top to the bottom, and the king's son, the new Chosroes,[4] arose and slew him.

9. And at the time of the emperor's death there were grave dissensions amongst the troops, and two parties were formed. And when the younger[5] Chosroes saw what had befallen, he took to flight and reached the Roman territory. And having made himself known to the Roman officials, he sent ambassadors to the emperor Maurice with the request that he should be permitted to remain under the Roman sway, and that he should make war on the

---

[1] Cf. Evagrius, *H. E.* vi. 20.   [2] The word here is purely Amharic.
[3] So restored by Zotenberg. See Evagrius, *H. E.* vi. 16–18.
[4] Text restored by Zotenberg.   [5] Text has ' elder'.

Persians and seize their kingdom, and make it (part of) the Roman
empire.   10. And the emperor Maurice betook himself to John,
patriarch of the city of Constantinople, in order to deliberate with
him.   And this John was an ascetic and eat no (animal?) food
whatever, and drank no wine, but supported himself sufficiently on
the produce of the field and on green vegetables.   11. And there
came together to him all the magistrates and officers in order to
deliberate with him regarding Chosroes, king of Persia, who had
come to them.   12. And John cried aloud to them all and said unto
them : 'This man who has murdered his father cannot benefit the
empire.   Nay it is Christ, our true God, who will war on our behalf
at all times against all the nations that attack us.   And as for this
man who has not been faithful to his father, how will he be faithful
to the Roman empire.'   13. But the emperor Maurice did not
accept the advice of the patriarch wherewith he advised him, and
likewise his officers, and he wrote forthwith to Domitian, (the son
of) his father's brother, who was bishop of Melitene, and to Narses,
commander of the forces in the east, and commanded him to take
all the Roman troops and set out and establish Chosroes, king of
Persia, and to annihilate all his adversaries.   14. And he gave them
the royal insignia and magnificent garments befitting his rank.
Now this Chosroes used to go to Golanduch to ask her if he should
become king of Persia or not.   And she said unto him : 'Thou
shalt conquer and shalt certainly become king of the Persians and
the Magi; but the Roman empire has been given to the emperor
Maurice.'

15. And Narses did as he had commanded, and he conducted the
accursed Chosroes back to the Persians, and he made war upon them,
and conquered them, and delivered the kingdom of the Magi into
the hand of this wretch.   16. And when he was established on the
throne he proved ungrateful to the Romans, who had been his
benefactors, and devised evil against the Romans.   17. And all the
magicians assembled by night in his house in order to prepare
poison to put in the food of the Roman troops and in the food of
their horses, with a view to destroying them all together with their
commander Narses.   18. But our Lord Jesus Christ inspired the
hearts of the members of the court with pity, and they went and
disclosed the matter to Narses the Roman commander.   When he
was acquainted with this plot he gave orders to all the troops, and

said unto them : 'When they offer you food do not eat it, but give
it to the dogs, and as for the fodder give it to other animals.'
19. And when the dogs had eaten they burst asunder in the midst,
and the cattle died.   And when Narses saw this he was very wroth
against Chosroes, and arose forthwith and marched and brought
back the Roman forces to their rulers (?).   And all the Romans
hated the emperor Maurice because of the calamities which had
befallen in his days.

CHAPTER XCVII. 1. There were three brothers in a city, in the
north of Egypt, named Aikelâh, i. e. Zâwjâ.   And the names of
the three brothers were Abaskîrôn, Menas, and Jacob.   2. Now
this Abaskîrôn was the eldest, and he was a Nasâha.[1]   And he had
a son named Isaac.   3. Now John the prefect of the city of
Alexandria had made them governors over many cities in Egypt.
Their own city Aikelâh was near the city of Alexandria.   4. And
these four men were in the enjoyment of great wealth, but not
being able to bear (it) they attacked the Blue Faction, and sacked
the two cities of Benâ and Bûsîr, without the permission of the
governor of the province.   Now the latter was a good, excellent,
and chaste man.   5. And these four men whom we have already
mentioned, shed much blood, and burnt the city of Bûsîr and the
public bath.   And the governor of the city of Bûsîr fled by night ;
for the inhabitants of the city of Aikelâh wished to kill him.
6. And he succeeded in making his escape from them, and proceeded to the city of Byzantium to the emperor Maurice, shedding
many tears, and he informed him of the death which the four men
had prepared for him.   And a second dispatch came to the emperor
from the governor of the city of Alexandria announcing these
events.   7. And when the emperor Maurice was apprised of these
things, he was very wroth, and gave orders to John the prefect of
the city of Alexandria to remove them from (their) office.   Now
these men mustered a large force of daring men provided with
horses and swords and weapons of war, and they seized a large
number of ships, in which grain was carried to the city of
Alexandria, and there arose a great famine in the city.   And (its
inhabitants) suffered greatly and sought to kill the prefect John.
But the faithful who loved Christ fought on his behalf because of
his good conduct.

[1] An Arabic word meaning ' scribe '.

8. And the inhabitants of the city wrote a letter and sent it to the emperor informing him regarding the troubles of the city. And the emperor removed the prefect John, and appointed in his stead Paul of the city of Alexandria. And the inhabitants of the city escorted John as he departed with every mark of honour. And he went and had an interview with the emperor and informed him regarding the deeds of violence wrought by the inhabitants of the city of Aikelâh, and he stayed for a short time with the emperor. 9. And the latter, however, appointed him and gave him full authority over the city of Aikelâh. And when the inhabitants of the city of Aikelâh heard what had befallen, and likewise of the return of John to the city of Alexandria, they stirred up disquiet and strife throughout all the land of Egypt alike on sea and land. 10. And they sent one of their number, the daring Isaac with his freebooters, and these went down to the sea, and seized a large number of ships which were on the sea and they broke (?) them up. And they proceeded to Cyprus and captured much booty.

11. And many people, that is, Tanânikûn, and Lakûrîn, and Elmatrîdîn Elmasr, and the Blue and Green Factions,[1] and the enemy of God from Bûsîr—all these mustered in the city of Aikelâh, and took counsel with Eulogius, Chalcedonian patriarch in the city of Alexandria, and with Ailas the deacon, and Mînâs the assistant, and Ptolemy the commander of the barbarians, but the inhabitants of the city of Aikelâh were not aware of this procedure. 12. They wanted to appoint a prefect in the room of John; for they said : ' This John has no respect of persons, and he hates injustice and he will ⟨not⟩ treat us as we wish. 13. Now the inhabitants of Aikelâh went on committing transgression after transgression, and they seized the grain-laden ships, and they got hold of the imperial taxes and forced the prefect of the city to send forward the taxes to them.

14. Now John quitted with honour the imperial presence and came to the city of Alexandria, and the (insurgent) chief of the city of Aikelâh heard of the arrival of John. And John mustered the forces of Alexandria, Egypt, and Nubia in order to attack the inhabitants of the city of Aikelâh. 15. And forthwith there came a general named Theodore, who had been with Aristomachus. Now this Theodore was a son of the commander Zechariah. And he

---

[1] The text as Zotenberg suggests = πράσσοντες, a corruption of πράσινοι.

sent a secret letter to John, (requesting him) to send him trained
troops who could shoot with the bow (lit. the arrow) and to release
from prison two men, namely (the one), Cosmas the son of Samuel,
and the other Bânôn the son of Ammôn. 16. And he commanded
Cosmas to proceed by land route and Bânôn by sea. Now this
Zechariah—a man of illustrious rank—was the lieutenant [1] of John
in the city of Bûsîr. 17. And (John) found (on his arrival) that
much devastation had been wrought in the city of Alexandria.
And he had a large number of the daring ones seized and punished,
and he captured a great number of ships, and inspired a great fear
in them (the rebels) on his arrival in the city of Alexandria.
18. And subsequently he had many great works constructed in the
sea at the cost of great exertions. And he did not return to
the city of Byzantium till he died. [2]

19. And when the general Theodore and his men came up they
burned the camp of the rebels, and they all advanced as far as
Alexandria, (even) the (full-grown) men, the youths who shot with
the bow, and some stone-slingers. 20. And he took with him the
five men whom he had released from prison, namely, Cosmas, the
son of Samuel, Bânôn, the son of Ammôn, and their companions,
in order to show the Egyptians those whom he had released from
imprisonment. 21. And when they came to the border of the river,
they marshalled the sturdy soldiers in boats and the cavalry on the
land. And the general passed over to the eastern bank of the river
with all his soldiers. 22. But Cosmas and Bânôn remained on the
western bank of the river with a numerous force. And they cried
aloud to the conspirators on the eastern bank of the river and said
unto them: 'Observe all ye people who have joined with those
rebels: do not war against the general; for the Roman empire is
neither enfeebled nor subdued; but through our compassion
towards you we have borne with you until now.' 23. And thereupon the people who had assembled along with those rebels broke
off from them and crossed the river and joined the Roman troops.
24. And they began an attack on the inhabitants of Aikelâh, and
they vanquished them. And the latter fled by night and gained a
small city named Abûsân, and not being able to remain there they

---

[1] An Arabic word نايب (Zotenberg), which may mean 'lieutenant' or
'vicar'.

[2] This sentence precedes the former in the text.

passed on to the great city ⟨of Alexandria⟩. 25. And the Roman
troops pursued them thither and captured the four men, Abaskîrôn,
Menas, Jacob, and Isaac, and put the four on a camel, and had
them conducted throughout all the city of Alexandria in the sight
of all men. 26. And next they cast them into prison with their
hands and feet loaded with chains. 27. And after a long interval
Constantine the patrician who had been appointed governor of the
city of Alexandria came and examined the case of the prisoners.
28. And when he became acquainted with the charges against them,
he had three of the brothers executed; but as for Isaac he had
him thrown into chains and transported for life to the island of
Atrôkû. 29. And as for their accomplices, some were condemned
to corporal punishment, others had their goods confiscated. And
the cities of Aikelâh and Abûsân were burnt with fire. And great
fear prevailed over all the land of Egypt, and its inhabitants dwelt
in the enjoyment of tranquillity and peace.

30. And about this time also there arose a rebel named Azarias
in the province of Akhmîm, who mustered a large force of Ethiopic
slaves and brigands and seized the imperial taxes without the
knowledge of the officers of the province. 31. But when the
inhabitants saw the warlike measures of these slaves and barbarians,
they feared them, and sent a dispatch to the emperor with information (on the matter). 32. And the emperor sent a distinguished
commander with a numerous force of Egyptians and Nubians to
attack Azarias. But before the attack was made, he fell into a
panic and fled, and gained the summit of an arid mountain which
resembled a citadel. 33. And the troops beleaguered that mountain
for a long time until the water and food of the rebels failed.
Thereupon the rebel Azarias died and likewise his followers through
hunger and thirst. Now they had already abandoned their horses.

34. And in the reign of this emperor also, when the governor
and commander in Alexandria was one named Menas, the son of
Maîn, there appeared (two) creatures in human form, one resembling
a man and the other a woman. 35. And all who travelled by river,
when they stopped near the bank, saw them clearly and wondered
greatly at the spectacle. And Menas likewise saw them and all
the officers and notables of the city. 36. And all who saw them
spake to them and said: 'We adjure you in the name of the God
who created you, show yourselves to us again.' And when they

heard the adjuration, they showed their face and hands and breasts. And all who saw them, said: ' This is the work of demons who dwell in the waters.'   37. But others said: ' This river is of two sexes, for there have appeared in it creatures such as have never been seen before.'   Others said: ' This is an evil thing for our country.'   Others said: ' The apparition of these creatures is a happy omen.'   All these were false, and their statements were without truth.

CHAPTER XCVIII.   1. And there was likewise in the reign of the emperor Maurice, a man named Paulinus in the city of Byzantium, a worshipper of impure demons, who falsely said: ' The emperor Maurice overlooks these practices.'   And God punished this magician and he lost his reason.   2. And he had a silver bowl which contained the blood of impure sacrifices to demons.   And he carried this cup and sold it to a silversmith.   And after the (silver)smith had bought this bowl, the abbot of a monastery saw it, and being greatly pleased with it bought the bowl and conveyed it to his monastery.   3. And he placed it full of water away from the altar, and gave orders to the brethren and said unto them : ' Each time ye take of the holy mysteries drink of the water in the bowl in order to cool the oblation which is for the body and blood of Christ our God.'   4. But the great King of Glory, our Lord Jesus Christ, did not approve that the vessels of demons should be mingled with the vessels of the holy altar of our God which are without blood, as the apostles say.   And thereupon that water became blood. 5. And when the brethren partook of the holy mysteries, they went forth from the sanctuary to take of that water for cooling according to the custom.   And when they saw this miracle that had been wrought in the silver bowl, they together with their Superior were seized with fear, and fell a-weeping.   And they resorted to self-examination but could find no evil that they had committed. 6. And thereupon they arose and took the silver bowl, filled as it was with blood, and brought it to John, patriarch of Constantinople, and they informed him of all that had befallen.   7. And John sent unto the man who had sold it and said unto him : ' Whence have you obtained this bowl, and from whom have you bought it ? ' And the man said: ' I bought it from Paulinus.'   8. And thereupon the patriarch and the priesthood and the faithful of the Christian Church recognized that the matter was from God.   And (the patriarch) wished to make known the apostasy and the infamy of the magician Paulinus: and forthwith with godly zeal they arose and fetched Paulinus to the palace of the emperor Maurice. 9. And the chief officer interrogated him in the presence of all the magistrates and senators regarding this matter, and he confessed in the presence of all, saying: ' I was accustomed to place in this bowl the blood of the sacrifices which I offered to demons.' 10. And they all passed judgement upon him that he should be burnt alive. And they proclaimed aloud regarding him by the voice of a herald three distinct proclamations. The first in these terms: ' Wherefore should Paulinus be saved, the enemy of God who to his own destruction prays to Apollo?' The next as follows: ' Thou hast lusted after a strange sin: and he has laboured much in that which benefits not his own soul.' And the third proclamation: ' Paulinus has sought of himself his own destruction. He has become the enemy of the Holy Trinity, and has not kept faithful to the true orthodox faith.' But those who followed him in his evil practices sought to save him.

11. And when the patriarch John was apprised of this movement, he went to the court and put off his priestly robe. Meanwhile all the people cried aloud and said: ' May the orthodox faith spread and prosper.' 12. And the patriarch said: ' If Paulinus the magician is not committed to the flames this very hour, I will resign my throne and close all the churches. And I will not permit any one to partake of the holy mysteries, until Christ has punished those who blaspheme His name.' 13. And the emperor feared that a tumult might be occasioned thereby. And so the patriarch did not return to his palace till he had burnt Paulinus alive. Now the emperor used to follow heathen practices; but when the emperor heard that he was censured (for so doing) he was very deeply grieved.

CHAPTER XCIX. 1. And at the outset of his reign he had ordained a law that they should inscribe at the beginning of all their writings the formula: ' In the name of our Lord Jesus Christ our God and Saviour.' He wished to profess his faith in Jesus Christ the Saviour of all the world. 2. And thereupon Domitian, the son of the emperor's brother, gave orders that force should be used to compel the Jews and Samaritans to be baptized and become Christians. But these proved false Christians. And likewise he forced heretics to be enrolled in the orders of the Church; for he was a true Chalcedonian.

CHAPTER C. 1. And likewise in the reign of the emperor Maurice there came a flood in the night on the east of the city of Esna, which is the capital of Rîf, while the inhabitants were asleep, and it destroyed many houses together with their inhabitants, and it carried them off and submerged them in the river. 2. And great havoc was wrought in the city and in (its) inhabitants. And likewise in the city of Tarsus in Cilicia the same befell; for the river, named Euphrates, which flows near it, rose at midnight and submerged one division of the city, named Antinoaea, and destroyed many buildings. 3. And a stone tablet was found in the river with the inscription: 'This river will destroy many of the buildings of the city.'

CHAPTER CI. 1. And likewise in the reign of this Maurice, the city of Antioch was troubled by a great earthquake and laid low. Now it had been laid low seven times. 2. And many roads (?) in the east were destroyed, and islands, and an innumerable multitude of men through the earthquake. 3. And likewise at that time the sun was eclipsed at the fifth hour of the day, and the light of the stars appeared. And there was a widespread alarm, and men thought that the end of the world was at hand. And all men wept and implored and prayed Christ our God to have mercy and compassion upon them. 4. Thereupon the light reappeared and the sun rose out of the darkness, and those who had come together said: 'This event is one that has taken place at the end of the cycle of 532 years.' 5. And they set themselves to calculate, and discovered, as they said, that it was the end of the twelfth cycle. But holy and righteous persons said: 'This chastisement has befallen the earth owing to the heresy of the emperor Maurice.

CHAPTER CII. 1. Now a certain event took place relating to a magistrate named Eutocius,[1] who had been deputed to a barbarous country. Now he possessed a silk embroidered (lit. sewn) garment, namely, a tunic, and he gave orders to his steward to fetch it to him. 2. And when he brought it to him, he found that the rats had eaten and destroyed it. And he was wroth with the steward, and cast him into a pit which was full of rats, and he closed the pit's mouth for many days, and (the rats) eat him and he died.

---

[1] So restored by Zotenberg.

3. And after many days he sought him, and found him dead and putrid. And he repented having killed the man for the sake of a garment. He practised good works, and gave much money to the poor, with much weeping addressing his prayers unto our Lady the holy Virgin Mary. 4. And likewise he went to holy places and visited the saints who abode there, confessing to them his sin, in order that he might hear the words of consolation. And these spoke to him in hostile terms in order to make him abandon the salvation of his soul. 5. And next he went to the convent of Sinai, and (there the monks) said unto him : ' There is no forgiveness '— therein they were deceived—' there is no forgiveness after baptism ' ; and they robbed him of (all) hope. 6. Now they remembered not the word which was written regarding David ; for when he had slain Uriah, (God) afterwards accepted his repentance, and restored him again to his first state. 7. And the restoration of Manasseh was brought about through repentance, after he had sacrificed to demons and slain Isaiah the prophet, and wrought countless evils. Yea, when he repented, God accepted him. 8. And this unfortunate man, when all hope was cut off,[1] went up a lofty acclivity and cast himself down and so died a violent death.

9. And shortly after, the Thracians rebelled and rose up against the emperor Maurice, and (their) four commanders set out against him. And when Maurice heard this news he began to distribute money among the inhabitants of Constantinople. Now they had been wont to call Maurice a heathen and a magician, and a person undeserving of the imperial throne. 10. And when the soldiers heard of these movements they took measures to wrest concessions from him touching their wage[2] and food, that is, the pay of the officers and chiefs. 11. But subsequently changing their plans they cast lots, and the lot fell upon Phocas, and marked him out as emperor. Now he was one of the four commanders of Thrace. 12. And the inhabitants of Constantinople were all of one mind, and cried out saying : ' Let us have a Christian emperor in this city.' And when Maurice heard that the inhabitants of the city wished to seize him, he went into the palace, and brought forth all (his) wealth, and placed it in a ship, and likewise his children and his wife, ⟨and⟩ they made for Bithynia.

CHAPTER CIII. 1. And Maurice wrought a noble deed during his

---

[1] Reading መተፉ፡ for መተሬ፡   [2] An Arabic word.

reign, and put a stop to the iniquities that had been practised by his imperial predecessors. 2. A certain captain of a ship set sail from Alexandria, having taken on board a considerable cargo of grain belonging to the emperor. But the ship was wrecked and the grain lost in the sea. And the governor of the province had him arrested and severely beaten, but no money was found upon him. 3. But the emperor Maurice gave orders for the captain of the vessel to be released, and thereupon published a decree, enacting that the captain of a vessel should not be subjected to punishment and made to render compensation when his ship was wrecked, but that the loss should be put down to the imperial revenue.

4. And after the flight of the emperor Maurice all the population came together to the patriarch, and by general consent they placed the imperial crown on Phocas in the church of S. John the Baptist.

5. And ⟨Phocas⟩ proceeded to the palace, and got ready his generals and officers and chariots, and sent them in pursuit of Maurice. 6. And whilst Maurice was proceeding by ship a strong wind rose against him and overturned the ship, and so he betook himself alone with his children to a small island near Chalcedonia. 7. And when the soldiers had learnt where he was, they proceeded to him according to the commands of Phocas, and put him to death with his five children in the twenty-second year of his reign. 8. And they stripped the empress Constantina and her two daughters and the wife of her son Theodosius of their imperial robes, and clothed them in servants' apparel, and placed them in a convent for virgins.

9. And when Phocas was firmly established in the empire, he sent ambassadors to Chosroes, king of Persia; but Chosroes refused to receive the ambassadors. Moreover, he was very wroth on account of the death of Maurice.

10. And certain persons accused †Alexander†,[1] who was one of the rulers—a discreet man and beloved by all the inhabitants of Constantinople, and they said to Phocas : ' This Alexander is desirous of slaying thee and becoming emperor in thy stead.' Now this †Alexander† had married a daughter of Maurice.[2] 11. And there-

---

[1] The Ethiopic is corrupt. Alexander occurs in the text, but seems quite wrong. On the probable events referred to see *Chron. Pasch.* 380; Bury, *Later Roman Empire*, ii. 86–92.

[2] Here we have a confused account of Germanus, the father-in-law of Theodosius, son of Maurice (?).

upon Phocas had †Alexander† and Kûdîs (= Elpidius?) and other officers thrown into chains and sent to the city of Alexandria to be imprisoned there. 12. Shortly after, Phocas sent orders to Justin the governor of Alexandria to execute †Alexander† and his companions.

CHAPTER CIV. 1. Owing to the great quantity of blood shed by Phocas great terror prevailed among all the officers (clergy?) of the province of the east.[1] 2. Now at that epoch no province was allowed to appoint a patriarch or any other ecclesiastical dignitary without his (the emperor's) authorization. 3. And the Orientals[2] assembled in the great city of Antioch. When the troops heard of these doings they were all enraged, and set out on horseback and made preparation for fighting, and they slew many people in the church (and continued the slaughter) till they had filled all the edifices with blood. 4. And this frightful massacre extended to Palestine and Egypt.

CHAPTER CV. 1. And there was a man named Theophilus, of the city of Meradâ in Egypt, the governor of five cities in the reign of Phocas. And the officers of the city and a large body of men revolted against him. (And) they attacked Theophilus and put him and his followers to the sword. 2. And they took the five cities by storm, i.e. Kertebâ, Sân, Bastâ, Balqâ, and Sanhûr. And David and Abûnakî, the envoys of the patriarch, informed Phocas (of these events). 3. And when Phocas heard, he was very wroth and sent a very malignantly-tempered general, named Bonosus, from the province of the east.[3] And he was like a fierce hyena. And he gave him full authority over the officers (?)[4] of the city of Antioch, that he might do unto them as they had done. 4. And when he came to Cilicia, he mustered a large body of men and marched against the officers (?) of the city of Antioch, and reduced them to submission, and by reason of the greatness of their fear of him they became like women before him. 5. And he punished them without mercy. Some of them he strangled, and others he

---

[1] Text is a transliteration of ἀνατολῆς (Zotenberg).

[2] Not so according to other chroniclers; it was the Jews caused these tumults. Cf. Cedrenus i. 712.

[3] Bonosus is called Κόμης 'Ανατολῆς in Cedrenus i. 712. According to Cedrenus, in this passage the leaders of this tumult in Antioch were Jews, who attacked the Christians.

[4] This and the following verses are full of confusions.

burnt, and others he drowned, and others he gave to wild beasts. And those who belonged to the factions he delivered to the sword. 6. And all with whom he wished to deal mercifully he sent into perpetual banishment. Upon the monks and convents of the nuns he perpetrated barbarities.

CHAPTER CVI. 1. And the following incident is an illustration of the conduct of the insensate Phocas. 2. He sent orders to the province of Cappadocia that there should be brought to him the wife of Heraclius the elder, who was the mother of the general Theodore, and the wife of Heraclius the younger, together with her daughter Fabia, a virgin.[1] 3. And he had them placed in the house of †Theodore† [2] (and treated) with distinction. Now †Theodoret† was of the family of the emperor Justinian. 4. And Phocas sought to dishonour Fabia. But she, using the stratagems of a woman, said: 'I am in the menstrual period'; and she showed him a cloth saturated with blood. And for this reason he let her go. 5. By the advice of Akrâsîs and Fîbâmôn, interpreters of dreams, this statement was made unto him.[3] 6. And when the elder Heraclius heard of these matters he thanked Akrâsîs, and let off Theodore, and took no action against him or his people.

CHAPTER CVII. 1. And they came to the city of Constantinople and informed Phocas of all that had been done. 2. At the same period came Heraclius, who distributed large sums of money among the barbarians of Tripolis and Pentapolis, and thereby prevailed on them to help him in the war. 3. Next he summoned the captain of his forces, named Bonakis,[4] with 3,000 men, and a large number of barbarians, and dispatched them to Pentapolis to wait for him there. 4. And he sent likewise Nicetas, the son of Gregory, with large subsidies to the prefect Leontius, who had been appointed to the province of Mareotis by Phocas, urging him to send salutations to Phocas and write to him in these terms: 'My Lord'. 5. Now Tenkerâ and Theodore the son of Menas, who had been governor of Alexandria in the reign of Maurice, had made a secret compact with Heraclius whereby they promised to give him the empire of Constantinople, and to slay Phocas, and compel the thousands (of troops) in Constantinople to submit to him.

[1] See note 4 on previous page.

[2] This seems corrupt for Theodora the wife of Justinian, who founded a convent for penitents.

[3] In the text this sentence precedes ver. 4.   [4] The text reads Kônâkis.

6. And this was done without the cognizance of Theodore the Chalcedonian patriarch of Alexandria, who had been appointed by Phocas. 7. But John the governor of the city was acquainted with his plot; for he was prefect of the palace and military commander in Alexandria. And Theodore also who was set over the grain supply (was acquainted with it). 8. These three wrote a letter to Phocas and informed him of all that had happened. But Phocas despised Heraclius. 9. Nevertheless he sent large sums of money to the †Apûlôn†[1] of the city of Manûf through the agency of the governor of the city of Constantinople, and he sent the latter to Egypt with a large military force; having first bound him by many an oath to defend his empire with fidelity, and to war against Heraclius in Egypt; and (he sent also) to Ptolemy the †Apûlôn† of the city of Athrîb, the governor of that city.

10. And next he sent orders to Qûsûm to leave the city of Antioch and repair to Alexandria. Now he had previously sent Bonosus by sea, with lions and panthers[2] and other wild beasts to be conducted to the city of Alexandria. 11. Now the emperors had heretofore destroyed them, but he re-established this custom. And he sent likewise instruments of torture of many kinds, chains and bonds, and much money and glorious garments.

12. And Bônâkîs,[3] the chief (captain) of Heraclius, (set out) and he saw Nicetas in Pentapolis as Heraclius had commanded. And he indeed had received troops from Leontius, who had been sent to the province of the Mareotis, and he had proceeded towards Nubia in Africa (?). 13. Now the prefect Leontius had come to terms with them. And when they had met the garrison of the city of Kabsên, they entered but did no violence to the garrison. And they set free all the prisoners that they might join them in the war. 14. And before they entered, they had prevailed on the inhabitants of the city to precede them (and) stir up a tumult on the river, named Pîdrâkôn, that is, the Dragon, which flows close to the great city of Alexandria on the west. 15. And when they had entered, they found the †Balalûn†,[4] the governor of Alexandria, with a large force of Egyptians arrayed with weapons of war. And

---

[1] This word is variously spelt in our text. I retain this spelling.
[2] An Amharic word.
[3] I have followed Zotenberg in reading Bonakis here. The text has ' John '.
[4] Called Apûlòn in ver. 9.

they said to him : ' Hearken to our words and flee from us and
preserve thy dignity, and remain neutral till thou seest the side which
is victorious ; and no calamity shall befall thee, and subsequently
thou shalt become the Administrator of Egypt; for behold the
days of Phocas are at an end.'   16. But he refused to comply with
this proposal and said : ' We will fight for the emperor unto death.'
And when they engaged they slew this misguided man, and cut off
his head, and suspending it on a lance they carried it into the city.
17. And not only none could withstand them, but many joined
their ranks.   And the prefect of the palace and Theodore who was
set over the corn supply withdrew into the church of S. Theodore
on the east of the city.   And Theodore the Chalcedonian patriarch
withdrew into the church of the holy Athanasius on the sea coast.
18. (And they did so) not only through fear of the soldiers (or ' war'),
but also of the inhabitants of the city; for they had kept under
guard Menas the coadjutor, the son of Theodore the vicar,[1] that is
the Adagshan,[2] in order to deliver him up to Bonosus when he
arrived.

19. And when the clergy (?) and the people of the city assembled
they were of one accord in their hatred of Bonosus,[3] who had already
sent the wild beasts and the instruments of torture.   20. And they
took the imperial taxes out of the hands of those who guarded
them, and openly rebelled against Phocas, and received Heraclius
with great honour, and took possession of the governor's palace
and established themselves therein.   21. And they suspended the
head of the Apûlôn on the gate for all that went in and out to see.
And they seized upon all the wealth consisting of gold and silver and
glorious garments which (Phocas) had sent to the Apûlôn.   22. And
he sent for his own troops and soldiers, and he sent likewise to
Pharos, and had the soldiers who were in the fleet arrested and
kept under a close guard.

23. And information was subsequently brought to Bonosus in the
city of Caesarea in Palestine that (the rebels) had captured the city
of Alexandria and slain the Apûlôn, and that the inhabitants of
that city hated him and were attached to Heraclius.   24. Now
previously to the arrival of Bonosus in Egypt, Bônâkîs met with

---

[1] See note on xcvii. 16.   [2] A corruption of a Coptic word.
[3] The text = Phons, which generally = Bonosus.   According to 10-11 it was
the emperor who sent them by means of Bonosus.

no reverse, but gained the mastery over all the prefects in Egypt. 25. And the Blues confiscated all the property of Aristomachus, the friend of the emperor, and the property of all the notables in the city of Manûf, and reduced them to such a degree of destitution that they were unable to pay taxes.

26. And all the people rejoiced because of the revolt against Phocas. And all the inhabitants of Nakius and the bishop Theodore and all the cities of Egypt joined the revolt. But Paul the prefect of the city of Samnûd alone did not join it. He was one of the prefects appointed by Phocas, and he was beloved by all the inhabitants of the city.

27. But the military commander they named Lîwnâkîs, by this name (*sic*), as he was a perverse and foolish man and ' a dog's head '. † And subsequently also Cosmas the son of Samuel, the friend of Paul, who was likewise one of their number, but who, being weak, was borne by two men † [1]—as for this man indeed whom they had released from prison, he was high spirited, and likewise those who were with him,[2] and he stirred up all the officers and made them submit to him. 28. And Paul was the first to resist and refuse to join the party of Heraclius, but he vacillated in his plans. 29. Indeed, all the province of Egypt was divided on the ground of the murder of the Aisâilîlûn. And Marcian, the prefect of the city of Athrîb ⟨likewise refused⟩; for he was a friend of theirs.

30. And Bonosus proceeded from the house of Ptolemais (?), and he sent his ships to the city of Athrîb. And Christodora the sister of Aisâllûn practised a system of espionage on those who threw off their allegiance to the emperor Phocas, and she refused to hearken to the message of Heraclius. 31. And all the troops of Egypt and of the east were expecting succour from the forces that were coming by land and sea. Now these were coming in ships by the two branches of the river, and they were to land as we have before said. 32. But the forces which came on horseback from the east were on the look out for Plato and Theodore. Now these were in the neighbourhood of the city of Athrîb and were alarmed at their arrival. 33. But before Paul and Cosmas the son of Samuel had . . . . .[3] the bishop Theodore and Menas, the scribe of the city

---

[1] The text is very confused. I have given so far as possible the general sense.
[2] The text needs no emendation here such as Zotenberg suggests.
[3] There seems to be a lacuna in the text here.

of Nakius, sent a message to Marcian the prefect and to the lady
Christodora, the sister of Aisâillûn, requesting them to cast down
the insignia[1] of Phocas and to submit to Heraclius. 34. But these
refused ; for they had heard news of Bonosus to the effect that he
had arrived at the city of Bîkûran. And when the party of Plato
heard this news, they sent a dispatch to Bônâkîs in Alexandria to
this effect : ' Hasten hither with thy forces ; for Bonosus has arrived
in the city of Farmâ.' 35. And when Bônâkîs had reached Nakius,
Bonosus likewise had already arrived at the city of Athrib, where he
found Marcian's troops ready for war. Christodora also, the sister of
Aillûs (sic), and the troops of Cosmas the son of Samuel (were
already there) by land. 36. And he marched to the small branch of
the river which proceeds from the main branch, and met with the
prefect Paul and his troops. 37. Then Bônâkîs came to attack
Bonosus, and they engaged on the east of the city of Manûf.
And in the engagement the forces of Cosmas the son of Samuel
prevailed and drove those of Bônâkîs into the river, and they took
Bônâkîs prisoner and slew him. 38. And Leontius the general
and Kûdis they put to the sword, and they surrounded[2] a large
body of troops, and took them prisoners and threw them into
chains. And when Plato and Theodore saw that Bônâkîs and
his men had been slain, they fled to a convent and concealed
themselves.

39. Then Theodore the bishop of Nakius and Menas the scribe
took the Gospels and proceeded to meet Bonosus, thinking that he
would have mercy upon them. And when Bonosus saw[3] Theodore
the bishop, he took him with him to the city of Nakius, but he
cast Menas into prison. 40. But Christodora and Marcian, the
prefect of Athrîb, informed him that it was the bishop that had
the insignia of Phocas thrown down from the gate of the city.
And when Bonosus saw the insignia of Phocas cast down upon the
ground, he gave orders for the beheading of the bishop. 41. But
as for Menas, he had him severely scourged, and required from him
the payment of 3,000 gold dînârs, and then he let him go. But
owing to the excessive scourging, he was attacked by a fever and

---

[1] An Arabic word, as Zotenberg points out.

[2] I have emended ግተፆሙ፡ into በገተፆሙ፡ Zotenberg emends into
ኢኣተተፆሙ፡ which is alike unsatisfactory in form and in meaning.

[3] I have emended the pronominal suffix.

died shortly afterwards. (He was so dealt with) at the instigation of Cosmas the son of Samuel.

42. And the three chief men of Manûf, Isidore, John, and Julian, and those who had concealed themselves in the convent of Atrîs, that is, Plato the friend of the emperor and Theodore the lieutenant, were delivered up to Bonosus by the monks. 43. And he had them arrested and thrown into chains and conducted to the city of Nakius, where he gave orders for them to be scourged and then beheaded in the place where the bishop had been put to death. 44. And he held an inquiry likewise regarding the troops who had fought under Bônâkîs. And such as had been soldiers of Maurice he sent into exile, but those who had been in the service of Phocas he called to account and put to death. 45. And the rest of the troops, seeing these things, fled and betook themselves to the city of Alexandria. And all the notables in Egypt mustered round Nicetas, the general of Heraclius, and assisted him because they detested Bonosus, and they informed Nicetas of all that he had done. 46. And Nicetas got together a numerous army of regulars, barbarians, citizens of Alexandria, the Green Faction,[1] sailors, archers, and a large supply of military stores. And they prepared to fight Bonosus in the environs of the city. 47. And Bonosus thus reflected : ' By what means can I get possession of the city and deal with Nicetas as I did with Bônâkîs.' 48. And he sent Paul of the city of Samnûd with his ships into the canal of Alexandria in order to co-operate with him. But Paul[2] was not able to approach the environs of the city ; for they hurled stones at him, and the ships took to flight. 49. And Bonosus likewise came with his troops and took up a position at Mîphâmônîs, i.e. the new Shabrâ. Next he marched with all his forces to the city of Demqârûnî, and was purposing to make a breach in the city on Sunday. Now these events took place in the seventh year of the reign of Phocas.

CHAPTER CVIII. 1. And there was a holy aged man, named Theophilus the confessor, who lived on the top of a pillar, near the banks of the river, and he was endowed with the spirit of prophecy. This old man lived thirty years on the top of the pillar. 2. Now Nicetas used to visit him frequently. And Theodore the general and Menas the coadjutor, and Theodosius, who were agents of

---

[1] So Zotenberg.   [2] The text wrongly reads Bonosus here.

Nicetas, informed him of the virtues of this holy man. 3. And Nicetas went to him and besought him and said: ' Who will be victor in this war ? '—for he feared lest evil should overtake him as it had done Bônâkîs. 4. And the holy man said to Nicetas : ' Thou shalt conquer Bonosus and overthrow the empire of Phocas, and Heraclius will become emperor this year.' 5. And Nicetas was guided by the prophecy of the aged man of God and said to the inhabitants of Alexandria : ' Fight no longer from the top of the wall but open the gate of Ôn and meet Bonosus in close encounter.' 6. And they hearkened to the words of Nicetas and put the troops in array and placed the catapults and engines for hurling stones near the gate. 7. And when a captain of Bonosus's troops advanced, a man smote him before he drew near to the gate, with a huge stone, and crushed in his jaw, and he fell from his horse and died forthwith. And another likewise was crushed. And when the battle pressed sore upon them they began to flee. 8. And Nicetas opened the second gate, which was close to the church of S. Mark the Evangelist, and he issued forth with his barbarian auxiliaries, and they went in pursuit of the fleeing troops and they put some of them to the sword. 9. And the inhabitants of Alexandria smote them with stones and pursued them and struck them with arrows and wounded them with grievous wounds. And some that sought to hide themselves from the violence of the battle fell into the canal and perished there. 10. And to the north of the city there were the qasabfârs,[1] that is, a plantation of roses and a hedge of thorns surrounding the plantation. And these stopped the fugitives. 11. And on the south side of the city also the fugitives were checked by a canal. And those who were pursued attacked each other, failing in the stress of danger to recognize their comrades. 12. Bonosus escaped with a few soldiers and took refuge in the city of Kariûn. And Marcian the prefect of Athrîb and the general Leontius, and Valens, and many men of distinguished names, were slain in the battle. 13. And when Nicetas saw that this victory was his through the prayers of the saints, and that the strength of the army of Bonosus was broken and that its numbers had become few, he sent Ptolemy, Eusebius, and other notables of the party of Heraclius to the river in order to fetch him

---

[1] As Zotenberg points out, this is the transliteration of two Arabic words, the first of which is translated by the Amharic word that follows.

all the wealth they could find, and collect for him many soldiers from all the cities of Egypt. 14. And the members of the Blue Faction, great and small, and the officers, protected and helped Nicetas in the city of Alexandria. 15. And when Paul and his companions were apprised of these events they remained secretly on board their ships and intended to desert Bonosus and go over to Nicetas. And the affairs of Bonosus grew (daily) worse, while those of Nicetas daily advanced in strength.

CHAPTER CIX. 1. And after his escape Bonosus stayed a few days in Nakius, and likewise his remaining troops. And he provided them with ships, and they destroyed many of the inhabitants of Alexandria. 2. And they proceeded towards Mareotis, and entered the canal of the Dragon which lies to the west of the city, and intended to harass the Alexandrians. But this unhappy man knew not that it is God who is strongest in warring. 3. And when Nicetas was apprised of this he had the qantarâ, that is, the bridge of Dafâshîr, cut away. Now it is near the church of S. Mînâs of the city of Mareotis. 4. And when Bonosus heard of this event, he was very grieved and purposed to slay Niketas by a treacherous device; for he said : 'If Nicetas dies, the army will be dispersed.' 5. And he had a soldier brought to him, and he persuaded him to go to Nicetas, boldly facing death, and he said unto him : 'Take thee a small sword, and put it in thy bosom, pretending that I have sent thee unto him, and that thou art to intercede on my behalf. And when thou comest near him smite him with this sword in his heart, that he may die. And if thou art able to escape, well and good ; but if thou diest on behalf of this nation I will take thy children and conduct them into the imperial palace, and I will give them money sufficient for all the days of their life.' 6. But one of his suite, named John, having heard this abominable project, sent and informed Nicetas. And this soldier rose thereupon, and took an imperial sword, and placed it in his bosom, and betook himself to Nicetas. 7. And when (the latter) saw him, he ordered his troops to surround him, and when they had stripped him, they found the sword in his bosom. And thereupon they beheaded him with the sword.

8. And Bonosus proceeded to the city of Dafâshîr and put many men to the sword. And when Nicetas was apprised of this event he pursued him with all haste. And when he came up to him,

Bonosus crossed the river and betook himself to the city of Nakius. 9. And after he crossed the river, Nicetas abandoned the pursuit and marched to the city (?) of Mareotis, and left considerable forces there to guard the route. And he marched likewise to the city of the upper [1] Manûf. 10. And when he drew near the city, the party of Bonosus who were there took to flight, and he captured the city, and Abrâis and his people were taken prisoners, and (the troops of Nicetas) burnt their houses and likewise the way (?) of the city. 11. And Nicetas directed a combined and powerful attack on the city of Manûf and compelled it to open its gates. Then all the cities of Egypt sent in their submission to him. 12. Next he crossed the river in pursuit of Bonosus, (who was) in the city of Nakius. And when Bonosus was apprised thereof he rose in the night and quitted the province of Egypt and betook himself to Palestine. 13. And he was driven also from this country by the people because of the abominable murders he had perpetrated among them formerly. And he went from thence to the city of Byzantium, and there met with Phocas, his friend, the assassin.

14. And all the land of Egypt fell under the power of Niketas, from the great city of Alexandria to the village of Theophilus the Stylite, who had predicted the accession of Heraclius to the imperial throne.

15. And Nicetas, moreover, had Paul of the city of Samnûd and Cosmas the son of Samuel arrested. He pardoned them and inflicted no punishment upon them, but sent them to Alexandria to be kept in custody there till the death of Bonosus. 16. And taking advantage of the war between Bonosus and Nicetas, the artisan guilds [2] of Egypt arose (and) perpetrated outrages on 'the Blues', and gave themselves shamelessly to pillage and murder. 17. And when Nicetas was apprised of these facts he had them arrested, and reproved them, and said unto them : ' Do no outrage henceforth to any one.' And he established peace amongst them. And he named prefects in all the cities and repressed plundering and violence, and he lightened their taxes for three years. And the Egyptians were very much attached to him.

18. And in regard to Rome it is recounted that the kings of (this) epoch had by means of the barbarians and the nations

---

[1] So Zotenberg, who takes 𝘡ω·ᒪ: as the faulty transliteration of an Arabic word.   [2] i. e. 'the Greens'.

and the Illyrians devastated Christian cities and carried off their
inhabitants captive, and that no city escaped save Thessalonica
only; for its walls were strong, and through the help of God the
nations were unable to get possession of it.   But all the province
was devastated and depopulated.   19. Then the armies of the east[1]
arose against Rome, and they took the Egyptians prisoners, who
were there, and who had fled from Egypt from fear of Bonosus.
These were Sergius the Apostate and Cosmas who had delivered up
his city.   20. Now these had denied the Christian faith and had
abandoned holy baptism, and had followed in the paths of the
pagans and idolaters.

21. And ⟨the Persians⟩ made themselves masters of the river
Euphrates and of all the cities of Antioch, and they plundered
them and left not a soldier surviving at that epoch.   22. And likewise the inhabitants of the district of Tripolis in Africa brought
blood-eating barbarians (into the country) out of affection to
Heraclius.   23. For they detested Phocas, and they attacked the
general Mardius and sought to slay him, and likewise two other
generals named Ecclesiarius and Isidore.   24. And when these
barbarians arrived they made war on the province of Africa, and
proceeded to join Heraclius the elder.   And the great prefect of
the district of Tripolis, named Kîsil, went to Nicetas with large
supplies in order to help him against Bonosus.

25. And Heraclius the elder sent his son Heraclius the younger
to the city of Byzantium with ships and a large force of barbarians
in order to attack Phocas.   And when he touched at the islands
and the various stations on the sea coast, many people, notably
those of the Green Faction, went on board with him.   26. And
Theodore the Illustrious, together with a large number of wise
senators, deserted Phocas and submitted to Heraclius.   27. And
seeing this the civilians and the soldiers who were with him followed his example and submitted to Heraclius and Cappadocian.
And all the people assailed Phocas with angry invectives, and
none stayed them.   And all these matters fell out in the city of
Constantinople.   28. And when Phocas was apprised of these facts,
and had learnt that everybody had made his submission to
Heraclius, he sent the imperial chariots to Bonosus in order that
he might march against him (Heraclius).   29. And other prefects

---

[1] Zotenberg emends the text and reads ' west '.

of the emperor got ready the Alexandrian ships in which corn had been brought from the land of Egypt to Constantinople. For Phocas had had these seized because of the revolt of the inhabitants of Alexandria.

CHAPTER CX. 1. And when at the suggestion of Nicetas, the patrician, the people accepted Heraclius as their emperor, the people of Africa lauded Heraclius in these terms: ' The emperor Heraclius will be like Augustus.' And all the people of Alexandria also and of the camp[1] spake in the same fashion. 2. And thereupon they began an engagement on the seashore, and the men of the chariots slew Bonosus. And they all with one voice in the Greek language cried aloud in praise of Heraclius the younger, the son of Heraclius the elder, and abused Phocas and Bonosus. 3. And, hearing these demonstrations, the Green Faction and the inhabitants of the city of Byzantium, who were on the sea, assembled their ships and pursued the ' Blues.' Now these latter were disquieted because of the accusation made against them, and subsequently took refuge in the church of S. Sophia. 4. And all the officers and senators had taken up a position near the palace, and they were lying in wait for Phocas. But when Phocas and Leontius the chamberlain became aware that they sought with evil intent to slay them as they had slain the depraved Bonosus, the two arose and seized all the money that was in the imperial treasury which had been amassed by Maurice, and likewise that which had been amassed by (Phocas) himself from the Roman nobles whom he had put to death, and whose property he had confiscated, and likewise the money of Bonosus, and they cast it into the waves of the sea, and so thoroughly impoverished the Roman empire. 5. And thereupon the senators and the officers and soldiers went in and seized Phocas, and took the imperial crown from his head, and (they seized) Leontius the chamberlain likewise, and conducted them in chains to Heraclius to the church of S. Thomas the Apostle, and they put both of them to death in his presence. 6. And they cut off the privy parts of Phocas, and tore off his skin right down to his legs because of the dishonour and shame he had brought on the wife of ⟨Photius⟩ because she was consecrated to the service of God, for he had taken her by force and violated her, although she was of an illustrious family. 7. And next they took the bodies of

---

[1] So manuscripts. Zotenberg emends and renders ' au château '.

Phocas and Leontius and Bonosus and they conveyed them to
the city of Constantinople, and they burnt them with fire, and
scattered the ashes of their bodies to the winds; for they were
detested by all men. 8. And thus the vision was accomplished
which Benjamin of the city of Antinoe had received from God,
and the inhabitants of Byzantium did not slight a detail in it.
9. On the contrary, they conducted Heraclius against his will to
the church of S. Thomas the Apostle and placed the imperial crown
on his head. When he had completed his prayers, he went and
entered into the palace, and all the †wise† congratulated him.

10. And after his accession to the imperial throne Heraclius
wrote a letter to Heraclius, his father, to inform him of all that
had happened, and likewise of his accession to the imperial throne.
11. Now Heraclius, his father, had seized the city of Carthage, the
imperial capital of Africa, and he was much concerned for his son
who had gone to Byzantium. But when he heard this news, he
rejoiced (thereat). 12. Now great uncertainty prevailed in the
churches because of the long duration of the war, and every one
was full of apprehension over the victory which had been won
over Bônâkîs, and the disquietude which had been occasioned in
regard to his (Heraclius's) son.

13. And subsequently Heraclius fell ill and quitted this world,
while he was at his post in his government. God alone knows
whom He appoints, and unto God be glory for ever.

Chapter CXI. 1. Now Theodore was commander-in-chief in
Egypt. And when the messengers of Theodosius the prefect of
Arcadia informed him regarding the death of John,[1] general of
the local levies, he thereupon turned with all the Egyptian troops
and his auxiliary forces and marched to Lôkjôn, which is an island.
2. Moreover he feared lest, owing to the dissensions prevailing
amongst the inhabitants of that district, the Moslem should come
and seize the coast of Lôkjôn and dislodge the communities of the
servants of God who were subjects of the Roman emperor. 3. And
his lamentations were more grievous than the lamentations of David
over Saul when he said: 'How are the mighty fallen, and the
weapons of war perished!'[2] For not only had John the general of

---

[1] John, Duke of Barca, who had been sent against the Moslem that had
invaded Egypt (so Zotenberg, comparing Nicephorus, *Brev. Hist.*, p. 17). See,
however, Butler's *Arab Conquest of Egypt*, p. 222 n.   [2] 2 Sam. i. 27.

the forces perished, but likewise John the general, who was of the city of Mârôs, had been slain in battle and fifty horsemen with him.

4. I will acquaint you briefly with what befell the former inhabitants of Fajûm.

5. John and his troops, the warriors whom we have just mentioned, had been appointed by the Romans to guard the district. Now these posted other guards near the rock of the city of Lâhûn in order to keep guard continually, and to give information to the chief of the forces of the movements of their enemies. 6. And subsequently they got ready some horsemen and a body of soldiers and archers, and these marched out to fight the Moslem, purposing to prevent the advance of the Moslem. 7. And subsequently the Moslem directed their march to the desert and seized a large number of sheep and goats from the high grounds without the cognizance of the Egyptians. 8. And when they reached the city of Bahnasâ, all the troops on the banks of the river came (to the succour) with John, but were unable on that occasion to reach Fajûm.

9. And the general Theodosius, hearing of the arrival of the Ishmaelites, proceeded from place to place in order to see what was likely to befall from these enemies. 10. And these Ishmaelites came and slew without mercy the commander of the troops and all his companions. And forthwith they compelled the city to open its gates, and they put to the sword all that surrendered, and they spared none, whether old men, babe, or woman. 11. And they proceeded against the general John. And he[1] took all the horses: and they hid themselves in the enclosures and plantations lest their enemies should discover them. Then they arose by night and marched to the great river of Egypt, to Abûît, in order to secure their safety. Now this matter was from God.

12. And the chief of the faction who was with Jeremiah informed the Moslem troops of the Roman soldiers who were hidden. And so these took them prisoners and put them to death. 13. And tidings of these events were brought to the general Theodosius, and to Anastasius, who were then twelve miles distant from Nakius. And they betook themselves immediately to the citadel of Babylon, and they remained there, sending the general Leontius to the city

---

[1] So manuscripts.

of Abûît.   14. Now he was obese in person, quite without energy
and unacquainted with warlike affairs.   And when he arrived he
found the Egyptian troops and Theodore fighting with the Moslem
and making sorties every day from the city of Fajûm in order to
⟨re⟩take the city.¹   And taking half the troops he returned to
Babylon in order to acquaint the governors (with the state of
affairs), and the other half of the troops remained with Theodore.

15. And Theodore sought with great diligence for the body of
John, who had been drowned in the river.   And with much
lamentation he had the body drawn forth in a net, and placed in
a bier and sent to the governors, who also (in turn) sent it to
Heraclius.

16. And such (of the Romans) as were in Egypt sought refuge
in the citadel of Babylon.   And they were also awaiting the arrival
of the general Theodore in order to join with him in attacking the
Ishmaelites before the rise of the river and the time of sowing,
when they could not make war lest their sowings should be destroyed
(and) they should die of famine together with their children and
cattle.

CHAPTER CXII.   1. Moreover, there prevailed great indignation
between Theodore the general and the governors owing to the
charges brought by the emperor.   2. And both ² Theodosius and
Anastasius went forth to the city of Ôn, on horseback, together
with a large body of foot soldiers, in order to attack 'Amr the son
of Al-Âs.³   Now the Moslem had not as yet come to know the
city of Misr.⁴   3. And paying no attention to the fortified cities
they came to a place named Tendunias,⁵ and embarked on the river.
4. And 'Amr showed great vigilance and strenuous thought in his
attempts to capture the city of Misr.   But he was troubled because
of his separation from (a part of) the Moslem troops, who being
divided into two corps on the east of the river were marching
towards a city named 'Ain Shams, i. e. Ôn, which was situated on
high ground.   5. And 'Amr the son of Al-Âs sent a letter to Omar
the son of Al-Khattâb in the province of Palestine to this effect:

---

¹ i. e. Bahnasâ (?).

² I have emended 𝕳·𝕳°𝕺𝕺·ᵢ (= ' all ') into 𝕳Ნ𝕌ᵖ𝕺𝕺·ᵢ = ' both '.

³ On 'Amr's parentage see Gibbon, v. 444 (ed. Bury).

⁴ This was the fortress, otherwise called Babylon.

⁵ Identified by Butler (*Arab Conquest of Egypt*, p. 217 *n.*) with Umm Dûnain.

' If thou dost not send Moslem reinforcements, I shall not be able
to take Misr.' 6. And he sent him 4,000 Moslem warriors. And
their general's name was Walwârjâ. He was of barbarian descent.
7. And he divided his troops into three corps. One corps he placed
near Tendunias, the second to the north of Babylon in Egypt;
and he made his preparations with the third corps near the city
of Ôn. 8. And he gave the following orders: ' Be on the watch,
so that when the Roman troops come out to attack us, you may
rise up in their rear, whilst we shall be on their front, and so having
got them between us, we shall put them to the sword.' 9. And
thus when the Roman troops, unaware (of this design), set out
from the fortress to attack the Moslem, these Moslem thereupon
fell upon their rear, as they had arranged, and a fierce engagement
ensued. And when the Moslem came in great numbers against
them, the Roman troops fled and betook themselves to the ships.
10. And the Moslem army took possession of the city of Tendunias;
for its garrison had been destroyed, and there survived only 300
soldiers. And these fled and withdrew into the fortress and closed
the gates. But when they saw the great slaughter that had taken
place, they were seized with panic and fled by ship to Nakius in
great grief and sorrow. 11. And when Domentianus of the city of
Fajûm heard of these events, he set out by night without informing
the inhabitants of (A)bûît that he was fleeing to escape the Moslem,
and they proceeded to Nakius by ship. 12. And when the Moslem
learnt that Domentianus had fled, they marched joyously and seized
the city of Fajûm and (A)bûît, and they shed much blood there.

CHAPTER CXIII. 1. And after the capture of Fajûm with all its
territory by the Moslem, 'Amr sent Abâkîrî [1] of the city of Dalâs
requesting him to bring the ships of Rîf in order to transport to
the east bank of the river the Ishmaelites who were upon the west.
2. And he mustered all his troops about him in order to carry on a
vigorous warfare. And he sent orders to the prefect George to
construct for him a bridge on the river of the city Qaljûb with
a view to the capture of all the cities of Misr, and likewise of
Athrîb and Kuerdîs. And people began to help the Moslem.
3. And (the Moslem) captured the cities of Athrîb and Manûf,
and all their territories. And he had moreover a great bridge

---

[1] Butler (*Arab Conquest of Egypt*, p. 235 *n.*) has shown that Abâkiri is the same
as Apa Cyrus, pagarch of Heracleopolis Magna.

constructed over the river near Babylon in Egypt to prevent the passage of ships to Nakius, Alexandria, and upper Egypt, and to make it possible for horses to cross from the western to the eastern bank of the river.   And so they effected the submission of all the province of Misr.   4. But 'Amr was not satisfied with what he had already done, and so he had the Roman magistrates arrested, and their hands and feet confined in iron and wooden bonds.   And he forcibly despoiled (them) of much of (their) possession, and he doubled the taxes on the peasants and forced them to carry fodder for their horses, and he perpetrated innumerable acts of violence. 5. And such of the governors as were in the city of Nakius fled and betook themselves to the city of Alexandria, leaving Domentianus with a few troops to guard the city.   And they sent orders also to Dares the chief officer in the city of Samnûd to guard the two rivers.   6. Then a panic fell on all the cities of Egypt, and all their inhabitants took to flight, and made their way to Alexandria, abandoning all their possessions and wealth and cattle.

CHAPTER CXIV.   1. And when those Moslem, accompanied by the Egyptians who had apostatized from the Christian faith and embraced the faith of the beast, had come up, the Moslem took as a booty all the possessions of the Christians who had fled, and they designated the servants of Christ enemies of God.   2. And 'Amr left a large body of his men †in† [1] the citadel of Babylon in Egypt, and marched in person towards the two rivers in the direction of the east against the general Theodore.   3. But the latter dispatched Jeqbarî and Satfârî to seize the city of Samnûd (and) fight with the Moslem.   And when they came to the body of local levies,[2] they all refused to war against the Moslem.   And they indeed gave battle and put to the sword many of the Moslem ⟨and of those⟩ who were with them.   4. And the Moslem were not able to inflict any injury on the cities which lay on the two rivers; because the water served as a rampart, and the horses could not enter them because of the deep water which surrounded them. 5. And so leaving them they marched towards the province of Rîf and arrived at the city of Bûsîr.   And they fortified this city and likewise the approaches which they had previously seized.

---

[1] See Butler, p. 268 n.

[2] The Ethiopic word here bears sometimes, as in this passage, the meaning militia, turba militaris, as in Dillmann's Lex.

6. And in those days the general Theodore went to Kalâdji, and besought him saying : ' Come back to us, come back to the side of Rome.' And Kalâdji, fearing lest they should put to death his mother and wife, ⟨who⟩ were concealed in Alexandria, gave Theodore a great sum of money. 7. And the general Theodore prevailed on Kalâdji, and the latter arose in the night, while the Moslem were asleep, and marching on foot with his men he came to the general Theodore. 8. And thence he proceeded to the city of Nakius and formed a junction with Domentianus in order to war against the Moslem.

9. And subsequently Sabendîs devised an excellent plan and so escaped out of the hands of the Moslem by night. And he betook himself to Damietta to the prefect John. 10. And he indeed sent him to Alexandria with a letter . . . confessing his fault to the governors with many tears in these words : ' I have done this deed because of the blow and the ignominy which John inflicted upon me without showing any consideration for (my) old age. For this reason I joined the Moslem. Heretofore I was a zealous servant of the Romans.'

CHAPTER CXV. 1. And 'Amr the chief of the Moslem spent twelve months [1] in warring against the Christians of Northern Egypt, but failed nevertheless in reducing their cities. 2. And in the fifteenth year of the cycle, during the summer, he marched on the cities of Sakâ and Tûkû-Dâmsis,[2] being impatient to subdue the Egyptians before the rise of the river. But he was unable to do them any hurt. 3. And in the city of Damietta they also refused to admit him, and he sought to burn their crops. 4. And he began to march back to the troops that were in the fortress of Babylon in Egypt. And he gave them all the †booty which he had taken from the city of Alexandria. 5. And he destroyed the houses of the Alexandrians who had fled †, and he took their wood and iron and gave orders for the construction of a road from the fortress of Babylon to the city of the two rivers, in order that they might burn that city with fire. 6. And the inhabitants of that city on hearing of this project took to flight with their possessions,

---

[1] So emended by Butler (p. 298 *n.*). Text = ' years '.

[2] So restored by Zotenberg. See Butler (p. 297, *n.* 2), who takes this word to be a compression of two distinct words, Tûkh (Mazid) and (Mit) Damsîs, which lies about nine miles due east of Tûkh Mazîd in the Delta.

and abandoned their city, and the Moslem burned that city with
fire. But the inhabitants of that city came by night and extinguished the fire. 7. And the Moslem marched against other
cities to war against them, and they despoiled the Egyptians of
their possessions and dealt cruelly with them. 8. But the generals
Theodore and Domentianus were unable to do any injury to the
inhabitants of the city on account of the Moslem who were amongst
them.

9. And 'Amr left lower[1] Egypt and proceeded to war against
Rîf. He sent a few Moslem against the city of Antinoe. And
when the Moslem saw the weakness of the Romans and the hostility
of the people to the emperor Heraclius, because of the persecution
wherewith he had visited all the land of Egypt in regard to the
orthodox faith, at the instigation of Cyrus the Chalcedonian
patriarch, they became bolder and stronger in the war. 10. And
the inhabitants of the city (Antinoe) sought to concert measures
with John their prefect with a view to attacking the Moslem; but
he refused, and arose with haste with his troops, and, having
collected all the imposts of the city, betook himself to Alexandria;
for he knew that he could not resist the Moslem, and ⟨he feared⟩
lest he should meet with the same fate as the garrison of Fajûm.
11. Indeed, all the inhabitants of the province submitted to the
Moslem, and paid them tribute. And they put to the sword all
the Roman soldiers whom they encountered. And the Roman
soldiers were in a fortress, and the Moslem besieged them, and
captured their catapults, and demolished their towers, and dislodged
them from the fortress. 12. And they strengthened the fortress of
Babylon, and they captured the city of Nakius and made themselves strong there.

CHAPTER CXVI. 1. And Heraclius was grieved by the death of
John the chief of the local levies, and of John the general who had
been slain by the Moslem, as well as by the defeat of the Romans
that were in the province of Egypt. 2. And in accordance with
the decree of God who takes away the souls of rulers,[2] and of men
of war as well as of kings, Heraclius fell ill with fever, and died
in the thirty-first year of his reign in the month Yakâtît[3] of the

---

[1] The text is a transliteration of an Arabic word (Zotenberg).

[2] 'The souls of rulers'—so the manuscripts.

[3] Sixth Abyssinian month, beginning on Feb. 7 according to the Gregorian
Calendar.

Egyptians, that is, February of the Roman months, in the fourteenth year of the lunar cycle, the 357th year of Diocletian. 3. And some said: 'The death of Heraclius is due to his stamping the gold coinage with the figures of the three emperors—that is, his own and of his two sons on the right hand and on the left—and so no room was found for inscribing the name of the Roman empire.' And after the death of Heraclius they obliterated those three figures.

4. And when Heraclius the elder died, Pyrrhus,[1] the patriarch of Constantinople, passed over Martina ⟨the daughter of⟩ his (i. e. Heraclius's) sister and her children, and nominated Constantine the son of the empress Eudocia, and made him head of the empire in succession to his father. And the two princes were treated with honour and distinction. 5. And David and Marinus seized Pyrrhus, the Roman Chalcedonian patriarch, and banished him to an island in the west of Africa, without any one being cognizant of what had been fulfilled; for no word of the saints falls (to the ground). 6. Now it happened that the great Severus, patriarch of Antioch, wrote to Caesaria the patrician to the following effect: 'No son of a Roman emperor will sit on the throne of his father, so long as the sect of the Chalcedonians bears sway in the world.'

7. And Constantine, the son of Heraclius, on his accession to the empire mustered a large number of ships, and entrusted them to Kîrjûs and Salâkriûs, and sent them to bring the patriarch Cyrus to him that he might take counsel with him as to the Moslem, that he should fight, if he were able, but, if not, should pay tribute;[2] and that he should meet him in the imperial city on the festival of the holy Resurrection, and to cause all the inhabitants of Constantinople to assemble to carry out the same object. 8. And next he sent orders to Theodore[3] to come to him and leave Anastasius[3] to guard the city of Alexandria and the

---

[1] Ethiopic gives ኢርስ፥ owing to a faulty transcription of the Arabic.

[2] The words 'should pay tribute' occur in the text before 'as to the Moslem'. The Ethiopic is ungrammatical and unintelligible. I restore the text as follows: ለእስላም፥ ወይኩን፥ እሙ፥ ይከል፥ ተጋብኦቸ፥ ወእሙ፥ ኢይከል፥ የሁብ፥ ጸባሕት፥ As it stands the text runs: ወየሁብ፥ ጸባሕት፥ ለእስላም፥ ወለእሙ፥ ከ፥ ይከል፥ ተጋብኦቸ፥ ወሟም፥ ኢይከል፥

[3] The text reads 'Anastasius . . . Theodore', but I have in concurrence with Butler's suggestion (op. cit. 303 n.) transposed them. He points out that Anastasius was actually governor of Alexandria prior to the return of Cyrus (see p. 573), and that Theodore was with Cyrus at Rhodes on his way back to Egypt (see cxx. 6 sq.).

cities on the coast. And he held out hopes to Theodore that he would send him a large force in the autumn in order to war with the Moslem. 9. And when in conformity to the command of the emperor they had prepared the ships for setting out, the emperor Constantine forthwith fell ill,[1] and was attacked by a severe malady, and he vomited blood, and when the blood was exhausted he forthwith died. And this malady lasted a hundred days, that is, all the days of his reign wherein he reigned after his father Heraclius. And people mocked at Heraclius and his son Constantine.

10. And the members of the party of Gaïnas assembled in the church in the city of Dafâshîr near the bridge of the Apostle S. Peter. Now Cyrus the patriarch had robbed the church of large possessions in the time of the persecution, without any authorization on the part of the magistrates. 11. And when the Gaïnites sought to lay hands on the patriarch Cyrus, Eudocianus, the brother of the prefect Domentianus, being immediately apprised (of their purpose), sent troops against them to shoot them with arrows and prevent them from carrying out their intention. Some of them were so severely smitten that they died, while two had their hands cut off without legal sentence. 12. And proclamation was made throughout the city by the voice of a herald in these terms: ' Let every one of you withdraw to his own church, and let no one do any violence to his neighbour in defiance of the law.' 13. But God, the Guardian of justice, did not neglect the world, but avenged those who had been wronged : He had no mercy on such as[2] had dealt treacherously against Him, but He delivered them into the hands of the Ishmaelites. 14. And the Moslem thereupon took the field and conquered all the land of Egypt. And after the death of Heraclius, the patriarch Cyrus on his return did not cease (his) severities and persecution against the people of God, but rather added violence to violence.

CHAPTER CXVII. 1. And 'Amr the chief of the Moslem forces encamped before the citadel of Babylon and besieged the troops that garrisoned it. 2. Now the latter received his promise that they should not be put to the sword, and on their side undertook to deliver up to him all the munitions of war—now these were con-

---

[1] Text reads ወደቀ: = ' he fell '. This I have emended into ደወየ: = ' fell ill '.

[2] Here I omit በእንተ: before H.

siderable.[1] 3. And thereupon he ordered them to evacuate the citadel. And they took a small quantity of gold and set out. And it was in this way that the citadel of Babylon in Egypt was taken on the second day after the (festival of the) Resurrection. 4. Thus God punished them because they had not honoured the redemptive passion of our Lord and Saviour Jesus Christ, who gave His life for those who believe in Him. Yea, it was for this reason that God made them turn their back upon them (i. e. the Moslem). 5. Now on that day of the festival of the holy Resurrection they released the orthodox that were in prison; but, enemies of Christ as they were, they did not let them go without first ill-using them; but they scourged them and cut off their hands. 6. And on that day these (unhappy ones) wept and their tears poured down their faces and they were spurned, even as it is written regarding those unclean persons: 'They have defiled the Church by an unclean faith, and they have wrought apostasies and deeds of violence like the sect of the Arians, such as neither pagan nor barbarian has wrought, and they have despised Christ and His servants, and we have not found any that do the like amongst the worshippers of false idols. 7. But God has been patient with the apostates and heretics who have undergone baptism a second time in submission to despotic emperors. Yet it is the same God who recompenses every man according to his deeds and does justice to him that has been wronged. 8. How then, is it not far better for us to endure patiently the trials and punishments which they inflict upon us? They indeed think to honour our Lord Christ by so doing, whereas they are found to be perverted in their faith. They have not indeed voluntarily apostatized, but they persecute those who agree not with them in faith. God forbid (such agreement)! for they are not servants of Christ: yet they think they are such in their thoughts.'

CHAPTER CXVIII. 1. Now the capture of the citadel of Babylon and of Nakius by the Moslem was a source of great grief to the Romans. 2. And when 'Amr had brought to a close the operations of war he made his entry into the citadel of Babylon, and he mustered a large number of ships, great and small, and anchored them close to the fort where he was.

3. And Menas, who was chief of the Green Faction, and Cosmas the son of Samuel, the leader of the Blues, besieged the city of Misr and

---

[1] I have emended the ungrammatical · በዘ·ኝ፦ into በዝኝ፦

harassed the Romans during the days of the Moslem. And fighting men had gone up with fear-inspiring boldness from the western bank of the river in ships, and these made expeditions by night.

4. 'Amr and the Moslem army, on horseback, proceeded by land till they came to the city of Kebrias of Abâdjâ. And on this occasion he attacked the general Domentianus. 5. But when the latter learnt of the approach of the Moslem troops, he embarked on a ship and fled [in a ship] and abandoned the army and their fleet. And he sought to enter the small canal which Heraclius had dug during his reign. But finding it closed he returned and entered the city of Alexandria. 6. Now when the soldiers saw that their commander had taken flight, they cast away their arms and threw themselves into the river in the presence of their enemies. 7. And the Moslem troops slaughtered them with the sword in the river, and none escaped save one man only, named Zechariah, a doughty man and a warrior. 8. And when the crews of the ships saw the flight of the troops, they too took to flight and returned to their own country. And thereupon the Moslem made their entry into Nakius, and took possession, and finding no soldiers (to offer resistance), they proceeded to put to the sword all whom they found in the streets and in the churches, men, women, and infants, and they showed mercy to none. 9. And after they had captured (this) city, they marched against other localities and sacked them and put all they found to the sword. And they came also to the city of †Sa†,[1] and there they found Esqûtâws and his people in a vineyard, and the Moslem seized them and put them to the sword. Now these were of the family of the general Theodore. 10. Let us now cease, for it is impossible to recount the iniquities perpetrated by the Moslem after their capture of the island of Nakius, on Sunday, the eighteenth day of the month Genbôt,[2] in the fifteenth year of the cycle, and also the horrors committed in the city of Caesarea in Palestine.

11. And the general Theodore, who was in command of the city, even the city of Kîlûnâs, quitted (this) city and proceeded to Egypt, leaving Stephen with the troops to guard the city and

---

[1] Since Sa = Sais, which being as far north as Damanhûr was beyond the range of the Arabs at this time, Butler (*op. cit.* 285 *n.*) reads Ṣaûnâ, which is given in the heading of the chapter.

[2] Ninth Abyssinian month, beginning on May 8 according to the Gregorian Calendar.

contend with the Moslem. 12. And there was a certain Jew with the Moslem, and he betook himself to the province of Egypt. And when with great toil and exertion they had cast down the walls of the city, they forthwith made themselves masters of it, and put to the sword thousands of its inhabitants and of the soldiers, and they gained an enormous booty, and took the women and children captive and divided them amongst themselves, and they made that city a desolation (lit. destitute). 13. And shortly after the Moslem proceeded against the country (city ?) of †Côprôs† and put Stephen and his people to the sword.

CHAPTER CXIX. 1. And Egypt also had become enslaved to Satan. A great strife had broken out between the inhabitants of Lower Egypt, and these were divided into two parties. Of these, one sided with Theodore, but the other wished to join the Moslem. 2. And straightway the one party rose against the other, and they plundered their possessions and burnt their city. But the Moslem distrusted them.

3. And 'Amr sent a large force of Moslem against Alexandria, and they captured Kariûn, which lies outside the city. And Theodore and his troops who were in that locality fled and withdrew into Alexandria. 4. And the Moslem began to attack them but were not able to approach the walls of the city; for stones were hurled against them from the top of the walls, and they were driven far from the city.

5. And the inhabitants of Misr were at variance with those of Lower Egypt, and their strife ran high, but after a short time they made peace. 6. But when their discord came to an end, Satan stirred up another in the city of Alexandria; for Domentianus the prefect and Menas the general were at variance with each other through lust for office and other motives. 7. Now the general Theodore took the side of Menas: he was moreover hostile to Domentianus because of his flight from Nakius and his abandonment of the troops. 8. And with Eudocianus, the elder brother of Domentianus, Menas was very wroth, because he had practised cruelties against the Christians during the season of the holy Passion in regard to the faith. 9. And Domentianus mustered a large force of the 'Blues'. And when Menas was apprised of this movement, he too mustered a large force of the 'Greens' and of the troops in the city. And thus these two kept up their hostility.

10. It was subsequently to this that Philiades the prefect of the province of Arcadia arrived. Now Domentianus had become the foe of Cyrus the patriarch, and he showed him ill will, though he was his brother-in-law, and though previously they had been mutual friends. But subsequently he came to hate him without any good ground. 11. And Menas also who cherished a spiritual friendship[1] for Philiades and was not neglectful of him but invited him frequently out of respect for the priesthood ; for Philiades was the brother of the patriarch George. Now (Menas) was merciful and Godfearing and was grieved on behalf of those that were oppressed. But Philiades was not loyal in friendship, but acted unjustly, (and) cherished in secret evil designs. 12. Now in the days of the general Theodore, when a discussion was raised regarding the city named Mâmûnâ, and regarding the pay of the troops and the lands on which it should be levied, this wicked man straightway spake and said : ' In place of twelve men, it will be better to have one ; then there will be one man to receive pay instead of [2] twelve, and so the tax in kind and the pay of the troops will be lessened.' And in this incident Menas found an occasion against Domentianus. 13. And all the troops loved and trusted him : for Menas loved the esteem of all men—not in order to receive idle praise, but by reason of his wisdom and modesty. 14. Now while he was present in the great church of Caesarion with all the people, all the inhabitants of the city gathered together against Philiades and sought to put him to death. But he took to flight and hid himself in a church. 15. And straightway the people proceeded to his dwelling and burnt it, and pillaged all his property, but they spared such persons as they found in the house, and did not slay them. 16. And when Domentianus was apprised (of these events) he sent a body of the ' Blues ' to attack them. And a great strife ensued amongst them, and six men were killed and many wounded. 17. And with great efforts and exertions Theodore established peace amongst them. And he deposed the general Domentianus, and appointed Artânâ chief of ten orders, who is named a decurion. And all the property which had been carried off as pillage from the house of Philiades was returned to him. It has been said that this strife and tumult originated in religious dissensions.

---

[1] I have transposed ለፍቅር፡ መንፈሳዊ፡ before ለእብልደስ፡ Cf. text four lines lower.   [2] I have here added ህየንት፡ before ፲መ፪፡

18. And after the death of Constantine, the son of Heraclius, they brought forward Heraclius, his brother on his father's side, though but an infant. But his accession to the empire was as idle as had been that of his brother who died. 19. And the patriarch Pyrrhus, seeing that Heraclius, who was still a child, had become emperor through the intrigues of Martina his mother, whilst he Pyrrhus was still in exile[1] .... 20. And after his accession to the empire he recalled Pyrrhus from exile by the advice of the Senate, and abolished the penal decree issued by his brother Constantine and his imperial predecessors; for they abolished it because of the unjust accusation of Philagrius the treasurer. 21. And it was through his agency that the churches were in tribulation: for he put an end to the gifts which the emperors were accustomed to make, and he confirmed the heavy charges (that were upon them).

22. And subsequently he appointed him ⟨Cyrus⟩ a second time to the city of Alexandria, and the priests who were with him. He gave him power and authority to make peace with the Moslem and check any further resistance against them, and to establish a system of administration suitable to the government of the land of Egypt. And he was accompanied by Constantine, a general of the army, who was master of the local levies. 23. And he had the army from the province of Thrace brought to the city of Constantinople, and he banished Philagrius the treasurer to the province of Africa where Pyrrhus had previously been in banishment. 24. And there were great dissensions, and the inhabitants of the city rose up against Martina and her children because of the banishment of Philagrius the treasurer; for he was greatly beloved.

Chapter CXX. 1. Now not only Cyrus the Chalcedonian patriarch desired peace with the Moslem, but also all the people and the patricians and Domentianus, who had enjoyed the favour of the empress Martina—(and so) all these assembled and took counsel with Cyrus the patriarch with a view to making peace with the Moslem.

2. And all the clergy began to stir up odium[2] against the empire of Heraclius the younger, declaring: 'It is not fitting that one derived from a reprobate seed should sit on the imperial throne: rather it is the sons of Constantine, who was the son of Eudocia,

---

[1] There is a lacuna here.

[2] Reading ደጸልፐ: instead of ይጸልፐ:

that should bear sway over the empire.' And they rejected the will of the elder Heraclius.

3. And when Valentinus was apprised that all men were united against Martina and her sons, he took large sums of money out of the treasury of Philagrius, and distributed them amongst the soldiers and officers, and prevailed on them to act against Martina and her sons. 4. And some of them gave over warring against the Moslem, and turned their hostilities against their own countrymen. 5. And thereupon they sent an envoy secretly to the island of Rhodes with this message to the troops with the patriarch Cyrus : 'Return to the imperial city and do not take sides with him.' 6. And they sent also to Theodore, the prefect of Alexandria, the following message : ' Do not hearken to the voice of Martina, and do not obey her sons.' And they sent likewise to Africa, and to every province under the sway of Rome.

7. And when Theodore the general heard this news, he was pleased and kept the matter secret, and set out by night without the cognizance of any, and purposed proceeding from the island of Rhodes to Pentapolis, and he told only the captain of the ship. 8. But the captain of the ship alleged (that he could not), saying : ' The wind is contrary to us.' And he entered Alexandria on the night of the seventeenth day of Maskaram,[1] on the day of the festival of the Holy Cross. 9. And all the inhabitants of Alexandria, men and women, old and young, gathered together to meet the patriarch Cyrus, rejoicing and giving thanks for the arrival of the patriarch of Alexandria. 10. And Theodore betook himself secretly with the patriarch to the Church of the monks of Tabenna and closed the door. And he sent for Mînâs and appointed him general, and banished Domentianus from the city. And all the inhabitants cried out : ' (Begone) from the city.'

11. Now before the arrival of Cyrus the patriarch, George had been highly esteemed by the governor Anastasius ; for he had received the dignity from Heraclius the younger (?), and, when he was advanced in years, he enjoyed universal authority : even the patriarch suffered him to enjoy his authority.

12. And when the patriarch Cyrus came to the great church of Caesarion, they covered all the way (with carpets) and chanted hymns

---

[1] First Abyssinian month, beginning on Sept. 10 according to the Gregorian Calendar.

in his honour (and the crowds increased) till the people trod each other down. And after great exertions they brought him to the Church. 13. Now he extolled highly the well in which the Holy Cross had been found. And he took also (to the Caesarion) the venerable cross from the Convent of the monks of Tabenna which he had received previously to his exile from the general John.[1] 14. And when they began to celebrate divine service on the day of the holy Resurrection, instead of chanting the psalm proper to the day of the Resurrection, which is: 'This is the day which the Lord has made; we will rejoice and be glad in it',[2] the deacon, desiring to praise the patriarch and to congratulate him on his return, gave out another psalm that was not proper (to the day). 15. And when the people heard it, they said: 'This is not the proper psalm: it is an evil augury for the patriarch Cyrus: he will not see a second festival of the Resurrection in the city of Alexandria.' 16. And all the congregation and the monks made predictions after this fashion in public: 'He has acted contrary to what is ordained in the Canons.' But none who heard any of these sayings believed them.

17. And subsequently the patriarch Cyrus set out and went to Babylon to the Moslem, seeking by the offer of tribute to procure peace from them and put a stop to war in the land of Egypt. And 'Amr welcomed his arrival, and said unto him: 'Thou hast done well to come to us.' And Cyrus answered and said unto him: 'God has delivered this land into your hands: let there be no enmity from henceforth between you and Rome: heretofore there has been no persistent strife with you.' 18. And they fixed the amount of tribute to be paid. And as for the Ishmaelites, they were not to intervene in any matter, but were to keep to themselves for eleven months. The Roman troops in Alexandria were to carry off their possessions and their treasures and proceed (home) by sea, and no other Roman army was to return. But those who wished to journey by land were to pay a monthly (?) tribute. 19. And the Moslem were to take as hostages one hundred and fifty soldiers and fifty civilians and make peace.

---

[1] I have transposed the clause 'which he had . . . from the general John' from the close of the preceding sentence, in accordance with Butler's (*op. cit.* 314 sq.) suggestion. That sentence refers to the discovery of the Holy Cross by Helena, the mother of Constantine the Great.

[2] Ps. cxviii. 24.

20. And the Romans were to cease warring against the Moslem, and the Moslem were to desist from seizing Christian Churches, and the latter were not to intermeddle with any concerns of the Christians. 21. And the Jews were to be permitted to remain in the city of Alexandria.

22. And when the patriarch had concluded this negotiation, he returned to the city of Alexandria, and he reported to Theodore and the general Constantine (the conditions of peace), to the intent that they should report them to the emperor Heraclius and support them before him. 23. And straightway all the troops and the people of Alexandria and the general Theodore came together to him and paid their homage to the patriarch Cyrus. And he acquainted them with all the conditions which he had made with the Moslem, and he persuaded them all to accept them. 24. And while things were in this condition, the Moslem came to receive the tribute, though the inhabitants of Alexandria had not yet been informed (of the treaty). And the Alexandrians, on seeing them, made ready for battle. 25. But the troops and the generals held fast to the resolution they had adopted, and said: 'We cannot engage in battle with the Moslem: rather let the counsel of the patriarch Cyrus be observed.' 26. Then the population rose up against the patriarch and sought to stone him. But he said unto them: 'I have made this treaty in order to save you and your children.' And plunged in much weeping and grief he besought them. 27. And thereupon the Alexandrians felt ashamed before him, and offered him a large sum of gold to hand over to the Ishmaelites together with the tribute which had been imposed on them.

28. And the Egyptians, who, through fear of the Moslem, had fled and taken refuge in the city of Alexandria, made the following request to the patriarch: 'Get the Moslem to promise that we may return to our cities and become their subjects. And he negotiated for them according to their request. And the Moslem took possession of all the land of Egypt, southern and northern, and trebled their taxes.

29. Now there was a man named Menas, who had been appointed prefect of Lower Egypt by the emperor Heraclius: he was a presumptuous man, unlettered and a deep hater of the Egyptians. Now after the Moslem had got possession of all the country, they

established him in his (former) dignity : and a man named Sînôdâ they appointed prefect of the province of Rîf : and another named Philoxenus as prefect of the province of Arcadia, that is, Fajûm. 30. Now these three men loved the heathen but hated the Christians, and compelled the Christians to carry fodder for the cattle, and they forced them to † carry †¹ milk, and honey, and fruit and leeks, and other things in abundance : Now all these were in addition to the ordinary rations. 31. (The Egyptians) carried out these orders under the constraint of an unceasing fear. (The Moslem) forced them to excavate (anew) the canal of Trajan, which had been destroyed for a long time, in order to conduct water through it from Babylon in Egypt to the Red Sea. 32. And the yoke they laid on the Egyptians was heavier than the yoke which had been laid on Israel by Pharaoh, whom God judged with a righteous judgement, by drowning him in the Red Sea with all his army after the many plagues wherewith He had plagued both men and cattle. 33. When God's judgement lights upon these Ishmaelites may He do unto them as He did aforetime unto Pharaoh ! But it is because of our sins that He has suffered them to deal thus with us.   Yet in His longsuffering our God and Saviour Jesus Christ will look upon us and protect us : and we also trust that He will destroy the enemies of the Cross, as saith the book which lies not.

34. And 'Amr subdued the land of Egypt and sent his men to war against the inhabitants of Pentapolis.   And after he had subdued them, he did not permit them to dwell there. And he took from thence plunder and captives in abundance. 35. And Abûljânôs the prefect of Pentapolis and his troops and the rich men of the province withdrew into the city of Dûshera—now its walls were strongly fortified—and they closed the gates. So the Moslem after seizing plunder and captives retired to their own country.

36. Now the patriarch Cyrus was greatly grieved on account of the calamities which had befallen the land of Egypt. For 'Amr had no mercy on the Egyptians, and did not observe the covenant they had made with him, for he was of a barbaric race. 37. And on the festival of Palm Sunday the patriarch Cyrus fell ill of a fever owing to excessive grief, and he died on the fifth day of

---

¹ The word 𐌰𐌸𐌻: (= 'to carry', the same word as is used in the preceding clause) can hardly be right. Zotenberg renders it by 'fournir', but it never has this meaning.

Holy Week, on the twenty-fifth of the month Magâbît.[1] 38. Thus he did not live to see the festival of the holy Resurrection of our Lord Jesus Christ as the Christians had predicted regarding him. Now this event took place in the reign of the emperor Constantine the son of Heraclius (II).

39. And after his (Heraclius II) death the Romans were plunged in war on account of the sons of the empress Martina; for they had excluded them from the imperial throne, and wished to make the sons of Constantine emperors (in their stead). 40. And Valentine who was leagued with Philagrius assisted them. And he drew over all the troops and marched to the city of Chalcedon; for he thought and said: 'Martina's strength lies in the fighting men which are with her sons.' And he prevailed on all to consent to the recall of Philagrius from exile. 41. And thereupon Heraclius the younger embarked on the imperial ships, accompanied by a great number of priests and monks and illustrious bishops, and passed over to Chalcedon. 42. And he made the following appeal to all the troops: 'Abandon not the duty of Christian integrity by becoming hostile to me; but make peace with God, and comply with the will of my father Heraclius; for he laboured much on behalf of this country.' 43. Moreover he alleged that he would take unto him his brother's son and make him his colleague in the empire and there would no longer be war or bloodshed between them. And he received the assent of all the patricians and said unto them: 'I will bring back Philagrius from exile.' 44. And when Valentine learnt that all the people had submitted to him and received his words in peace, he took Domentianus and other patricians with him and placed the imperial crown on the younger Constantine, one of the sons of Constantine, the son of Heraclius the elder, whom Heracleonas had taken unto him (as colleague). And all the people dispersed without strife. 45. But they (the rebels) did not suffer this peace to be permanent. Shortly after they had raised Constantine to the imperial throne, the hatred of the two emperors grew in strength, that is, of Heraclius II and Constantine the younger. For Satan sowed dissensions between Heraclius II and the army. 46. And straightway the troops in the province of Cappadocia began to commit atrocities: moreover they produced

[1] Seventh Abyssinian month, beginning on Mar. 9 according to the Gregorian Calendar.

a letter to the following effect : 'This letter was sent by Martina and Pyrrhus the patriarch of Constantinople to David the Matarguem (urging him) to make a vigorous war, and to take Martina to be his wife, and to put down the sons of Constantine (III), who had been emperor with Heraclius (II) his brother.' [1]

47. And when the inhabitants of Byzantium heard this news, they said : 'This project is concerned with Kubratos, chief of the Huns, the nephew of Organa, who was baptized in the city of Constantinople, and received into the Christian community in his childhood and had grown up in the imperial palace.' 48. And between him and the elder Heraclius great affection and peace had prevailed, and after Heraclius's death he had shown his affection to his sons and his wife Martina because of the kindness (Heraclius) had shown him. 49. And after he had been baptized with life-giving baptism he overcame all the barbarians and heathens through virtue of holy baptism. Now touching him it is said that he supported the interests of the children of Heraclius and opposed those of Constantine. 50. And in consequence of this evil report all the soldiers in Constantinople and the people rose up, and Jûtâlîjûs, the son of Constantine, named Theodore became the chief of their forces. And he was a doughty warrior like his father. 51. And when they had made preparations to fight with David the Matarguem, the latter fled and took refuge in a fortress of Armenia. And (Jûtâlîjûs) pursued him and, since none could render him aid, cut off his head and had it sent round all the cities of the east. 52. And next he marched with a large force to the city of Byzantium and he captured the palace, and he had Martina and her three sons, Heraclius, David, and Marinus, escorted forth with insolence, and he stripped them of the imperial crown, and he had their noses cut off, and he sent them in exile to Rhodes. 53. And the patriarch Pyrrhus was deposed without having recourse to a council, and he was removed from the Church and sent in banishment to Tripoli where Philagrius was. And Philagrius indeed was brought back from banishment. 54. And the youngest son of Martina was castrated, through fear, as they said, of his becoming emperor when he grew up. But the child could not endure the great wound, and straightway died. And the second of her sons was a deaf-mute, and so was unfit for the throne. For

---

[1] MSS. to be followed here : text wrongly emended by Zotenberg.

this reason they did him no injury.   55. And they set at naught
the will of Heraclius the elder, and they made Constans, the son
of Constantine, emperor.   And they appointed Paul of the city of
Constantinople in the room of the patriarch Pyrrhus.

56. ⟨All these events⟩ and the separation of Egypt and Alexandria during the reign of Heraclius the emperor of the Chalcedonians
(fell out) as they are recorded in the letters of the great Severus
the patriarch of Antioch, which he wrote to the Patrician in the
reign of the emperor Anastasius, wherein he prophesied against
the Roman empire in these terms : ' No son shall sit on his father's
throne so long as the creed of the Chalcedonians prevails, who say
that there were two natures in Christ after they became one, a
creed which we cannot profess.   Their doctrine that the manhood
and the Godhead are two distinct natures after having become
united, we believers cannot teach.   It is not fitting that we should
speak as the heretics.'   57. Or according to the statement of
Gregory : 'We recognize God the Word to be of one nature
derived from two.   For God was united to the flesh and became
one Substance.   The Godhead indeed is not converted into the
manhood, nor the manhood into the other nature, but the Word
which became flesh had become unchangeable, and no change can
affect the Word.   But the Word which has become flesh is one
divine Substance.   58. But this union is a marvel.   That which is
invisible has become visible : the Creator has been born and we
have seen Him : He has healed us by His wounds ! '   59. But we
should cease giving citations from the words of the illustrious
Fathers of the Church, who have been learned in investigation :
for the Romans do not believe in aught now save the Passion.
60. But for those who welcome the flavour of true knowledge
I will set it forth briefly.   When they rejected the orthodox faith,
which is our faith, in like manner were they rejected from the
imperial throne.   And there has followed the undoing of all
Christians that are in the world, and we have not experienced the
mercy and compassion of our Lord Jesus Christ.

61. And in those days there arose great troubles through Valentine;
for he had assumed the imperial robes and sought to make himself
emperor.   But when the people of Constantinople heard, they arose
against him, and straightway he put off the (imperial) robes.
62. And forthwith they seized him and conducted him before the

emperor Constans. And he sware a terrible oath to this effect: 'I have not done this with any evil intent, but in order to contend against the Moslem.' 63. And when they heard this statement, they set him free and made him commander-in-chief of the army, and arranged with him that he should give his daughter in marriage to the emperor. And on that occasion they had her proclaimed through the voice of the herald by the imperial name of Augusta.

64. And the evil-doer Valentine accused Arcadius the archbishop of the island of Cyprus. Now this man was an ascetic in purity of life, and well known (as such) unto all men. And (Valentin) said touching him: 'He was an ally of Martina and the patriarch Pyrrhus, and a foe of the new emperor Constans.' 65. And (the emperor), acting on this evil counsel, sent from Constantinople a numerous band of soldiers to fetch in great ignominy Arcadius the archbishop. But by the command of God he found (his) consummation and died after the manner of all men. 66. But Cyrus the Chalcedonian patriarch in Alexandria was excessively grieved when he heard (of these events)—the exile of Martina and her sons who had brought him back from exile, the deposition of Pyrrhus the patriarch of Constantinople, the restoration of Philagrius his enemy, the death of the archbishop Arcadius, and the triumph and power of Valentine. 67. And for these reasons he wept unceasingly; for he feared lest he should suffer the same fortune that had befallen him previously. And in the midst of this grief he died according to the law of nature. And his chief grief was due to the Moslem, who had refused his request on behalf of the Egyptians. 68. And before he died he wrought the works of the apostates and persecuted the Christians; and for this reason God, the righteous Judge, punished him for the evils he had wrought.

69. And the general Valentine and his troops were not able to give any assistance to the Egyptians; but the latter, and particularly the Alexandrians, were very hard pressed by the Moslem. And they were not able to bear the tribute which was exacted from them. And the rich men of the city (country ?) concealed themselves ten months in the islands.

70. And subsequently Theodore the governor and Constantine the commander-in-chief of the army, and the remaining troops, and likewise those which had been hostages in the hands of the

Moslem, set out and embarked, and came to Alexandria. 71. And after the festival of the Cross they appointed Peter the deacon to be patriarch on the twentieth of Hamlê,[1] on the festival of the holy Theodore the martyr, and placed him on the patriarchal throne.

72. On the twentieth of Maskaram,[2] Theodore and all his troops and officers set out and proceeded to the island of Cyprus, and abandoned the city of Alexandria. And thereupon 'Amr the chief of the Moslem made his entry without effort into the city of Alexandria. And the inhabitants received him with respect; for they were in great tribulation and affliction.

CHAPTER CXXI. 1. And Abba Benjamin, the patriarch of the Egyptians, returned to the city of Alexandria in the thirteenth year after his flight from the Romans, and he went to the Churches, and inspected all of them. 2. And every one said : 'This expulsion (of the Romans) and victory of the Moslem is due to the wickedness of the emperor Heraclius and his persecution of the Orthodox through the patriarch Cyrus. This was the cause of the ruin of the Romans and the subjugation of Egypt by the Moslem.

3. And 'Amr became stronger every day in every field of his activity. And he exacted the taxes which had been determined upon, but he took none of the property of the Churches, and he committed no act of spoliation or plunder, and he preserved them throughout all his days. And when he seized the city of Alexandria, he had the canal drained in accordance with the instructions given by the apostate Theodore. 4. And he increased the taxes to the extent of twenty-two *batr* of gold till all the people hid themselves owing to the greatness of the tribulation, and could not find the wherewithal to pay. And in the second year of the lunar cycle came John of the city of Damietta.

5. He had been appointed by the governor Theodore, and had lent his aid to the Moslem in order to prevent their destruction of the city. Now he had been appointed prefect of the city of Alexandria when 'Amr entered it. And this John had compassion on the poor, and gave generously to them out of his possessions. And seeing their affliction he had mercy upon them, and wept over their lot. 6. 'Amr deposed Menas and appointed John in his stead.

---

[1] 'Mensis Abyssinorum undecimus qui xxv° Junii sec. Calend. Jul., vii° Jul. sec. Cal. Greg. incipit' (Dillmann, *Lexicon*, 71).

[2] This month begins on the 10th of Sept. according to the Calendar of Gregory.

Now this Menas had increased the taxes of the city, which 'Amr had fixed at 22,000 gold dinars, and the sum which the apostate Menas got together was 32,057 gold dinars—he appointed for the Moslem.[1] 7. And none could recount the mourning and lamentation which took place in that city : they even gave their children in exchange for the great sums which they had to pay monthly. And they had none to help them, and God destroyed their hopes, and delivered the Christians into the hands of their enemies. 8. But the strong beneficence of God will put to shame those who grieve us, and He will make His love for man to triumph over our sins, and bring to naught the evil purposes of those who afflict us, who would not that the King of Kings and Lord of Lords should reign over them, (even) Jesus Christ our true God. 9. As for those wicked slaves, He will destroy them in evil fashion : as saith the holy Gospel : ' As for Mine enemies who would not that I should reign over them, bring them unto Me.' 10. And now many of the Egyptians who had been false Christians denied the holy orthodox faith and lifegiving baptism, and embraced the religion of the Moslem, the enemies of God, and accepted the detestable doctrine of the beast, this is, Mohammed, and they erred together with those idolaters, and took arms in their hands and fought against the Christians. 11. And one of them, named John, the Chalcedonian of the Convent of Sinai, embraced the faith of Islam, and quitting his monk's habit he took up the sword, and persecuted the Christians who were faithful to our Lord Jesus Christ.

CHAPTER CXXII.   1. And now let us glorify our Lord Jesus Christ and bless His holy name at all times ; for unto this hour He hath preserved us Christians from the errors of the erring heathen, and from the transgressions of the apostate heretics. 2. And may He also strengthen and help us to endure tribulation through hope in His divinity.   And He will make us worthy to receive, with a face not put to shame, the inheritance of His eternal (and) incorruptible Kingdom in heaven.   And (let us bless) His Father, (pre-eminently) good, and the Holy Lifegiving Spirit for ever and ever, Amen.

CHAPTER CXXIII.   1. (Herewith) ends this blessed book which John the rector bishop of Nikius composed for the profit of the soul.

[1] The Ethiopic is irregular.

Now it contains divine mysteries and heavenly marvels which have befallen apostates from the faith. 2. At one time the earth quaked on account of the denial (of the faith), and the great city of Nicaea was destroyed. At another it rained fire from heaven : at another the sun was darkened from the hour of dawn till evening. 3. On a certain occasion the rivers rose and overwhelmed many cities ; while on another houses were overthrown and many men perished and went down to the depths of the earth. 4. And all these things fell out because they divided Christ into two natures, whilst some of them made Him (merely) a created being. 5. Also the Roman emperors lost the imperial crown, and the Ishmaelites and Chuzaeans won the mastery over them, because they did not walk in the orthodox faith of our Lord Jesus Christ, but divided the indivisible.

6. The transcription of this book began on the twenty-eighth day of Hamlê, and was finished on Monday on the twenty-second day of Teqmet,[1] at the sixth hour of the day, when the sun was in the sign of Scorpion, and the moon in the sign of Aquarius. 7. And the course of the sun was then in (its) 195th degree, and its zenith was at eighty-seven degrees thirty minutes. And the day was eleven hours, and the night thirteen. And the day increased and the night decreased daily by twenty minutes. 8. And the dominion of Elgûfr from Manâzel was then, in the 7594th year of the world, the 1947th year of Alexander, the 1594th year of the Incarnation of our Lord Jesus Christ, the 1318th year of the Martyrs, the 980th year of Hagar according to the solar reckoning, but the 1010th year according to the lunar reckoning: four years seven months and eight days after the accession of Malak Sagad the younger, son of Malak Sagad the elder, who was named Jakob when he received the grace of baptism: eight years three months and five days after the accession of the Godloving queen Malak Môgasâ, who was named Mârjâm Senâ on receiving the grace of baptism.

9. We have translated this book with great care from Arabic into Ge'ez, even poor I, the most worthless amongst men and the vilest amongst the people, and the deacon Gabriel the Egyptian, son of the martyr John Kolobos,[2] by the order of Athanasius

---

[1] This month begins on the 10th of October according to the Gregorian Calendar.

[2] i. e. 'the small'.

commander-in-chief of the army of Ethiopia, and by the order of the queen Mârjâm Senâ. 10. God grant that it may serve to the salvation of the soul and the preservation of the body. And praise be unto Him, who has given us power to begin and to finish (this work), for ever and ever. Amen and amen. So be it. So be it.

INDEX I

PROPER NAMES

(This index does not include the proper names in the table of contents
of the book, pp. 1–14.)

* Butler (*Arab Conquest of Egypt*, p. 22) points out that Dim is a prefix in ancient Egyptian meaning town, and that accordingly Demqârûnî is merely a Coptic form of Kariûn, which was thirty-eight kilometres from Alexandria. If Butler is right, then there must have been two towns named Kariûn; for in our author 119[3] Kariûn is said to lie outside Alexandria. Further, we must suppose that the translator has wrongly transliterated the word as Demqârûnî instead of Demkârûnî. The text seems to favour the idea that there were two towns so named.

INDEX II

BIBLICAL QUOTATIONS

DANIEL CHWOLSON

DAS LETZTE PASSAMAHL CHRISTI

UND DER TAG SEINES TODES

NACH DEN
IN ÜBEREINSTIMMUNG GEBRACHTEN BERICHTEN DER
SYNOPTIKER UND DES EVANGELIUM JOHANNIS

NEBST ANHANG ÜBER DAS VERHÄLTNIS DER JUDEN, PHARISÄER
UND SADDUCÄER
ZU CHRISTUS, NACH RABBINISCHEN QUELLEN ERLÄUTERT

VERMEHRTE AUFLAGE,
MIT DREI BEILAGEN, ERGÄNZUNGEN UND
VERBESSERUNGEN ENTHALTEND

APA - ORIENTAL PRESS
AMSTERDAM

SOLOMON SCHECHTER & CHARLES TAYLOR

THE WISDOM OF BEN SIRA

PORTIONS OF

THE BOOK ECCLESIASTICUS

HEBREW TEXT, EDITED
FROM MANUSCRIPTS IN THE CAIRO GENIZAH
COLLECTION, AND ANNOTATED,
WITH AN ENGLISH TRANSLATION, AN INTRODUCTION
AND AN APPENDIX
CONTAINING ADDITIONAL MATERIAL AND NOTES

WITH ADDITION OF

TALMUDICAL FRAGMENTS IN THE BODLEIAN LIBRARY

EDITED, WITH INTRODUCTION, BY
SOLOMON SCHECHTER & SIMEON SINGER

APA - PHILO PRESS
AMSTERDAM

FRIEDRICH SCHULTHESS

LEXICON SYROPALAESTINUM

ADIUVANTE
ACADEMIA LITTERARUM REGIA BORUSSICA EDIDIT

WÖRTERBUCH
DER CHRISTLICH–SYRISCHEN SPRACHE
AUS DEN BIBLISCHEN
BÜCHERN UND SYRISCH–PALÄSTINENSISCHEN
SCHRIFTEN DES
FRÜHMITTELALTERS ZUSAMMENGESTELLT

APA - ORIENTAL PRESS
AMSTERDAM

ERIC OTTO WINSTEDT

COPTIC TEXTS ON ST THEODORE

THE GENERAL (STRATELATES, †c306),
ON ST THEODORE THE EASTERN (THE ORIENTAL)
AND ON CHAMOUL AND JUSTUS

EDITED FROM VARIOUS MANUSCRIPTS, TRANSLATED AND ANNOTATED,
ACCOMPANIED BY INTRODUCTIONS AND
INDEXES OF NAMES AND SAHIDIC, BOHAIRIC AND GREEK WORDS

APA - PHILO PRESS
AMSTERDAM

APA / POSTBUS 122 / NL-3600 AC MAARSSEN / HOLLAND

SIR ERNEST A. WALLIS BUDGE

BARALÂM AND YĔWÂSĔF
[BARLAAM AND JOSAPHAT]

BEING THE ETHIOPIC VERSION OF A CHRISTIANIZED RECENSION
OF THE
BUDDHIST LEGEND OF THE BUDDHA AND THE BODHISATTVA

ETHIOPIC TEXT, EDITED
FROM TWO MANUSCRIPTS IN THE BRITISH MUSEUM
AND TRANSLATED INTO ENGLISH

WITH AN EXTENSIVE CRITICAL AND HISTORICAL INTRODUCTION
ON THE TRANSMISSION
OF THIS ROMANCE IN VARIOUS VERSIONS FROM ASIA TO AFRICA AND EUROPE
WITH NOTES, A LIST OF BIBLE PASSAGES, AND AN INDEX

REPRINT OF THE EDITION CAMBRIDGE 1923.
CXXII, 351; XVI, 246* pages; 75 plates. 2 volumes bound in one.
Cloth bound, 8vo. (ISBN 90 6022 481 7)
(Reprint authorized by Cambridge University Press, London)

APA / POSTBUS 122 / NL-3600 AC MAARSSEN / HOLLAND

AUGUST DILLMANN

ETHIOPIC GRAMMAR

ORTHOGRAPHY AND PHONOLOGY, MORPHOLOGY AND SYNTAX OF THE ETHIOPIC LANGUAGE, ALSO IN COMPARISON WITH OTHER SEMITIC LANGUAGES

WITH

A GENERAL INTRODUCTION AND AN INDEX OF PASSAGES

SECOND EDITION,
ENLARGED AND IMPROVED, EDITED BY CARL BEZOLD
TRANSLATED,
WITH ADDITIONS, BY JAMES A. CRICHTON

* * *
* *
*

REPRINT OF THE EDITION LONDON 1907.
XXXI, 581 pages and 9 folding tables.
Cloth bound, 8vo, jacket. (ISBN 90 6022 271 7)

APA / POSTBUS 122 / NL-3600 AC MAARSSEN / HOLLAND

GEORG STEINDORFF

LEHRBUCH DER KOPTISCHEN GRAMMATIK

SCHRIFT- UND LAUTLEHRE, FORMENLEHRE,

SATZBAU UND DIE SÄTZE

MIT ERGÄNZUNGEN UND BERICHTIGUNGEN VERMEHRT,

UND EINER BIBLIOGRAPHIE

HERAUSGEGEBEN VON HANS BONNET

Neudruck 1981 der Auflage Chicago 1951, mit Ergänzungen.
XX, 250 Seiten / pages. (APA-Philo Press)
Broschiert / Softbound, 8vo. (ISBN 90 6022 251 2)
Reprinted by permission of The University of Chicago Press

APA / POSTBUS 122 / NL-3600 AC MAARSSEN / HOLLAND

SIR ERNEST A. WALLIS BUDGE

THE CONTENDINGS
OF
THE APOSTLES

(MAṢHAFA GADLA ḤAWÂRYÂT)

BEING
THE ETHIOPIC VERSION OF THE HISTORIES OF THE LIVES,
MARTYRDOMS AND DEATHS
OF THE TWELVE APOSTLES AND EVANGELISTS

ETHIOPIC TEXTS,
EDITED FROM MANUSCRIPTS IN THE BRITISH MUSEUM, WITH
AN ENGLISH TRANSLATION AND AN INDEX

VOLUME I: THE ETHIOPIC TEXT
VOLUME II: THE ENGLISH TRANSLATION

* * * * *

REPRINT OF THE EDITION LONDON 1899; 1935. 2 VOLUMES.
XXII, 602*; XVI, 599 pages; 2 plates.
Cloth bound, 8vo. (ISBN 90 6022 482 5)
Volume I: Ethiopic text (ISBN 90 6022 483 3)
Volume II: Translation, Index (ISBN 90 6022 484 1)

APA   /   POSTBUS 122   /   NL-3600 AC MAARSSEN   /   HOLLAND

SIR HERBERT THOMPSON

A

COPTIC PALIMPSEST

CONTAINING
JOSHUA, JUDGES, RUTH, JUDITH, AND ESTHER
IN THE SAHIDIC DIALECT

COPTIC TEXT, EDITED FROM A SEVENTH CENTURY MANUSCRIPT
IN THE BRITISH MUSEUM
WITH A SHORT CRITICAL INTRODUCTION AND TEXTUAL NOTES

* * *
* *
*

REPRINT 1979 OF THE EDITION LONDON 1911.
XIII, 386 pages and 2 plates.
Paper bound, 8vo. (ISBN 90 6022 420 5) (APA-Philo Press)
Reprinted by arrangement with Oxford University Press, London

APA / POSTBUS 122 / NL-3600 AC MAARSSEN / HOLLAND